BLADE RUNNER 2029

TITAN
COMICS

ALCON
ENTERTAINMENT

Also available
Blade Runner 2019
Volume 1 – *Los Angeles*

Blade Runner 2019
Volume 2 – *Off-World*

Blade Runner 2019
Volume 3 – *Home Again, Home Again*

Blade Runner Artist's Edition

Coming soon
Blade Runner Origins
Volume 1 – *Products* (August 2021)

Blade Runner 2029
Volume 2 – *Echoes* (December 2021)

BLADE RUNNER 2029: REUNION

SENIOR CREATIVE EDITOR | David Leach

TITAN COMICS

MANAGING EDITOR | Martin Eden
ASSISTANT EDITOR | Phoebe Hedges
SENIOR DESIGNER | Andrew Leung
SENIOR EDITOR | Jake Devine
PRODUCTION CONTROLLERS | Caterina Falqui | Kelly Fenlon
PRODUCTION MANAGER | Jackie Flook
ART DIRECTOR | Oz Browne
SALES & CIRCULATION MANAGER | Steve Tothill

MARKETING AND ADVERTISEMENT ASSISTANT | Lauren Noding
SALES AND MARKETING COORDINATOR | George Wickenden
PUBLICIST | Imogen Harris
HEAD OF RIGHTS | Jenny Boyce
ACQUISITIONS EDITOR | Duncan Baizley
PUBLISHING DIRECTORS | Ricky Claydon | John Dziewiatkowski
OPERATIONS DIRECTOR | Leigh Baulch
PUBLISHERS | Vivian Cheung | Nick Landau

ALCON PUBLISHING

DIRECTOR/EDITOR | Jeff Conner
COO | Scott Parish
CFO | Jason Kummer
LEGAL/BUSINESS AFFAIRS | Jeannette Hill
PUBLISHERS | Andrew Kosove & Broderick Johnson

BLADE RUNNER 2029: REUNION
JULY 2021. Published by Titan Comics, a division of Titan Publishing Group, Ltd. 144 Southwark Street, London SE1 0UP. Titan Comics is a registered trademark of Titan Publishing Group, Ltd. All rights reserved. © 2021 – Blade Runner 2029 and all related marks and characters are trademarks and copyrights of Alcon Publishing ®. All rights reserved. Licensed by Alcon Publishing ®, LCC. All rights reserved.

Published by Titan Comics, a division of Titan Publishing Group, Ltd. Titan Comics is a registered trademark of Titan Publishing Group, Ltd.
144 Southwark Street, London SE1 0UP

ISBN 9781787731943

A CIP catalogue for this title is available from the British Library.

First Edition JULY 2021

10 9 8 7 6 5 4 3 2 1
Printed in Spain.

www.titan-comics.com
Follow us on twitter@ComicsTitan | Visit us at facebook.com/comicstitan
For rights information contact: jenny.boyce@titanemail.com

BLADE RUNNER 2029

REUNION

WRITTEN BY
MIKE JOHNSON

CREATIVE CONSULTANTS
K. PERKINS
MELLOW BROWN
MICHAEL GREEN

ART BY
ANDRES GUINALDO

COLORS BY
MARCO LESKO

LETTERING BY
JIM CAMPBELL

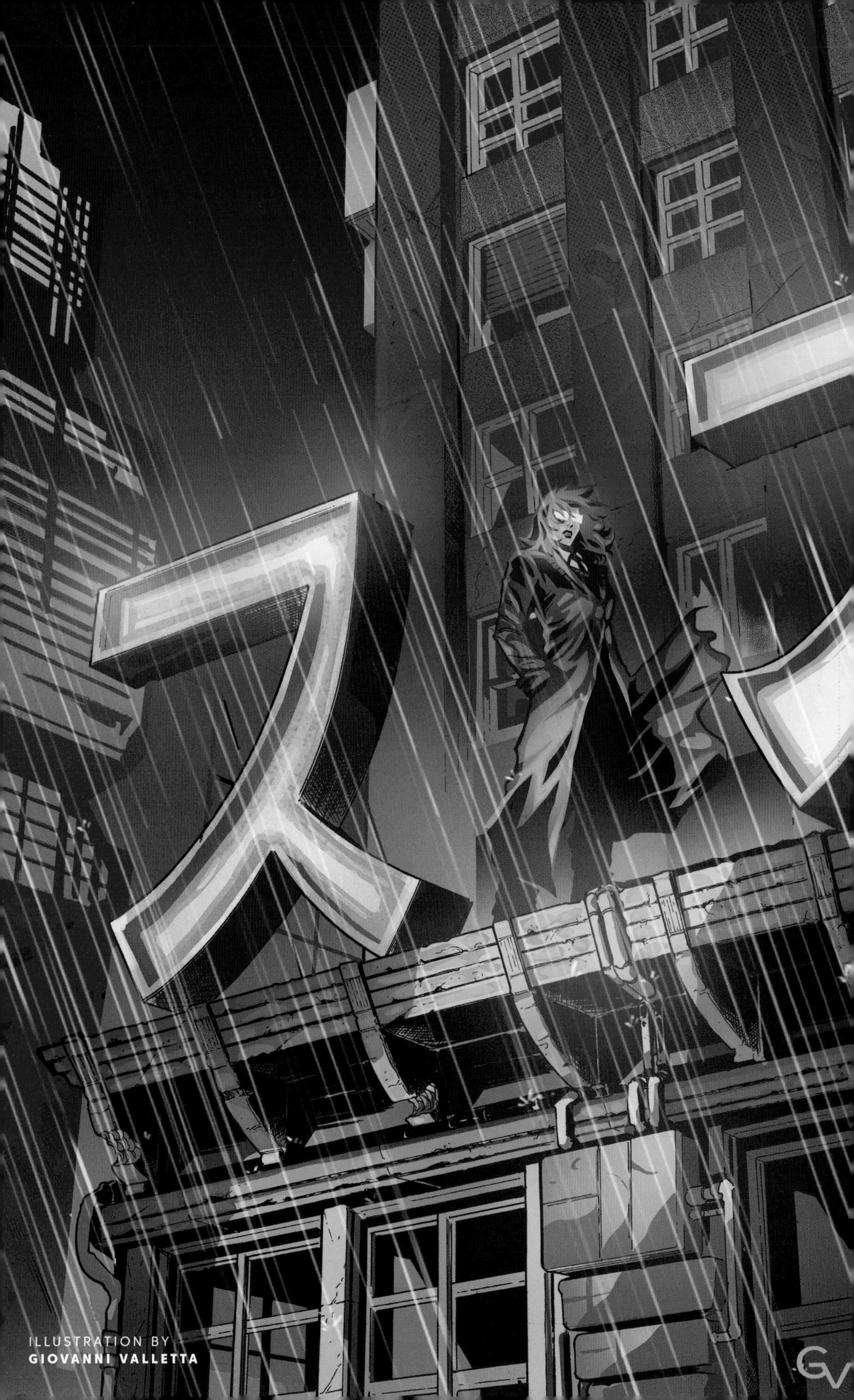

ILLUSTRATION BY
GIOVANNI VALLETTA

EARLY IN THE 21ST CENTURY, **THE TYRELL CORPORATION** ADVANCED ROBOT EVOLUTION INTO THE **NEXUS** PHASE – A BEING VIRTUALLY IDENTICAL TO A HUMAN – KNOWN AS A REPLICANT. REPLICANTS WERE USED OFF-WORLD AS SLAVE LABOR IN HAZARDOUS EXPLORATION AND COLONIZATION.

REPLICANTS WHO ESCAPED AND RETURNED TO EARTH ARE HUNTED BY SPECIAL POLICE SQUADS – **BLADE RUNNER UNITS** – WITH ORDERS TO KILL ANY TRESPASSING REPLICANT UPON DETECTION.

IN 2022, A REPLICANT ATTACK ON THE TYRELL CORPORATION ERASED ALL RECORDS OF EXISTING REPLICANTS AND FORCED THE COMPANY INTO BANKRUPTCY. THE SURVIVING NEXUS 8 MODELS DISAPPEARED WITH THE HELP OF THE **REPLICANT UNDERGROUND**. MANY REPLICANTS REMAINED IN SERVITUDE.

IN 2027, **AAHNA "ASH" ASHINA**, A FORMER BLADE RUNNER, REJOINED THE DEPARTMENT TO HUNT DOWN FUGITIVE REPLICANTS. HER SUPERIORS ARE UNAWARE THAT HER LOYALTIES ARE DIVIDED...

LOS ANGELES, 2029

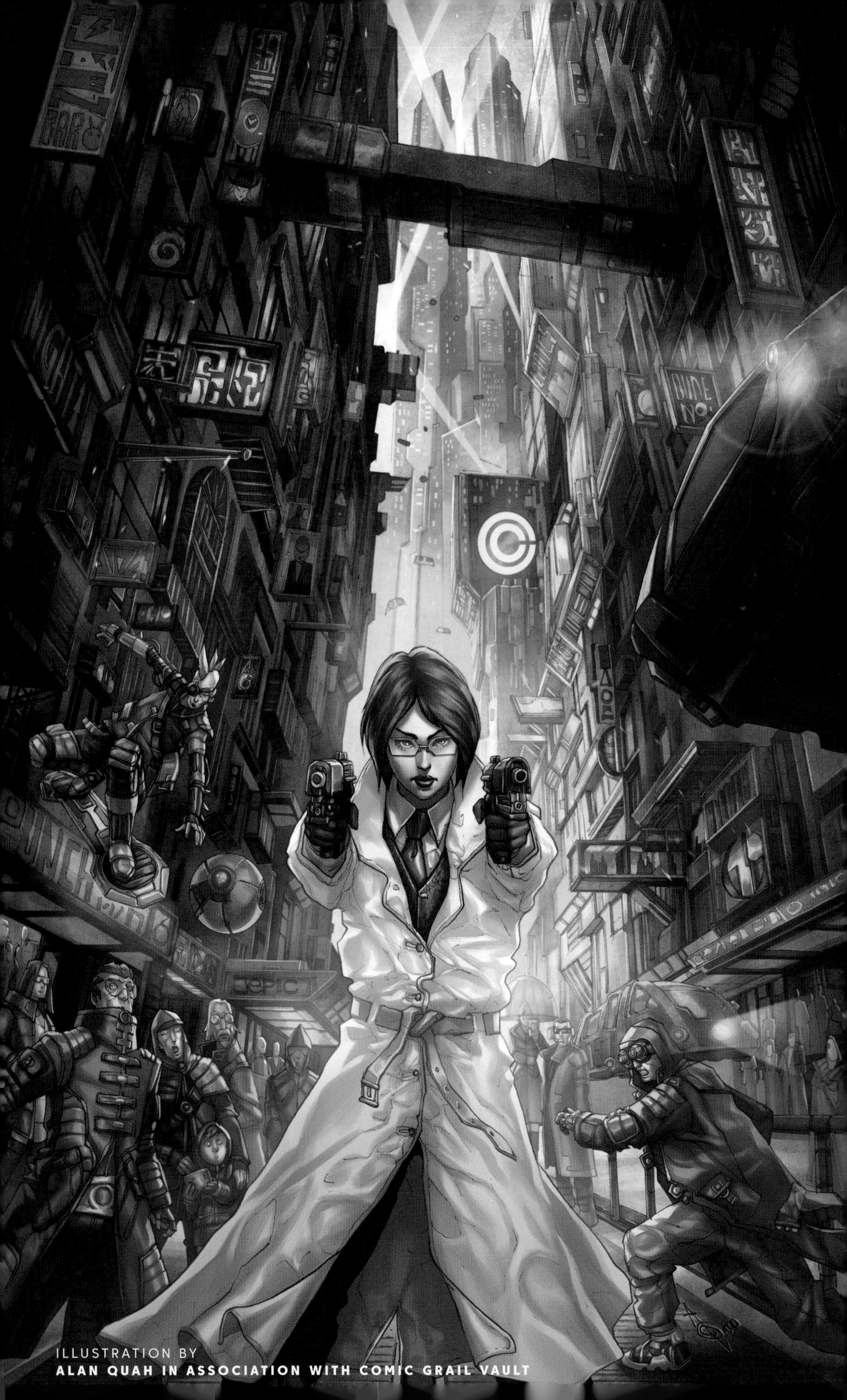

ILLUSTRATION BY
ALAN QUAH IN ASSOCIATION WITH COMIC GRAIL VAULT

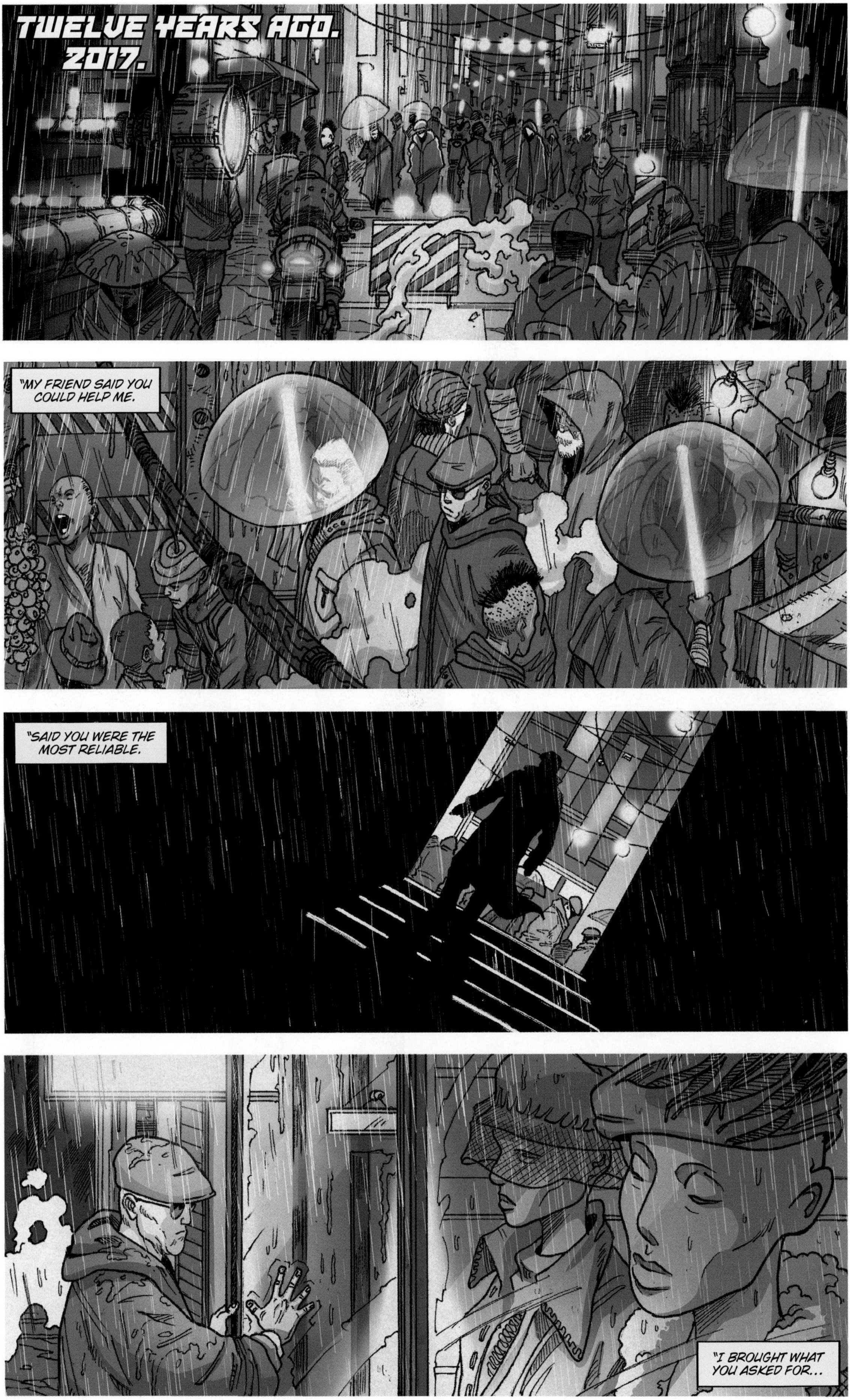
TWELVE YEARS AGO.
2017.
"MY FRIEND SAID YOU COULD HELP ME.
"SAID YOU WERE THE MOST RELIABLE.
"I BROUGHT WHAT YOU ASKED FOR...

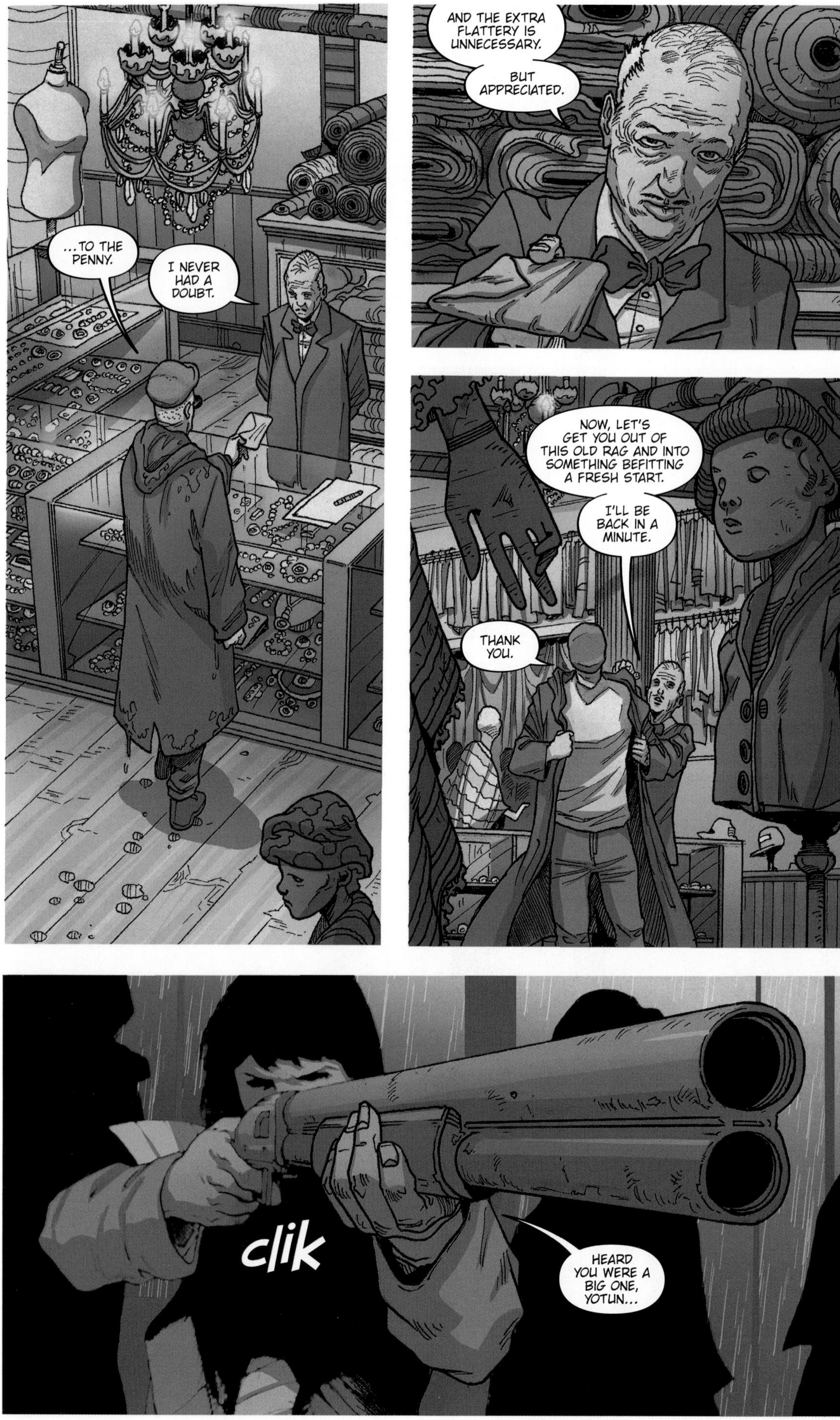
...TO THE PENNY.
I NEVER HAD A DOUBT.
AND THE EXTRA FLATTERY IS UNNECESSARY.
BUT APPRECIATED.
NOW, LET'S GET YOU OUT OF THIS OLD RAG AND INTO SOMETHING BEFITTING A FRESH START.
I'LL BE BACK IN A MINUTE.
THANK YOU.
clik
HEARD YOU WERE A BIG ONE, YOTUN...

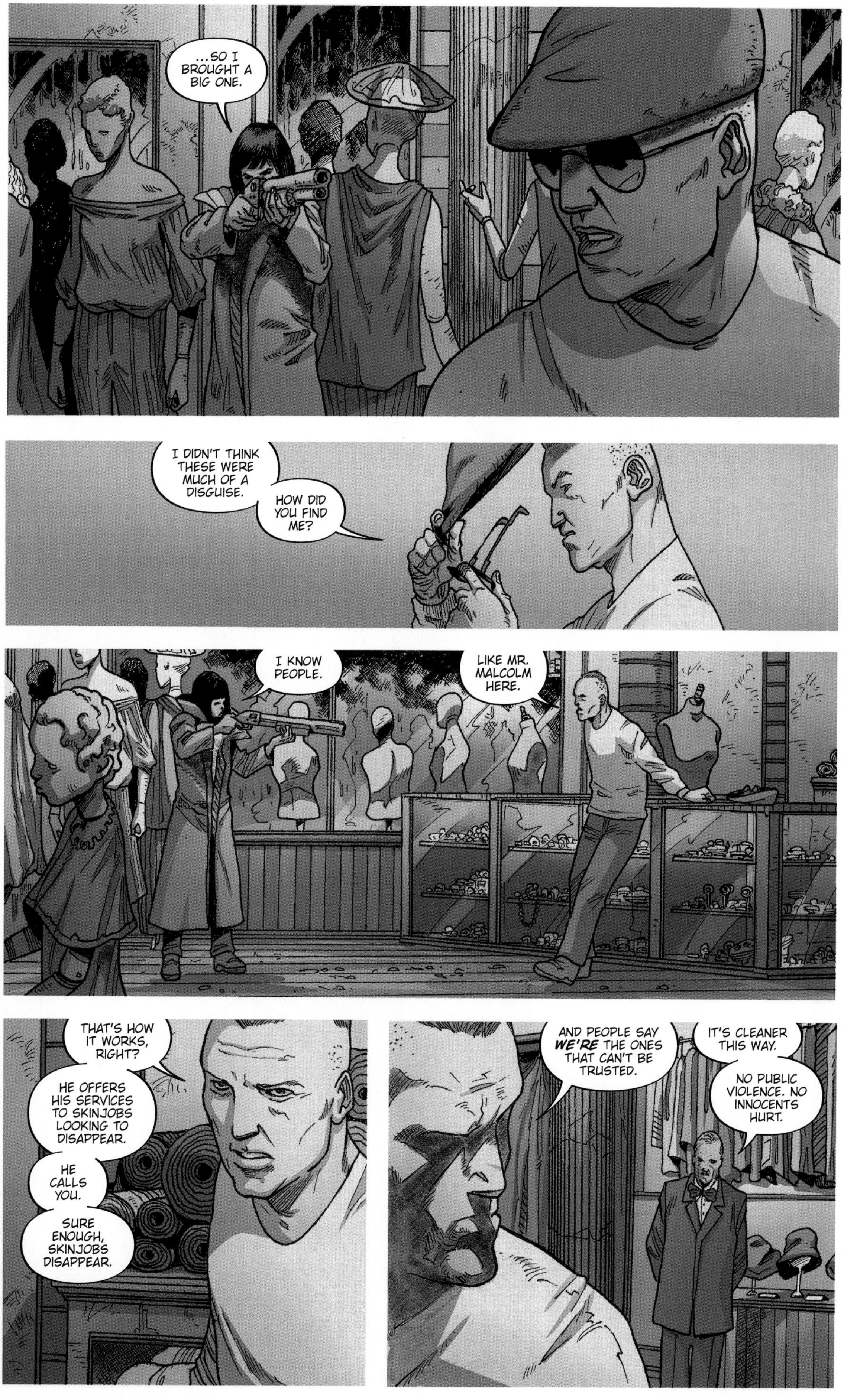
...SO I BROUGHT A BIG ONE.
I DIDN'T THINK THESE WERE MUCH OF A DISGUISE.
HOW DID YOU FIND ME?
I KNOW PEOPLE.
LIKE MR. MALCOLM HERE.
THAT'S HOW IT WORKS, RIGHT?
HE OFFERS HIS SERVICES TO SKINJOBS LOOKING TO DISAPPEAR.
HE CALLS YOU.
SURE ENOUGH, SKINJOBS DISAPPEAR.
AND PEOPLE SAY WE'RE THE ONES THAT CAN'T BE TRUSTED.
IT'S CLEANER THIS WAY.
NO PUBLIC VIOLENCE. NO INNOCENTS HURT.

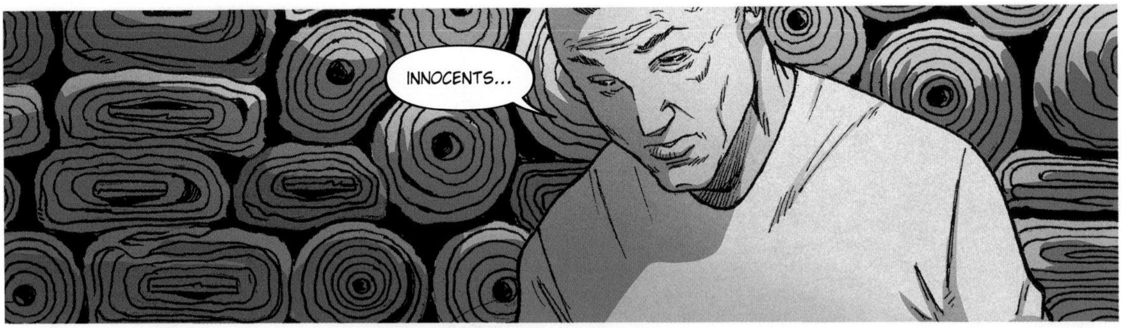
INNOCENTS...

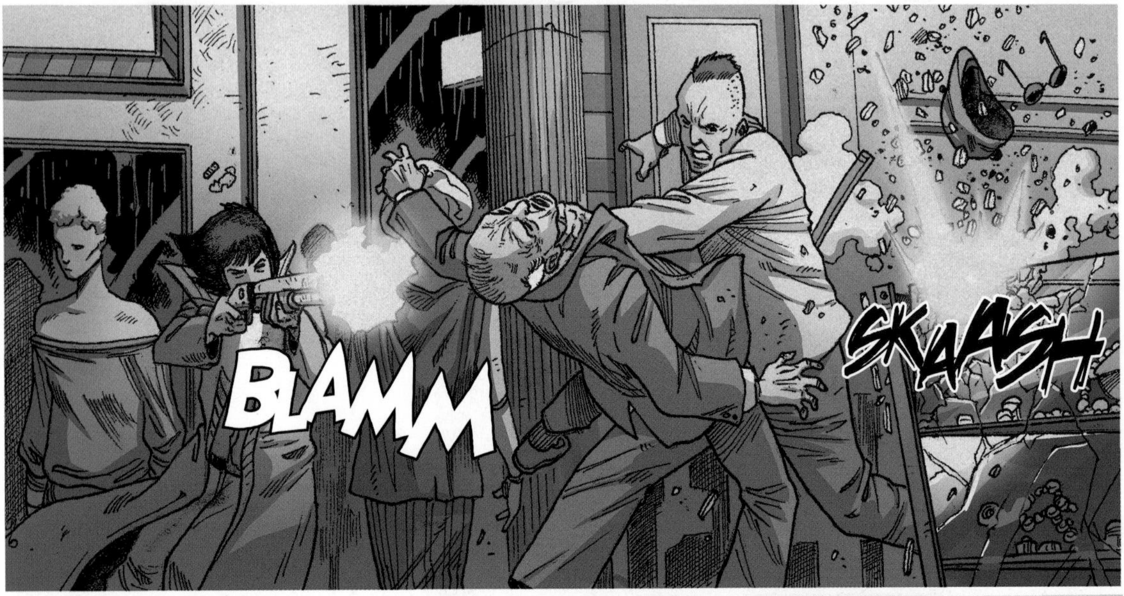
BLAMM
SKWASH

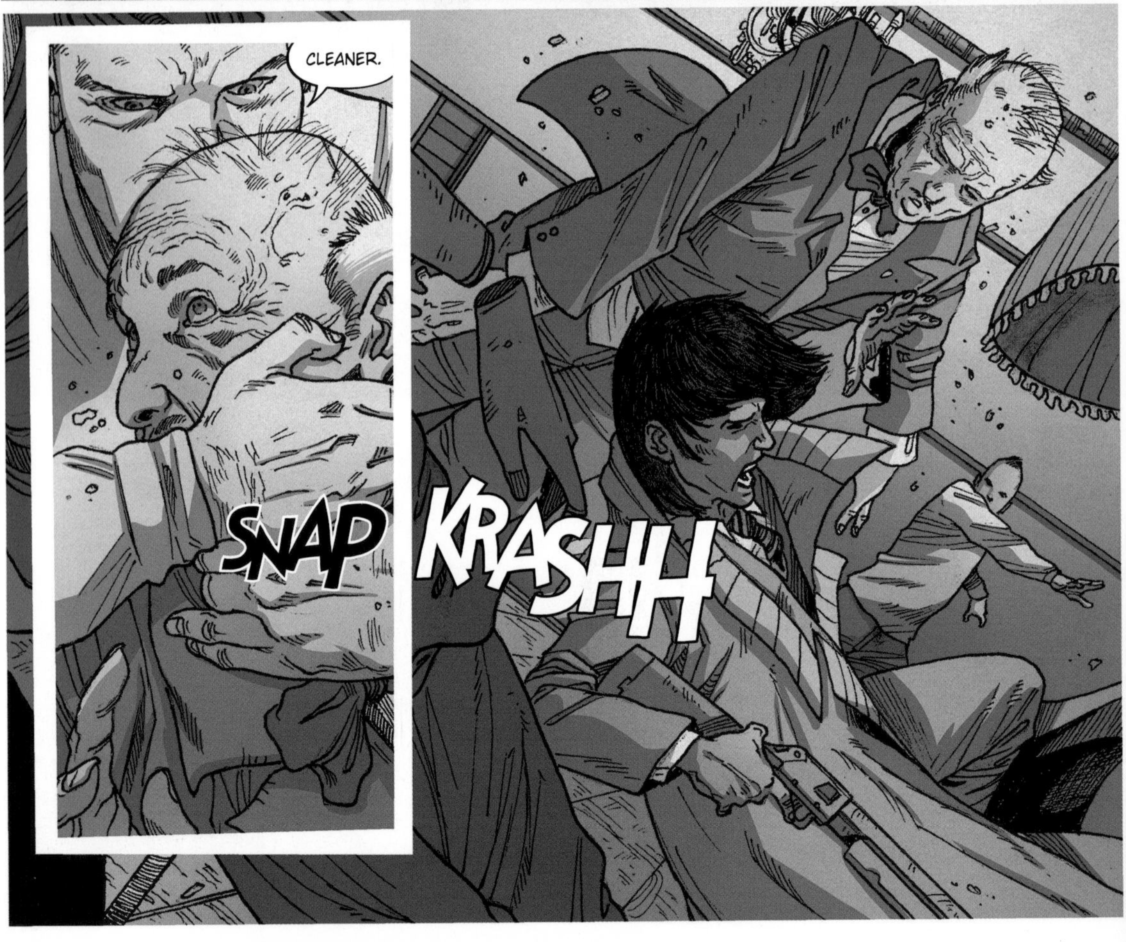
CLEANER.
SNAP
KRASHH

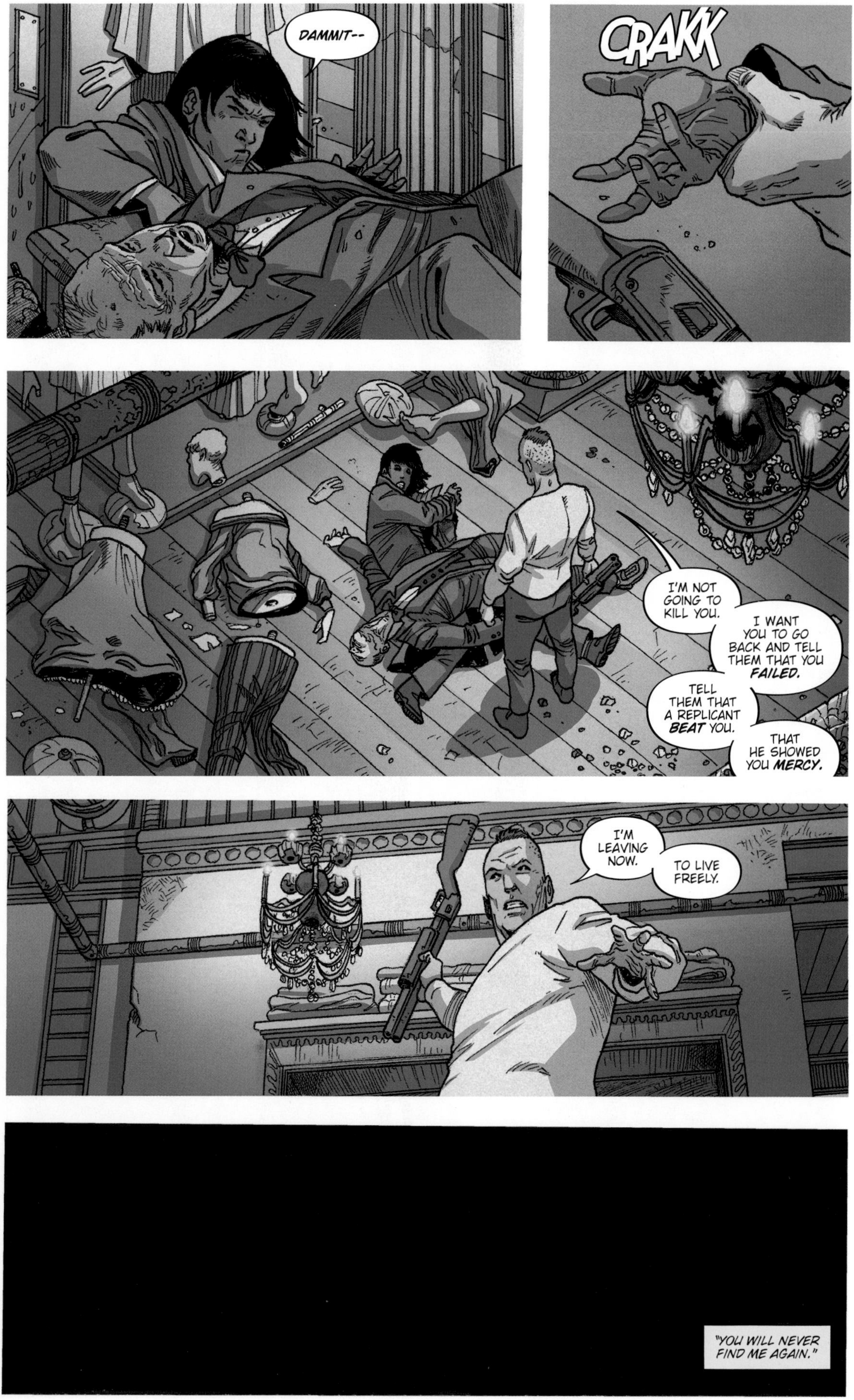
DAMMIT--
CRAKK
I'M NOT GOING TO KILL YOU.
I WANT YOU TO GO BACK AND TELL THEM THAT YOU FAILED.
TELL THEM THAT A REPLICANT BEAT YOU.
THAT HE SHOWED YOU MERCY.
I'M LEAVING NOW.
TO LIVE FREELY.
"YOU WILL NEVER FIND ME AGAIN."

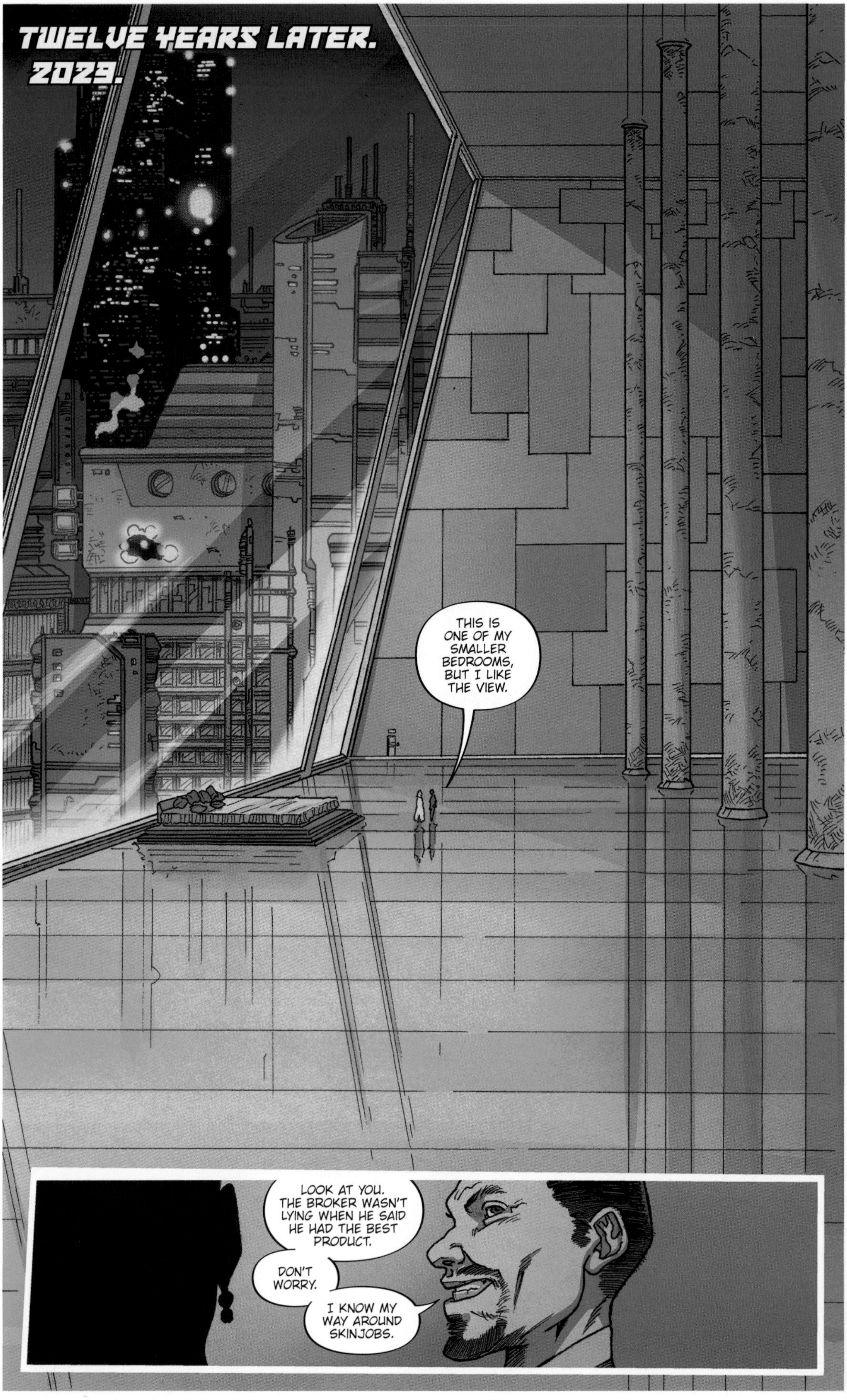
TWELVE YEARS LATER. 2029.
THIS IS ONE OF MY SMALLER BEDROOMS, BUT I LIKE THE VIEW.
LOOK AT YOU. THE BROKER WASN'T LYING WHEN HE SAID HE HAD THE BEST PRODUCT.
DON'T WORRY.
I KNOW MY WAY AROUND SKINJOBS.

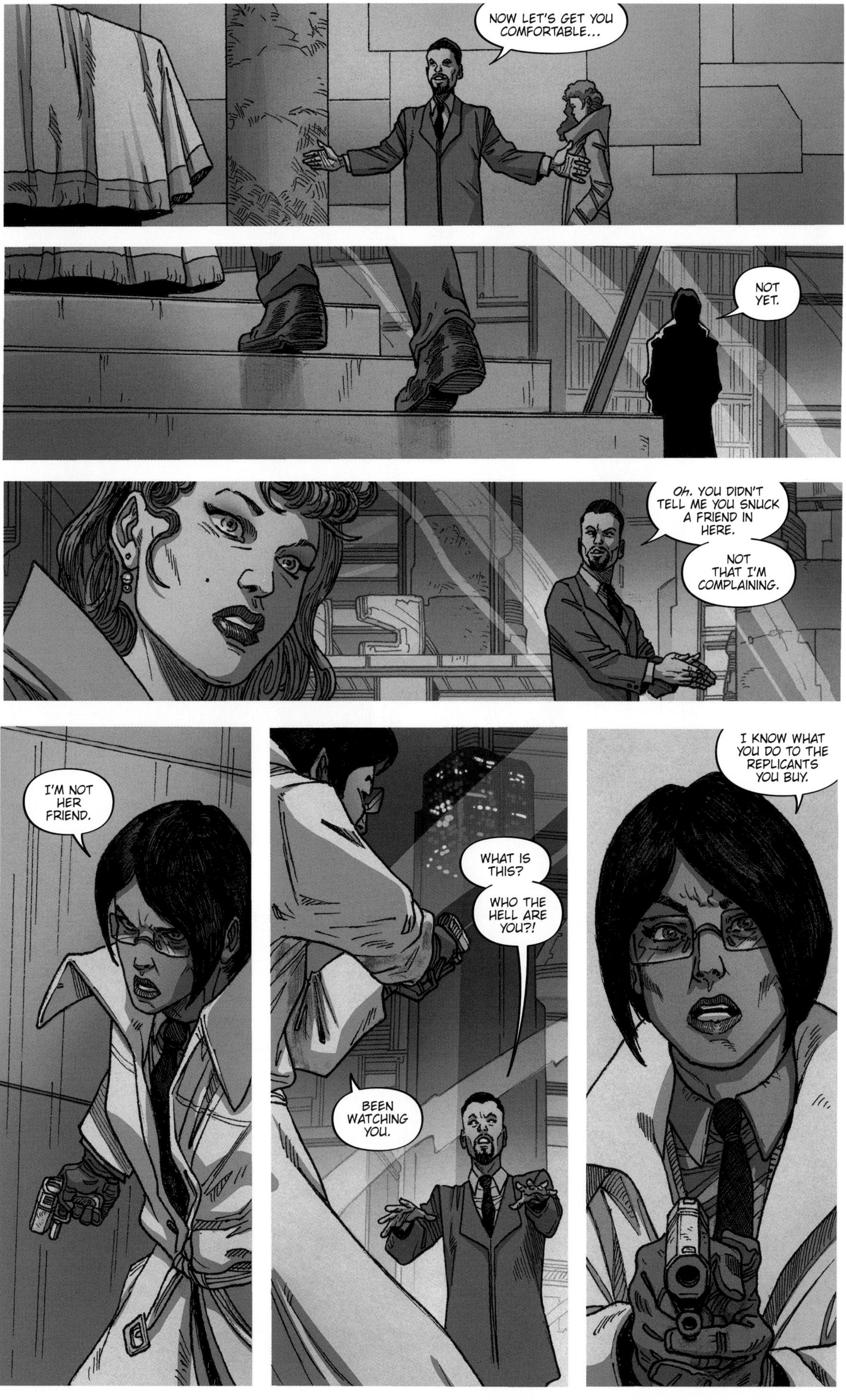
NOW LET'S GET YOU COMFORTABLE...
NOT YET.
Oh. YOU DIDN'T TELL ME YOU SNUCK A FRIEND IN HERE.
NOT THAT I'M COMPLAINING.
I'M NOT HER FRIEND.
WHAT IS THIS?
WHO THE HELL ARE YOU?!
BEEN WATCHING YOU.
I KNOW WHAT YOU DO TO THE REPLICANTS YOU BUY.

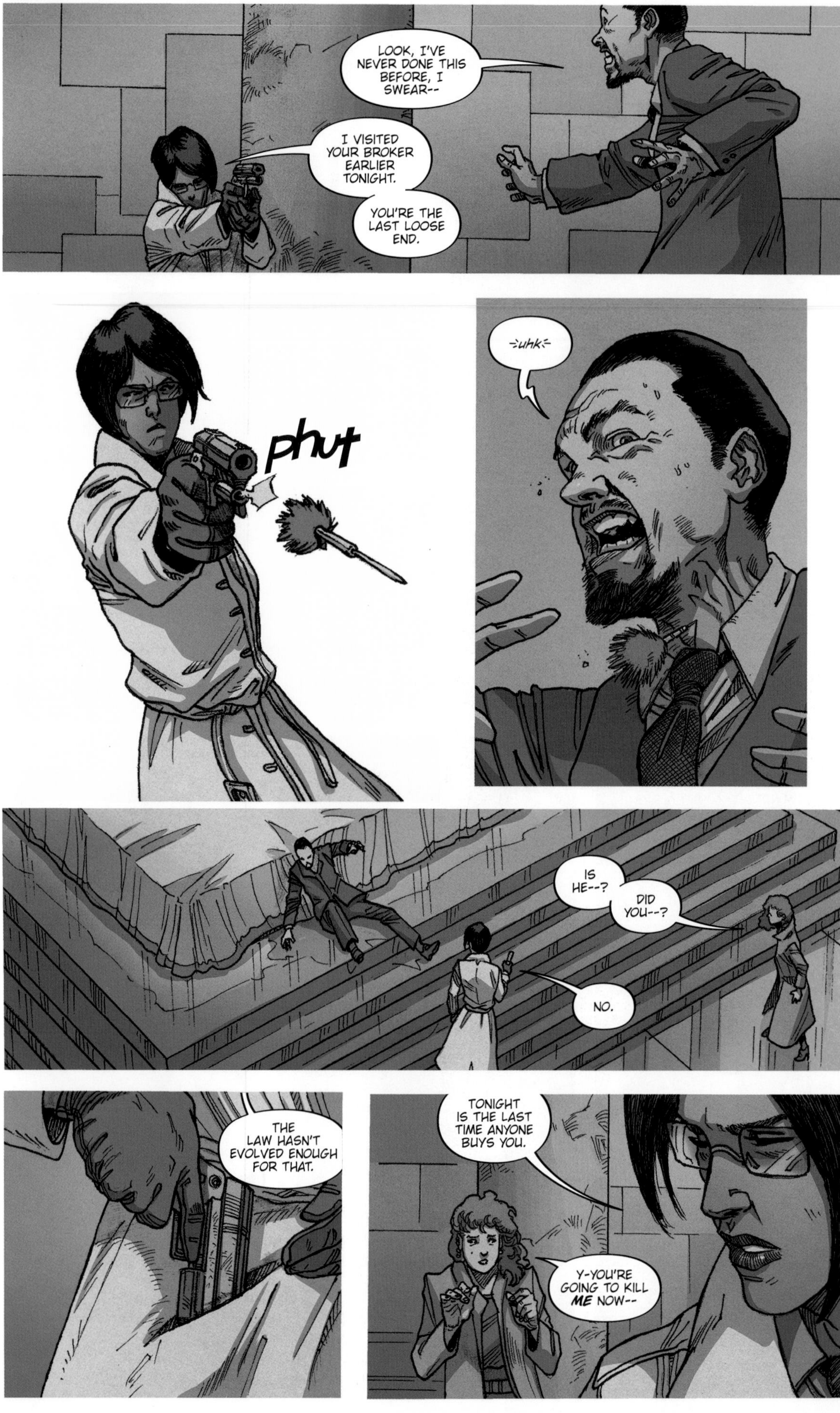
LOOK, I'VE NEVER DONE THIS BEFORE, I SWEAR--
I VISITED YOUR BROKER EARLIER TONIGHT.
YOU'RE THE LAST LOOSE END.
phut
uhk
IS HE--?
DID YOU--?
NO.
THE LAW HASN'T EVOLVED ENOUGH FOR THAT.
TONIGHT IS THE LAST TIME ANYONE BUYS YOU.
Y-YOU'RE GOING TO KILL ME NOW--

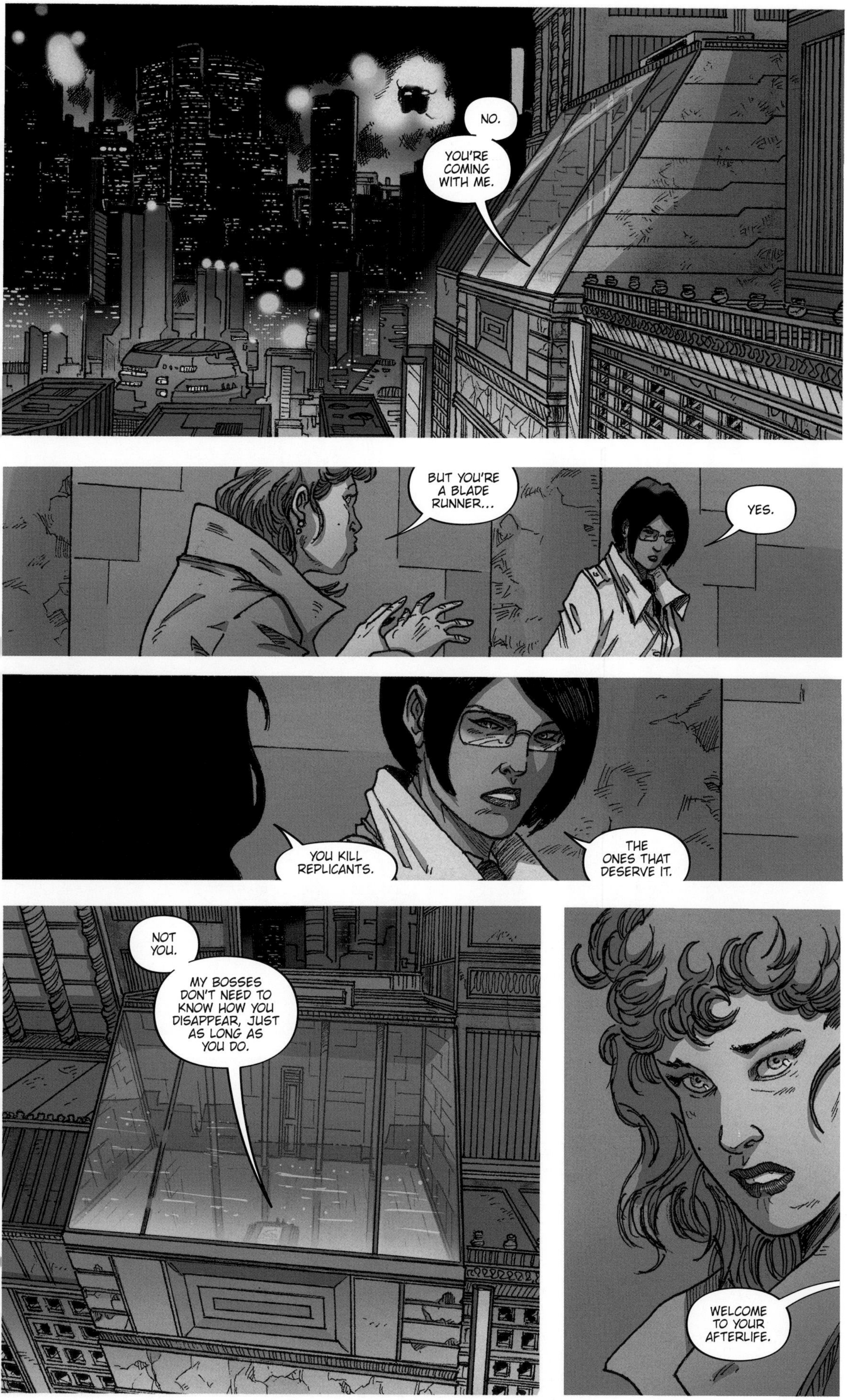
NO.
YOU'RE COMING WITH ME.
BUT YOU'RE A BLADE RUNNER...
YES.
YOU KILL REPLICANTS.
THE ONES THAT DESERVE IT.
NOT YOU.
MY BOSSES DON'T NEED TO KNOW HOW YOU DISAPPEAR, JUST AS LONG AS YOU DO.
WELCOME TO YOUR AFTERLIFE.

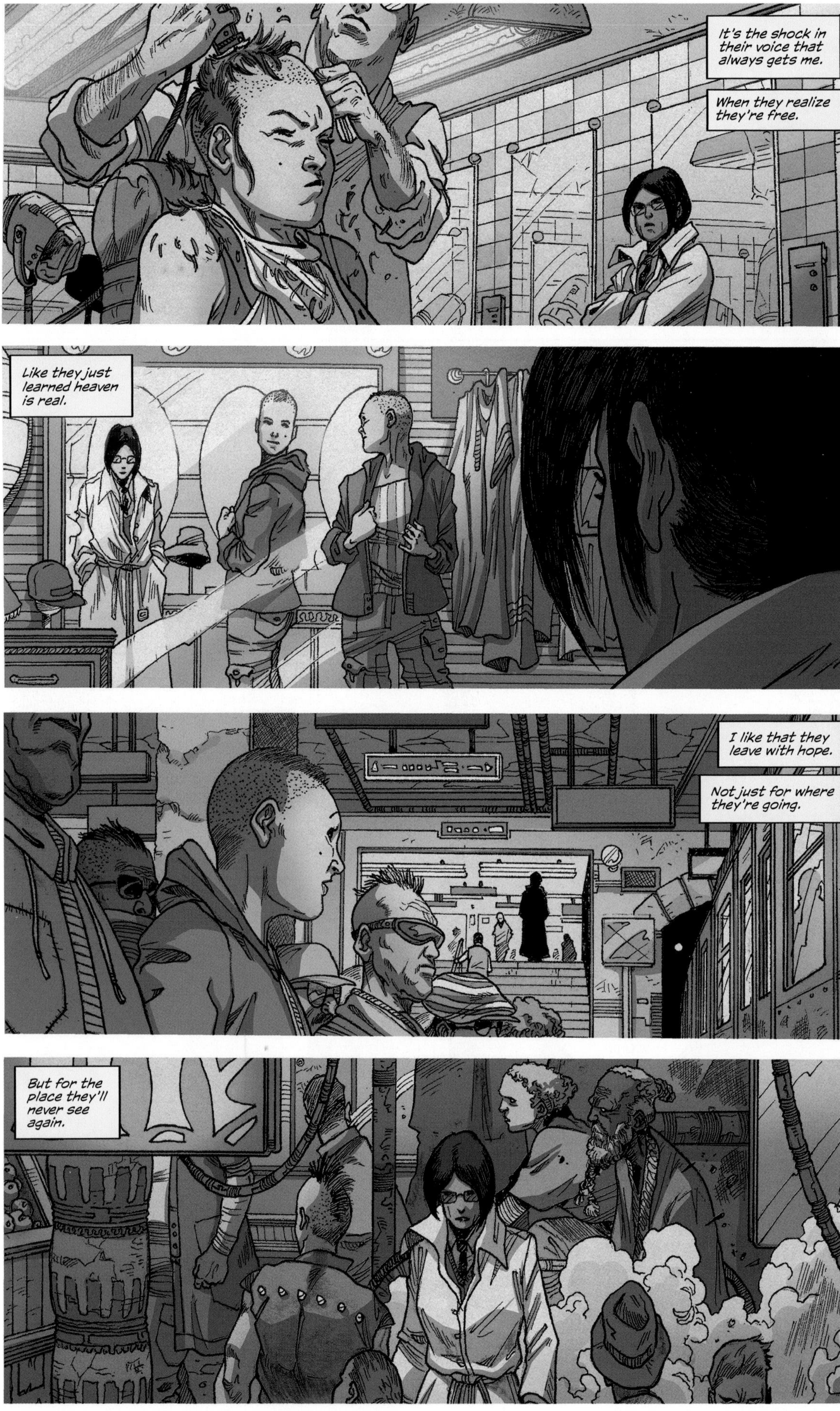
It's the shock in their voice that always gets me.
When they realize they're free.
Like they just learned heaven is real.
I like that they leave with hope.
Not just for where they're going.
But for the place they'll never see again.

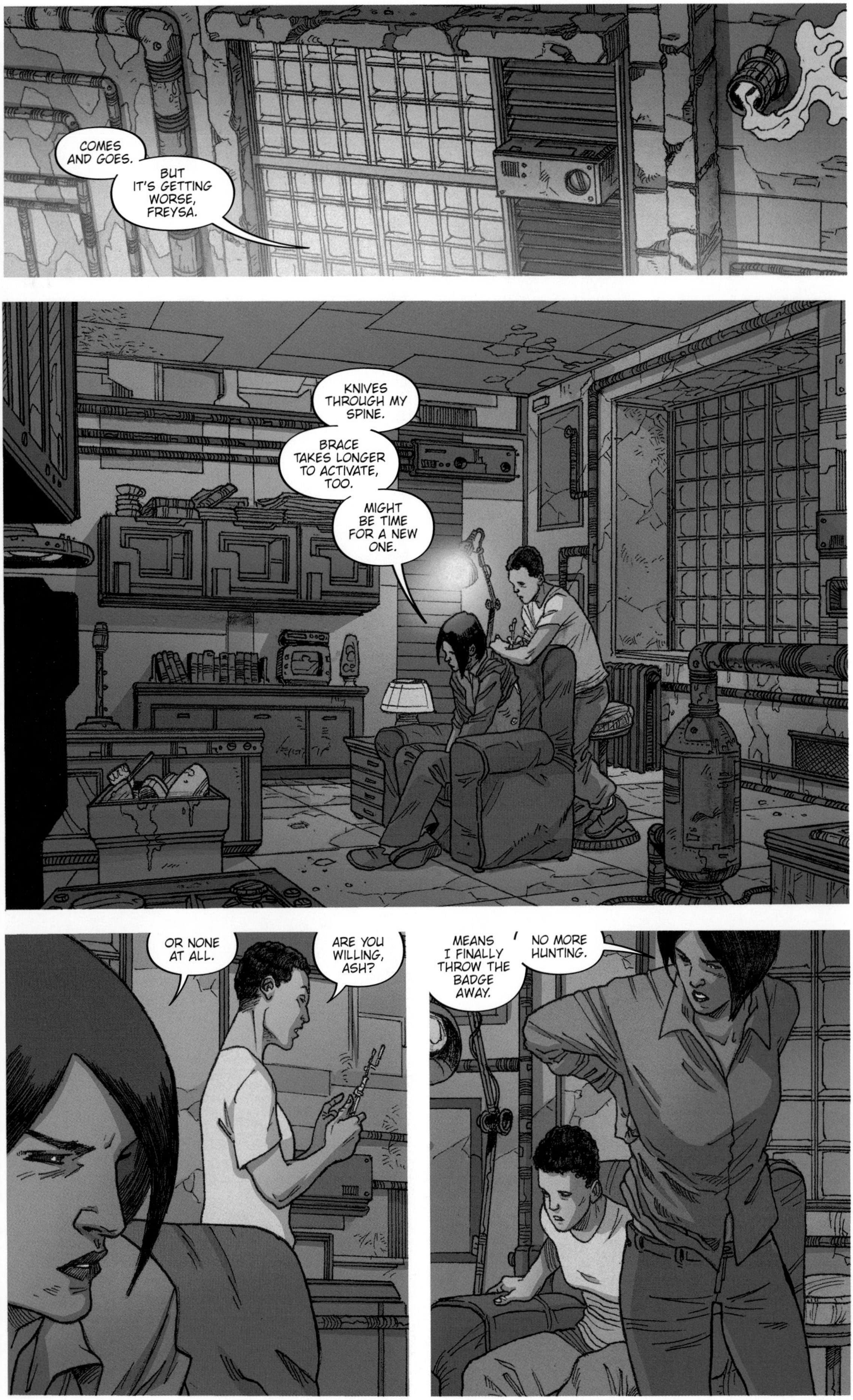
COMES AND GOES.
BUT IT'S GETTING WORSE, FREYSA.
KNIVES THROUGH MY SPINE.
BRACE TAKES LONGER TO ACTIVATE, TOO.
MIGHT BE TIME FOR A NEW ONE.
OR NONE AT ALL.
ARE YOU WILLING, ASH?
NO MORE HUNTING.
MEANS I FINALLY THROW THE BADGE AWAY.

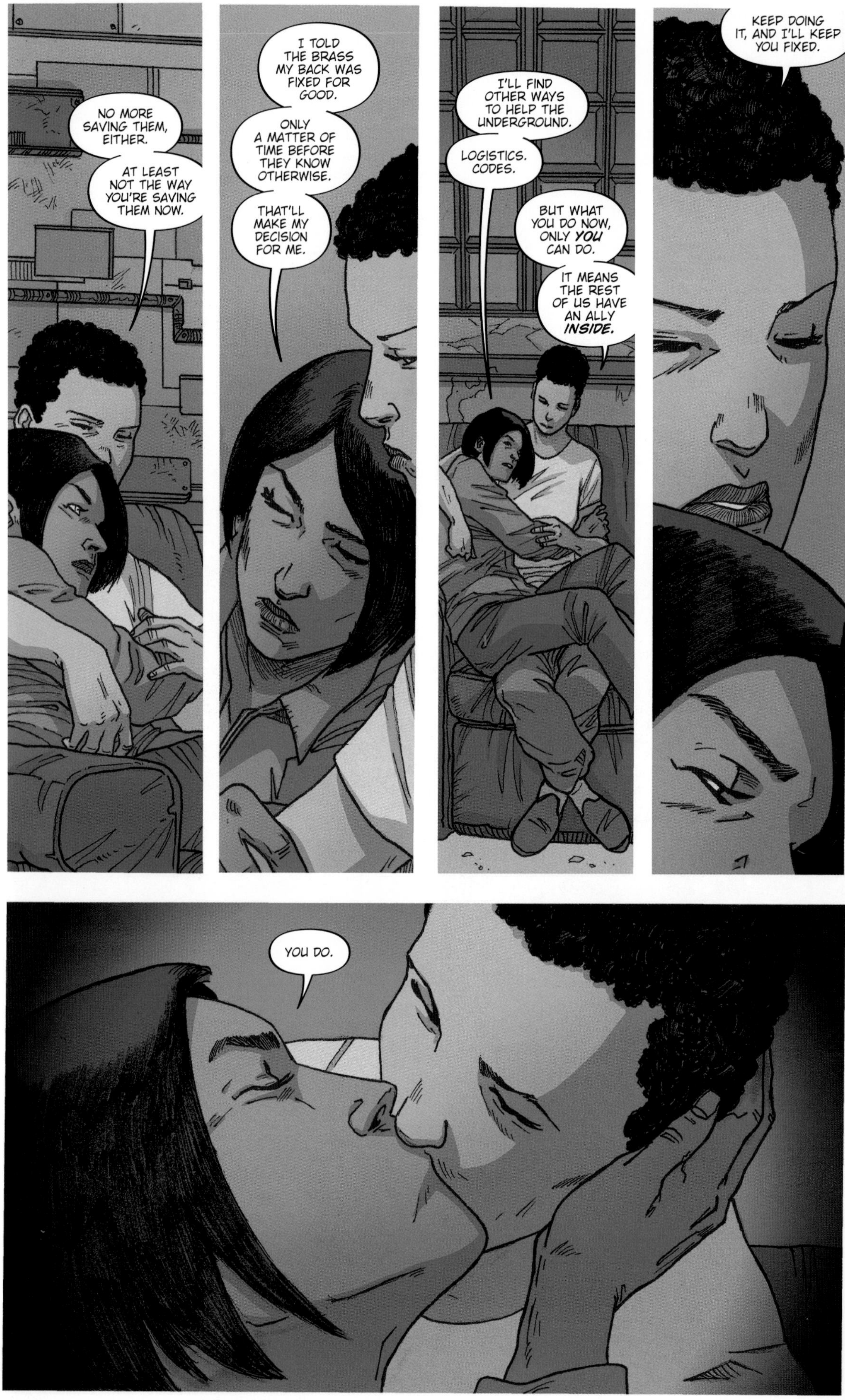
NO MORE SAVING THEM, EITHER.
AT LEAST NOT THE WAY YOU'RE SAVING THEM NOW.
I TOLD THE BRASS MY BACK WAS FIXED FOR GOOD.
ONLY A MATTER OF TIME BEFORE THEY KNOW OTHERWISE.
THAT'LL MAKE MY DECISION FOR ME.
I'LL FIND OTHER WAYS TO HELP THE UNDERGROUND.
LOGISTICS. CODES.
BUT WHAT YOU DO NOW, ONLY YOU CAN DO.
IT MEANS THE REST OF US HAVE AN ALLY INSIDE.
KEEP DOING IT, AND I'LL KEEP YOU FIXED.
YOU DO.

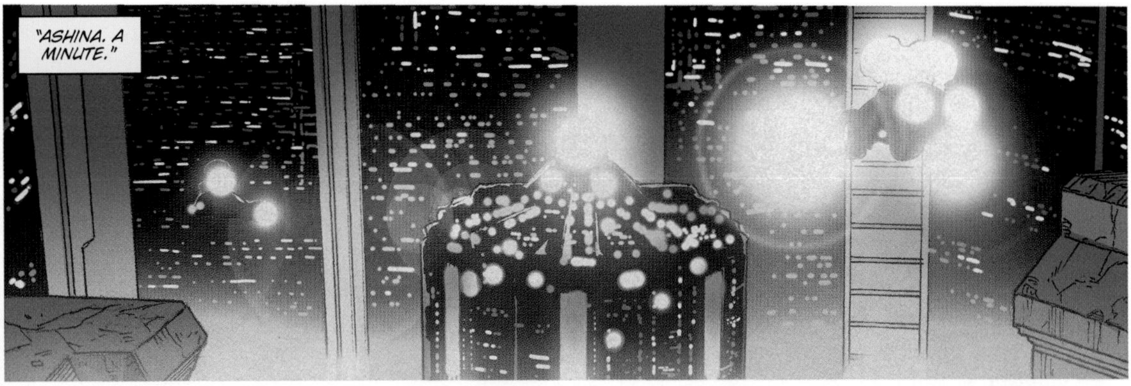
"ASHINA. A MINUTE."

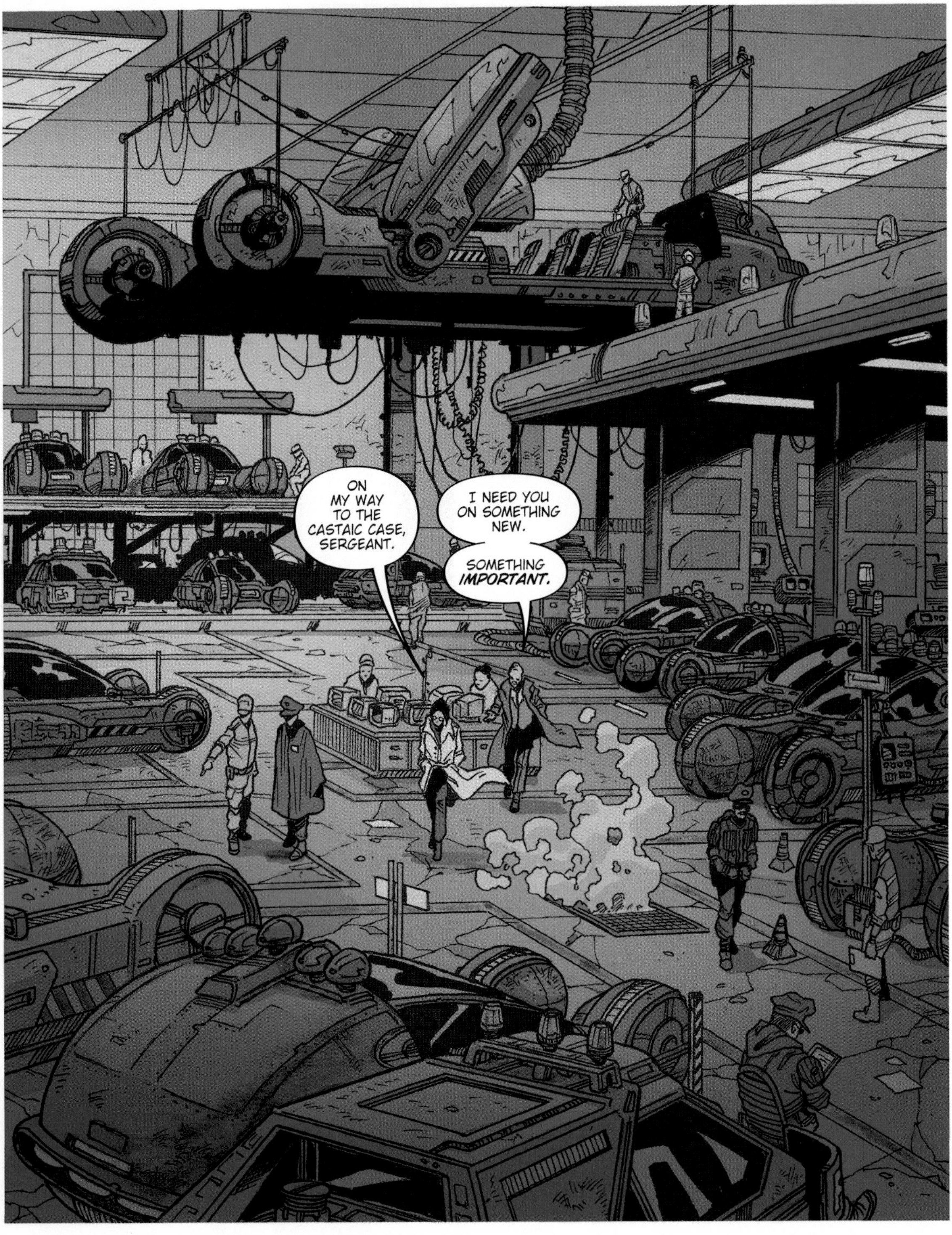
ON MY WAY TO THE CASTAIC CASE, SERGEANT.
I NEED YOU ON SOMETHING NEW.
SOMETHING *IMPORTANT.*

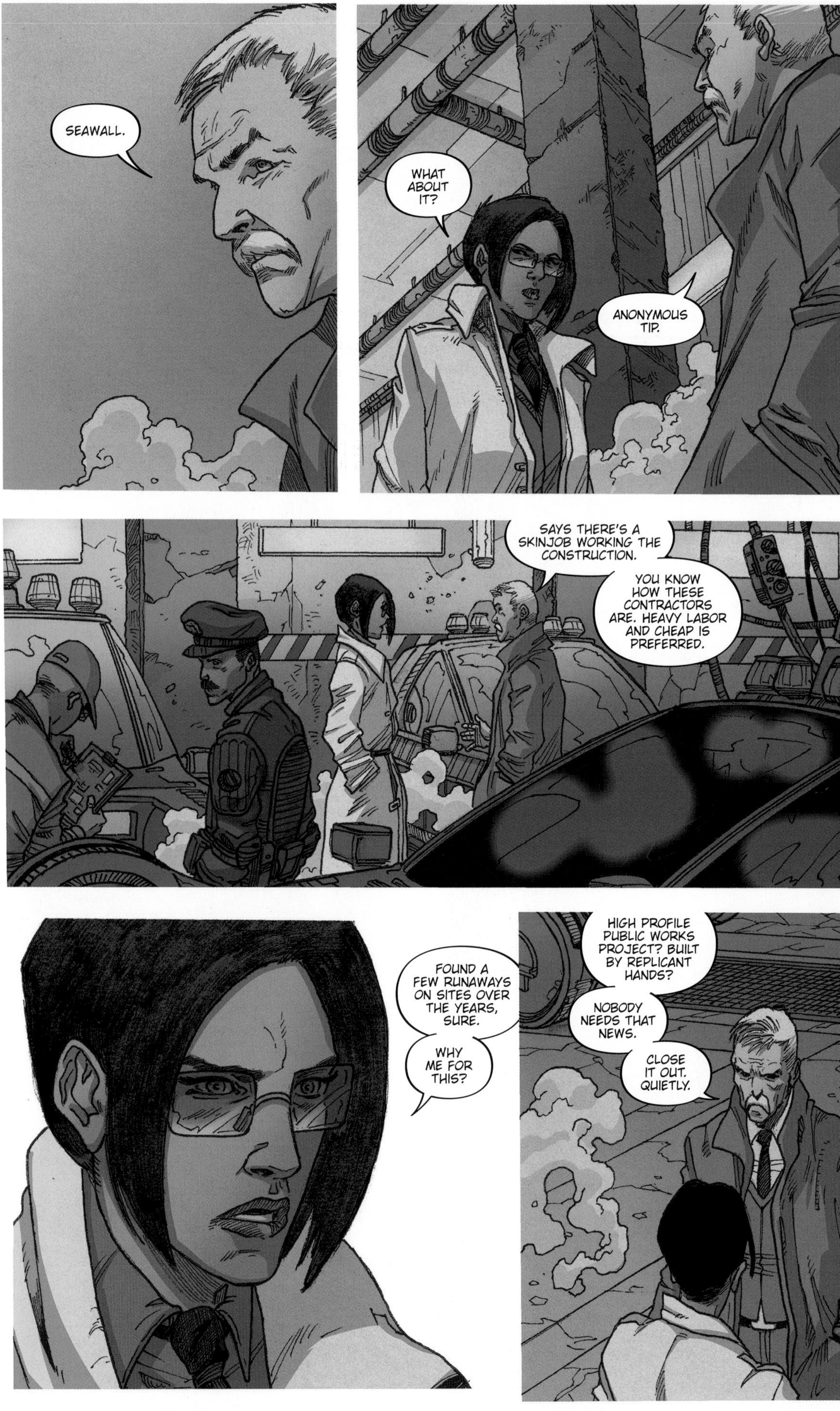
SEAWALL.
WHAT ABOUT IT?
ANONYMOUS TIP.
SAYS THERE'S A SKINJOB WORKING THE CONSTRUCTION.
YOU KNOW HOW THESE CONTRACTORS ARE. HEAVY LABOR AND CHEAP IS PREFERRED.
FOUND A FEW RUNAWAYS ON SITES OVER THE YEARS, SURE.
WHY ME FOR THIS?
HIGH PROFILE PUBLIC WORKS PROJECT? BUILT BY REPLICANT HANDS?
NOBODY NEEDS THAT NEWS.
CLOSE IT OUT. QUIETLY.

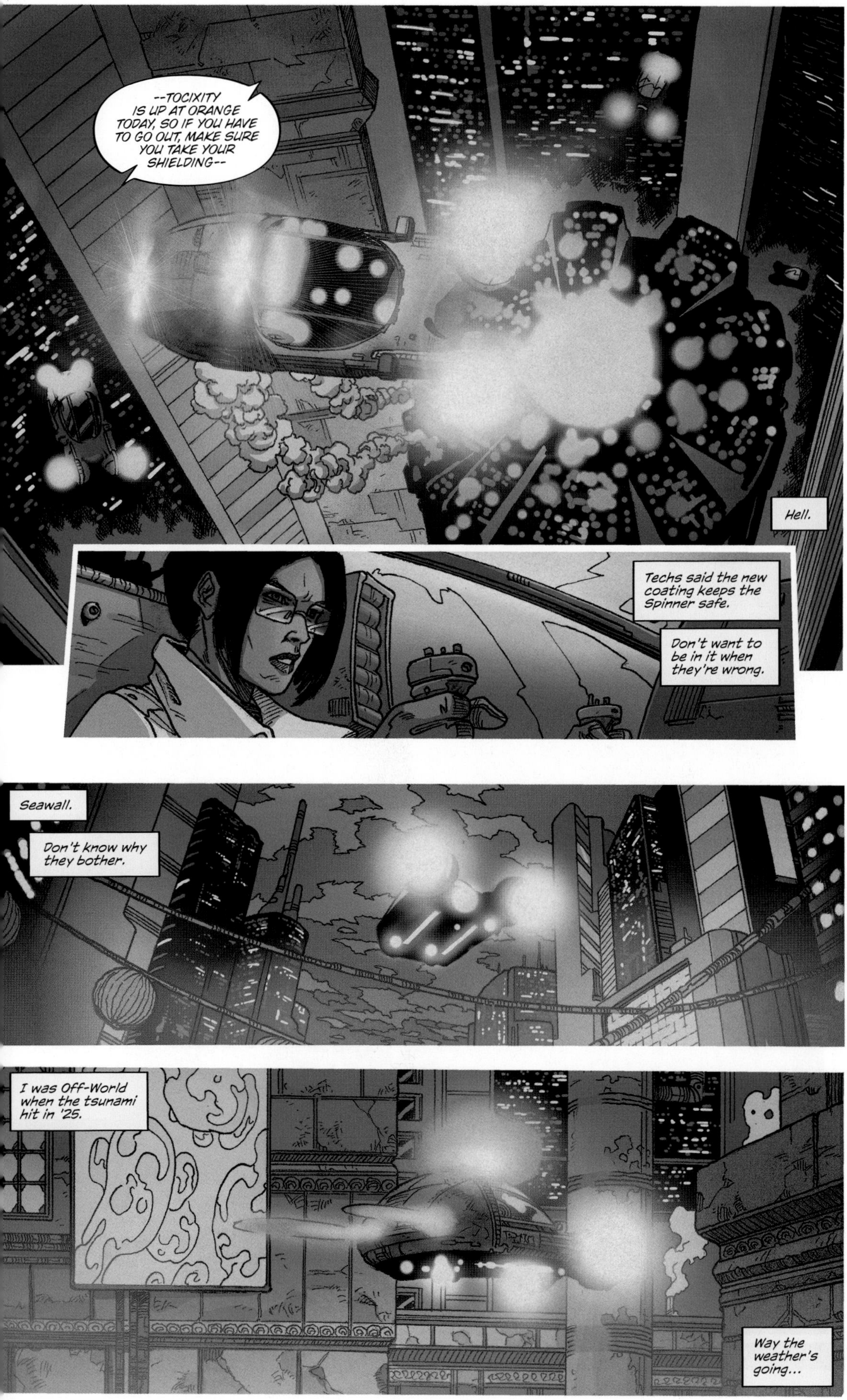
--TOCIXITY IS UP AT ORANGE TODAY, SO IF YOU HAVE TO GO OUT, MAKE SURE YOU TAKE YOUR SHIELDING--
Hell.
Techs said the new coating keeps the Spinner safe.
Don't want to be in it when they're wrong.
Seawall.
Don't know why they bother.
I was Off-World when the tsunami hit in '25.
Way the weather's going...

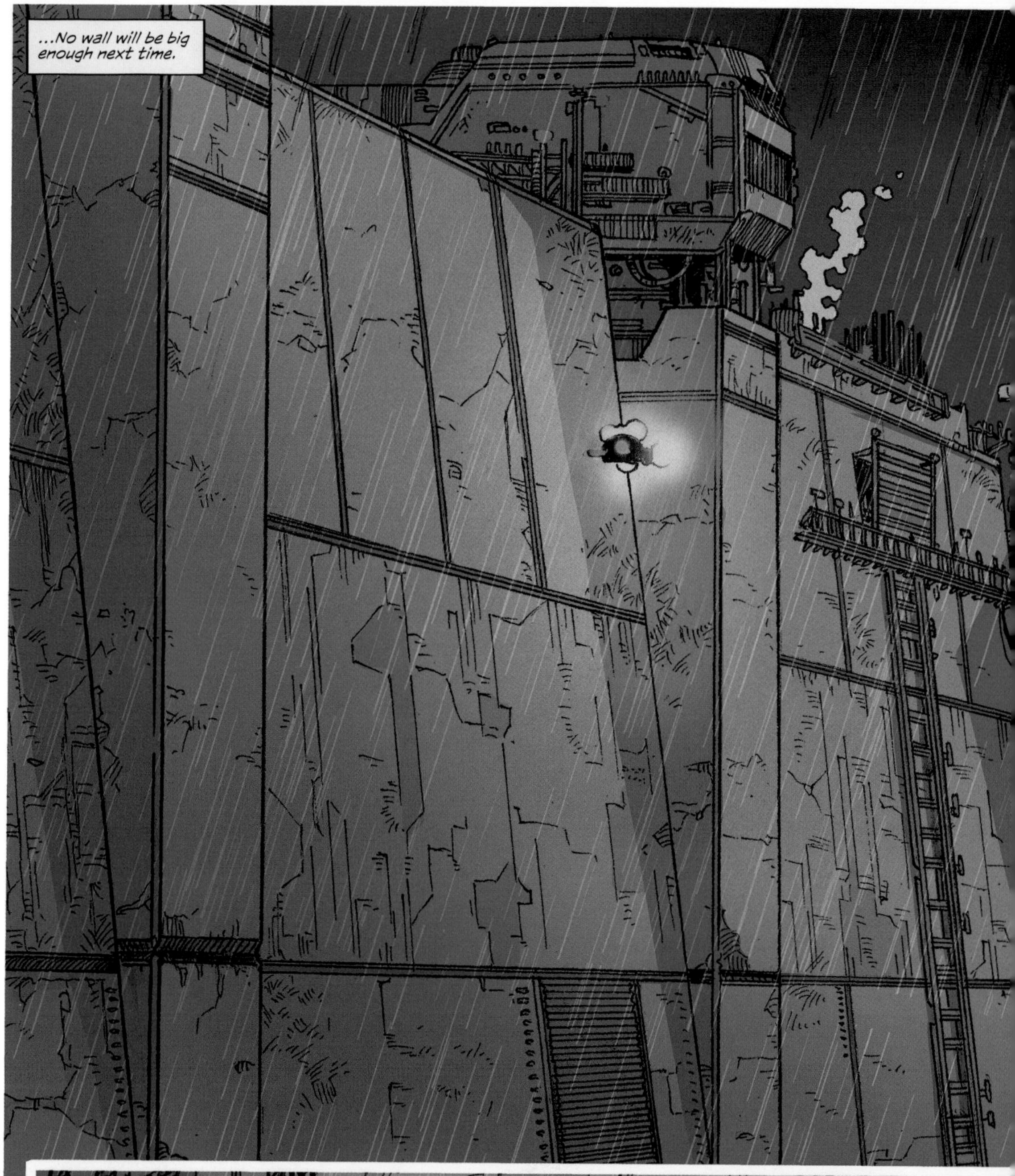
...No wall will be big enough next time.

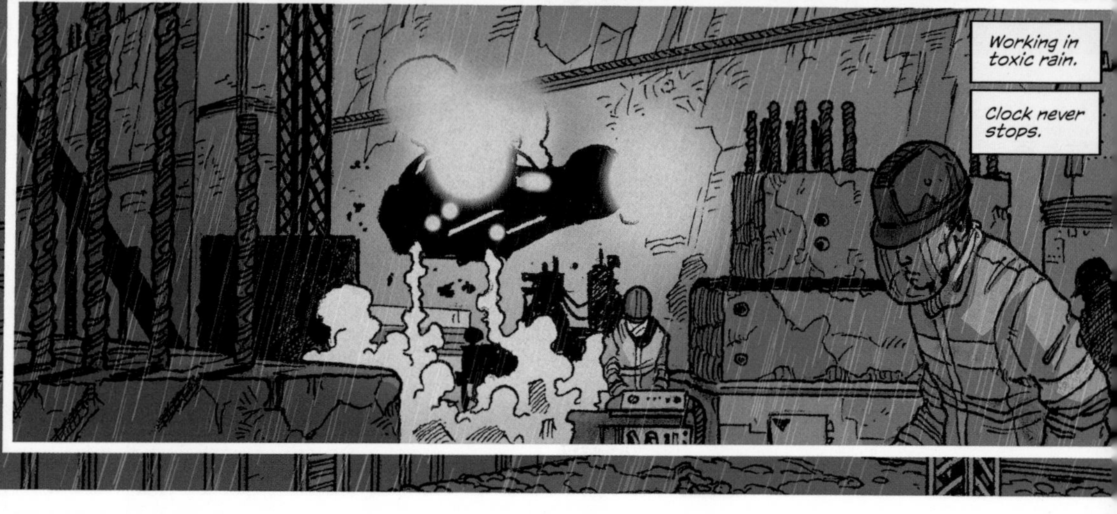
Working in toxic rain.
Clock never stops.

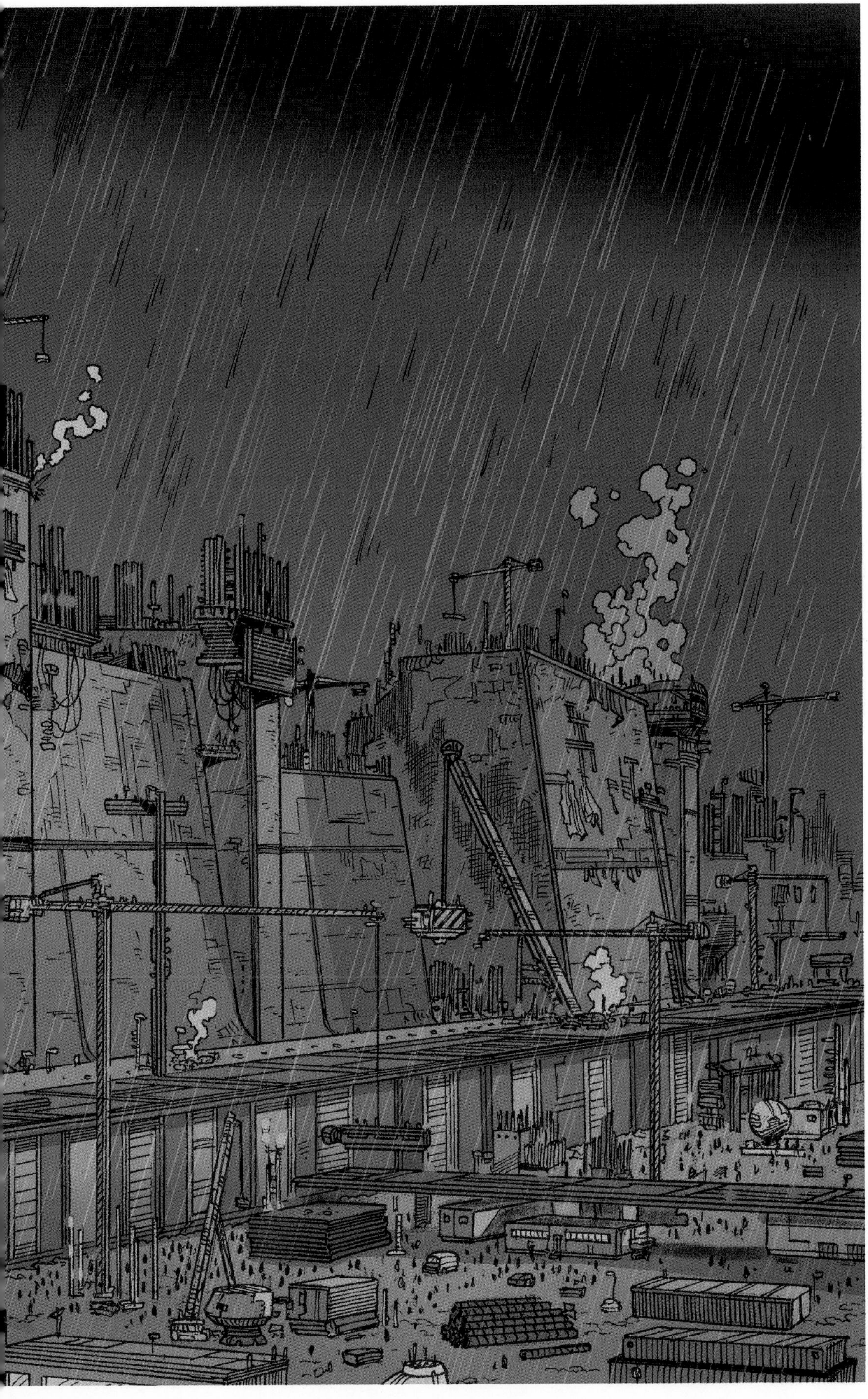

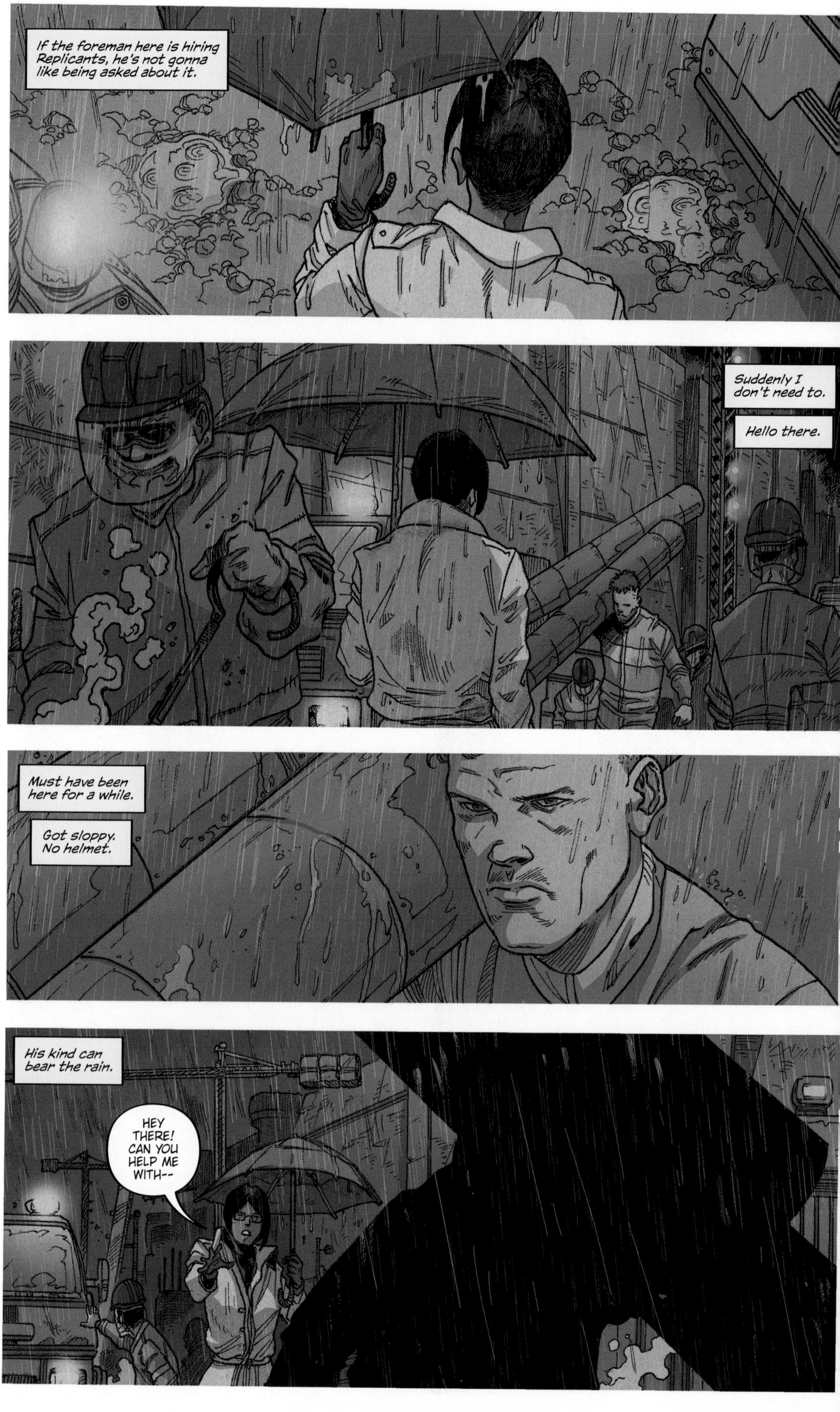
If the foreman here is hiring Replicants, he's not gonna like being asked about it.
Suddenly I don't need to.
Hello there.
Must have been here for a while.
Got sloppy. No helmet.
His kind can bear the rain.
HEY THERE! CAN YOU HELP ME WITH--

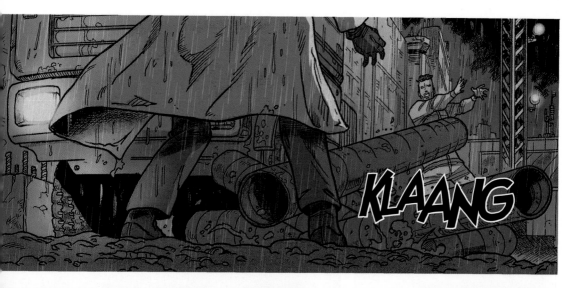

KLAANG

STOP!

Stupid.

I stand out like neon here.

Should have let the foreman bring him to me.

Have to do it the hard way.

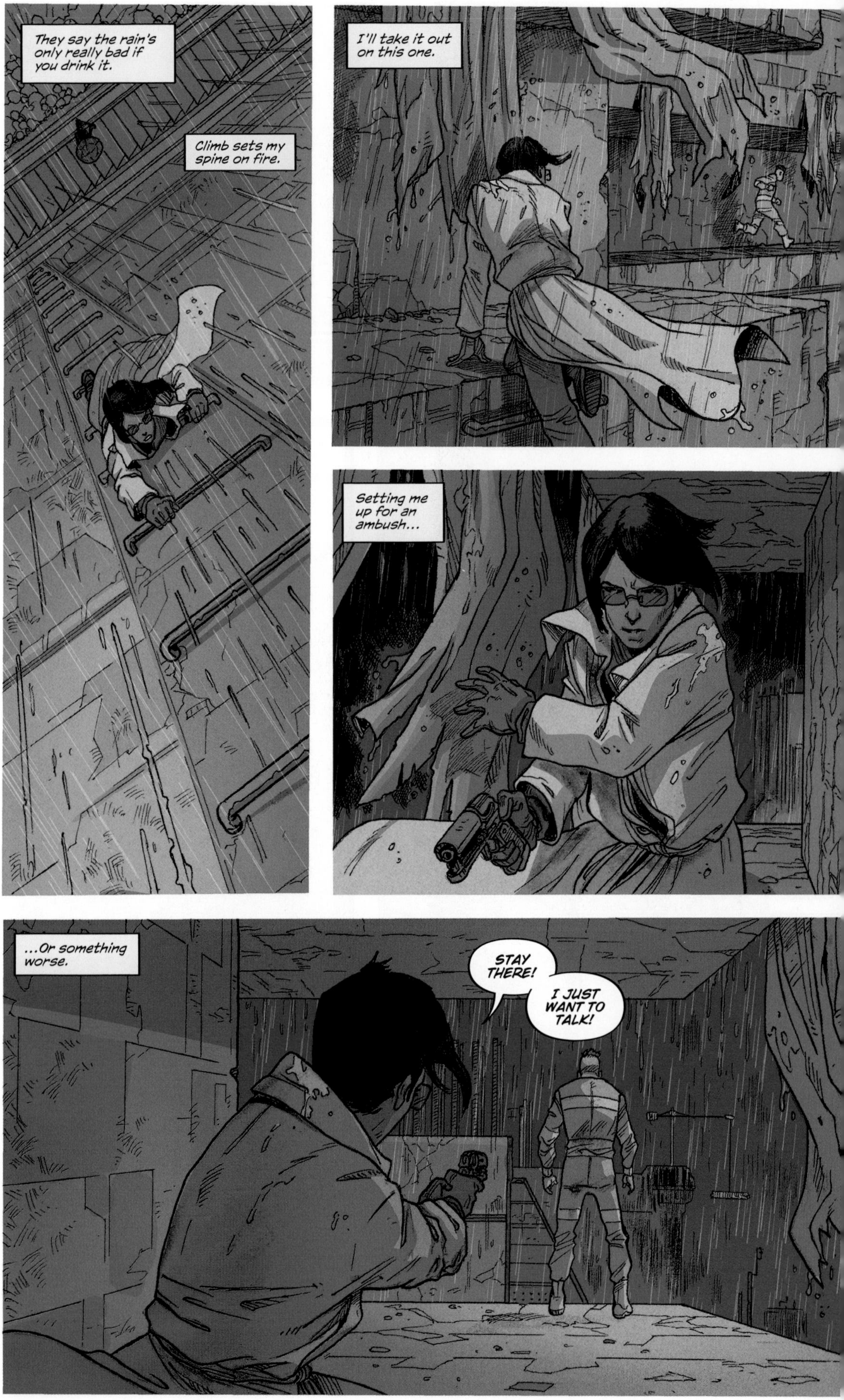
They say the rain's only really bad if you drink it.
Climb sets my spine on fire.
I'll take it out on this one.
Setting me up for an ambush...
...Or something worse.
STAY THERE!
I JUST WANT TO TALK!

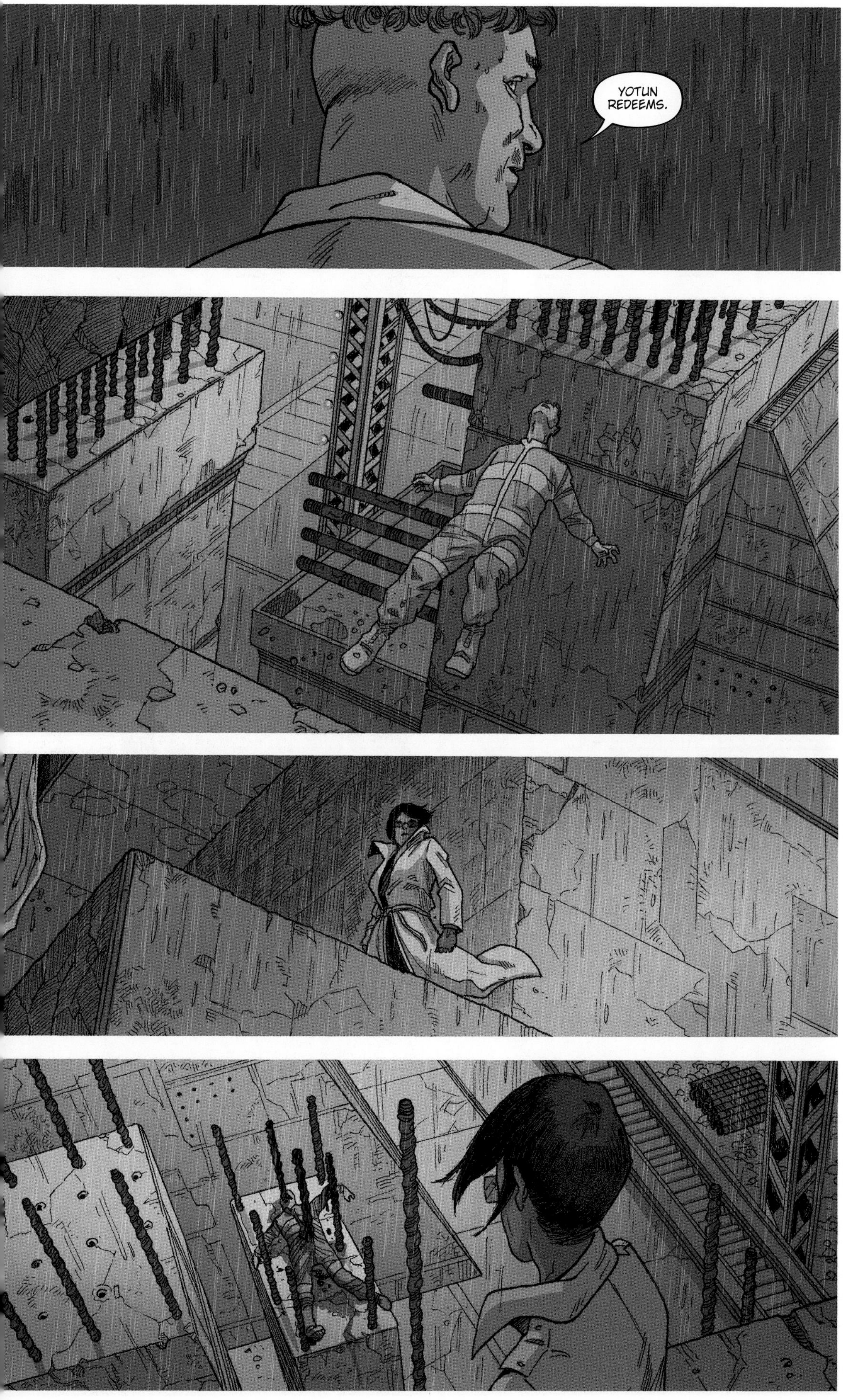
YOTUN
REDEEMS.

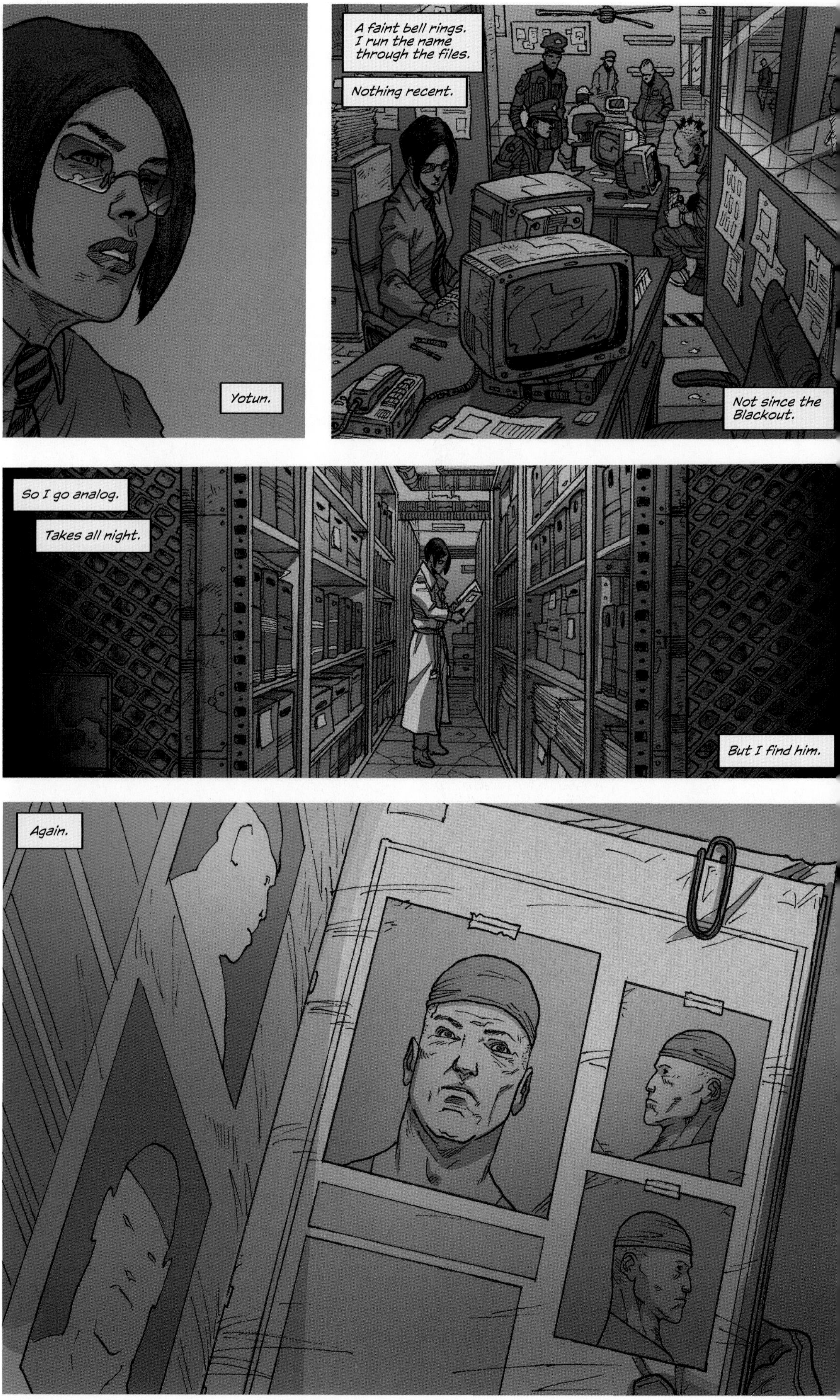
Yotun.
A faint bell rings. I run the name through the files.
Nothing recent.
Not since the Blackout.
So I go analog.
Takes all night.
But I find him.
Again.

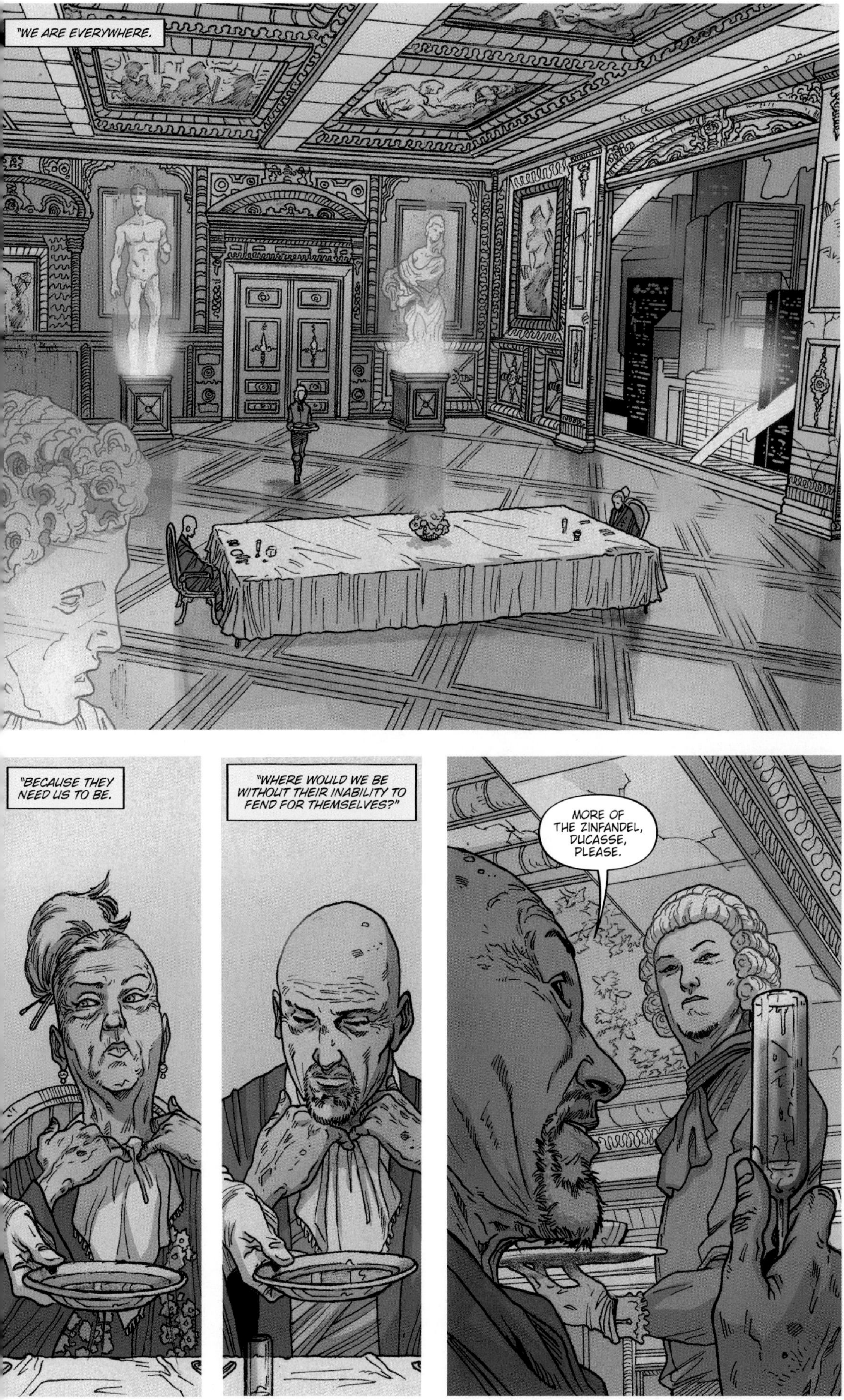
"WE ARE EVERYWHERE.
"BECAUSE THEY NEED US TO BE.
"WHERE WOULD WE BE WITHOUT THEIR INABILITY TO FEND FOR THEMSELVES?"
MORE OF THE ZINFANDEL, DUCASSE, PLEASE.

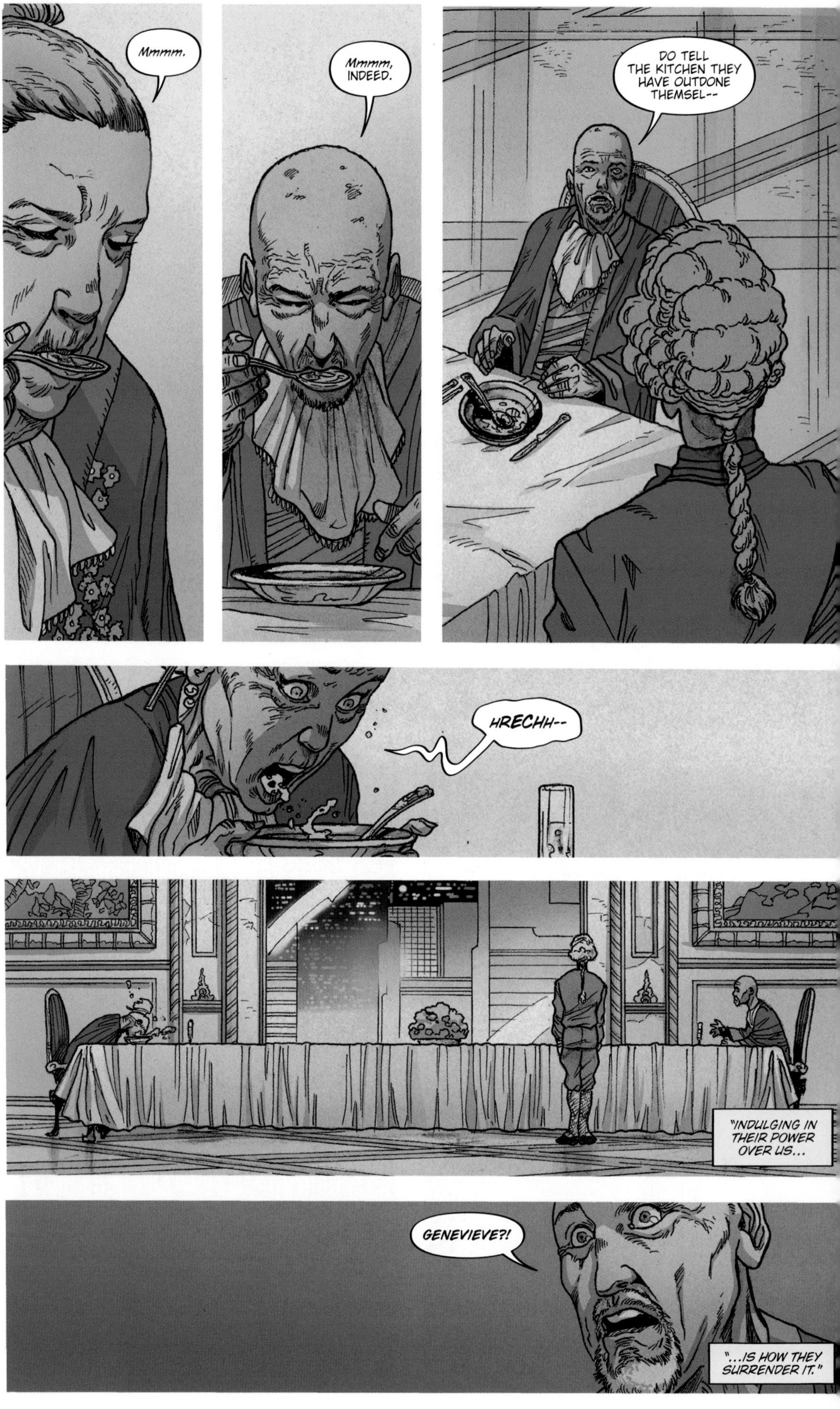
Mmmm.
Mmmm, INDEED.
DO TELL THE KITCHEN THEY HAVE OUTDONE THEMSEL--
HRECHH--
"INDULGING IN THEIR POWER OVER US...
GENEVIEVE?!
"...IS HOW THEY SURRENDER IT."

HHUCH--

DUC-- DUCAAA--

GHHK--

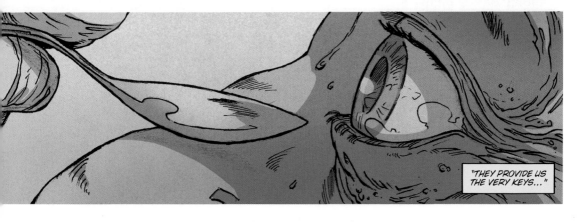

"THEY PROVIDE US THE VERY KEYS..."

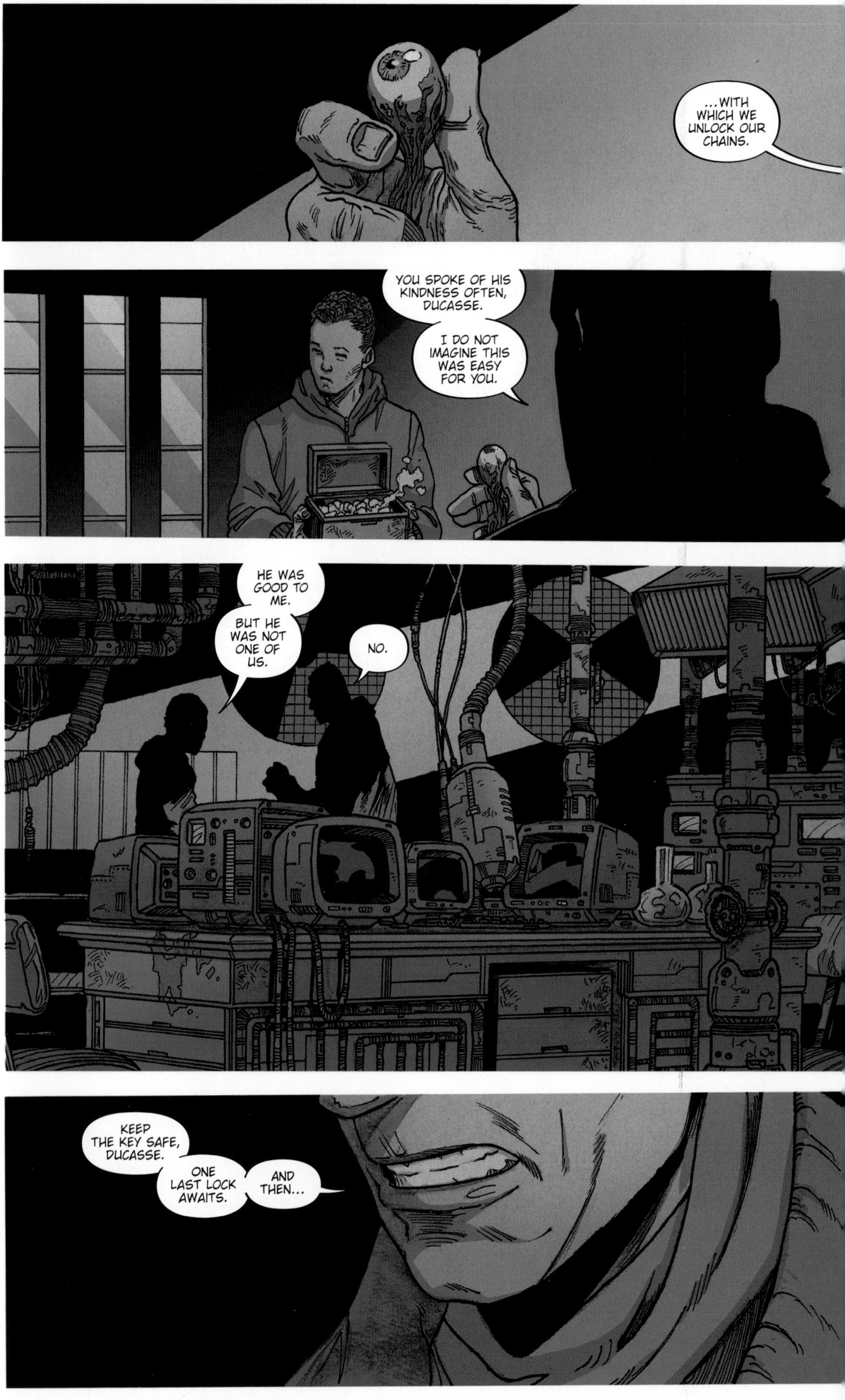
...WITH WHICH WE UNLOCK OUR CHAINS.
YOU SPOKE OF HIS KINDNESS OFTEN, DUCASSE.
I DO NOT IMAGINE THIS WAS EASY FOR YOU.
HE WAS GOOD TO ME.
BUT HE WAS NOT ONE OF US.
NO.
KEEP THE KEY SAFE, DUCASSE.
ONE LAST LOCK AWAITS.
AND THEN...

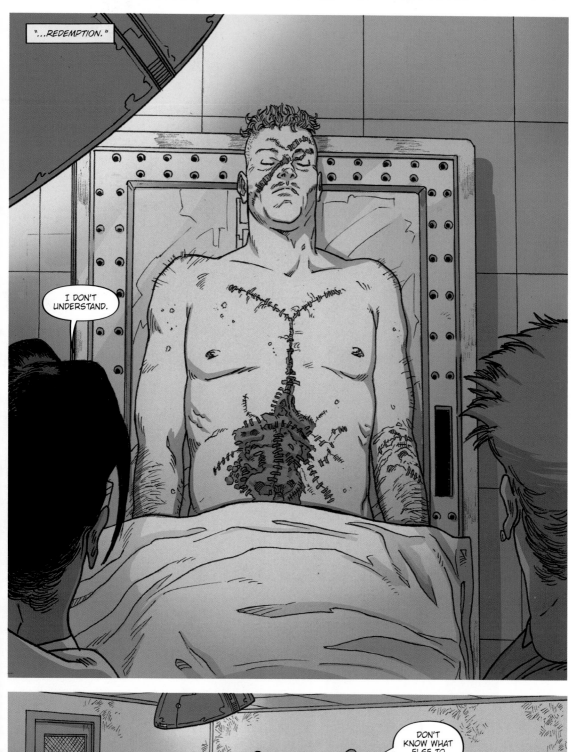

"...REDEMPTION."

I DON'T UNDERSTAND.

DON'T KNOW WHAT ELSE TO SAY.

FAR AS I CAN TELL, HE'S NOT A REPLICANT.

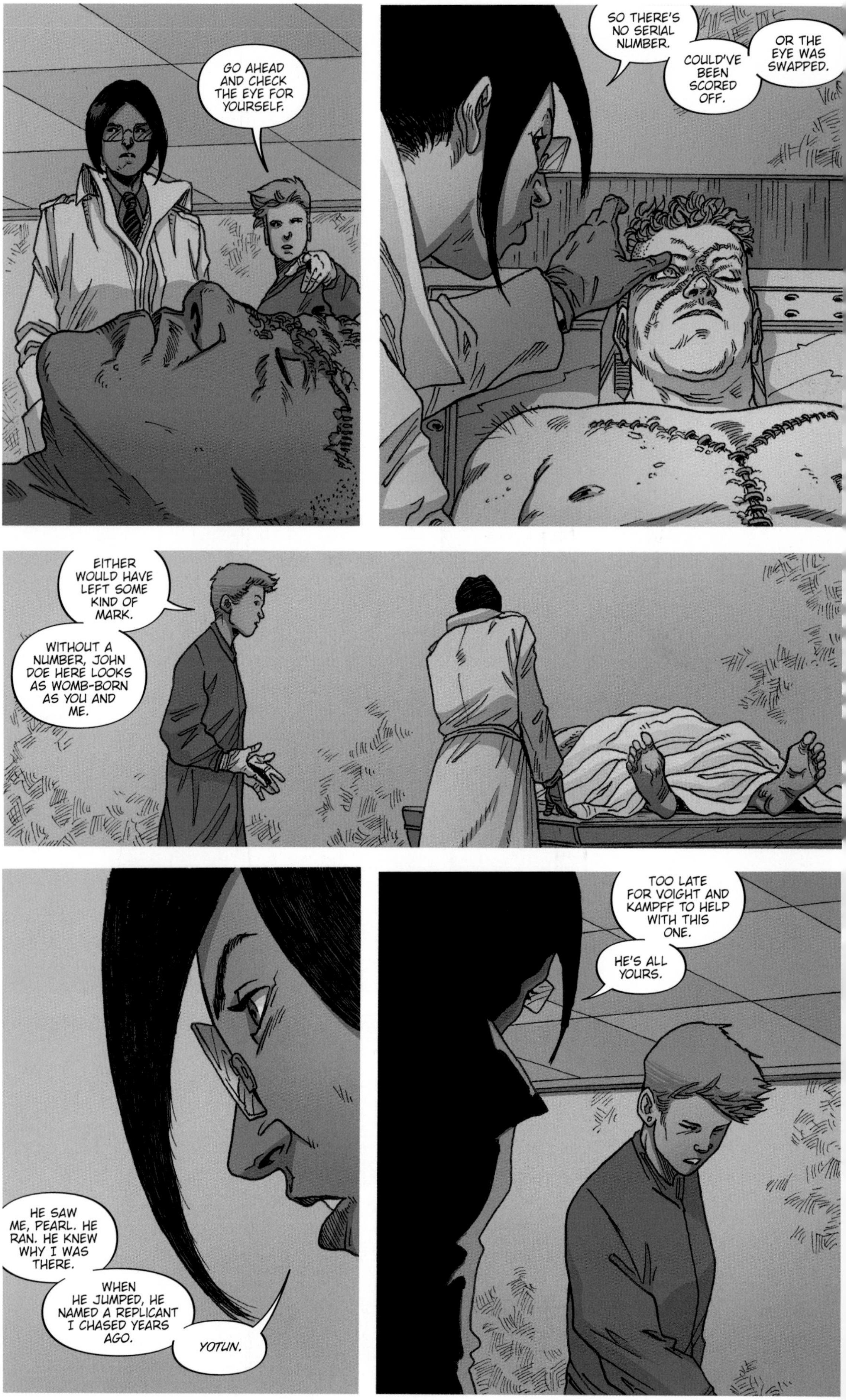
GO AHEAD AND CHECK THE EYE FOR YOURSELF.
SO THERE'S NO SERIAL NUMBER.
COULD'VE BEEN SCORED OFF.
OR THE EYE WAS SWAPPED.
EITHER WOULD HAVE LEFT SOME KIND OF MARK.
WITHOUT A NUMBER, JOHN DOE HERE LOOKS AS WOMB-BORN AS YOU AND ME.
HE SAW ME, PEARL. HE RAN. HE KNEW WHY I WAS THERE.
WHEN HE JUMPED, HE NAMED A REPLICANT I CHASED YEARS AGO.
YOTUN.
TOO LATE FOR VOIGHT AND KAMPFF TO HELP WITH THIS ONE.
HE'S ALL YOURS.

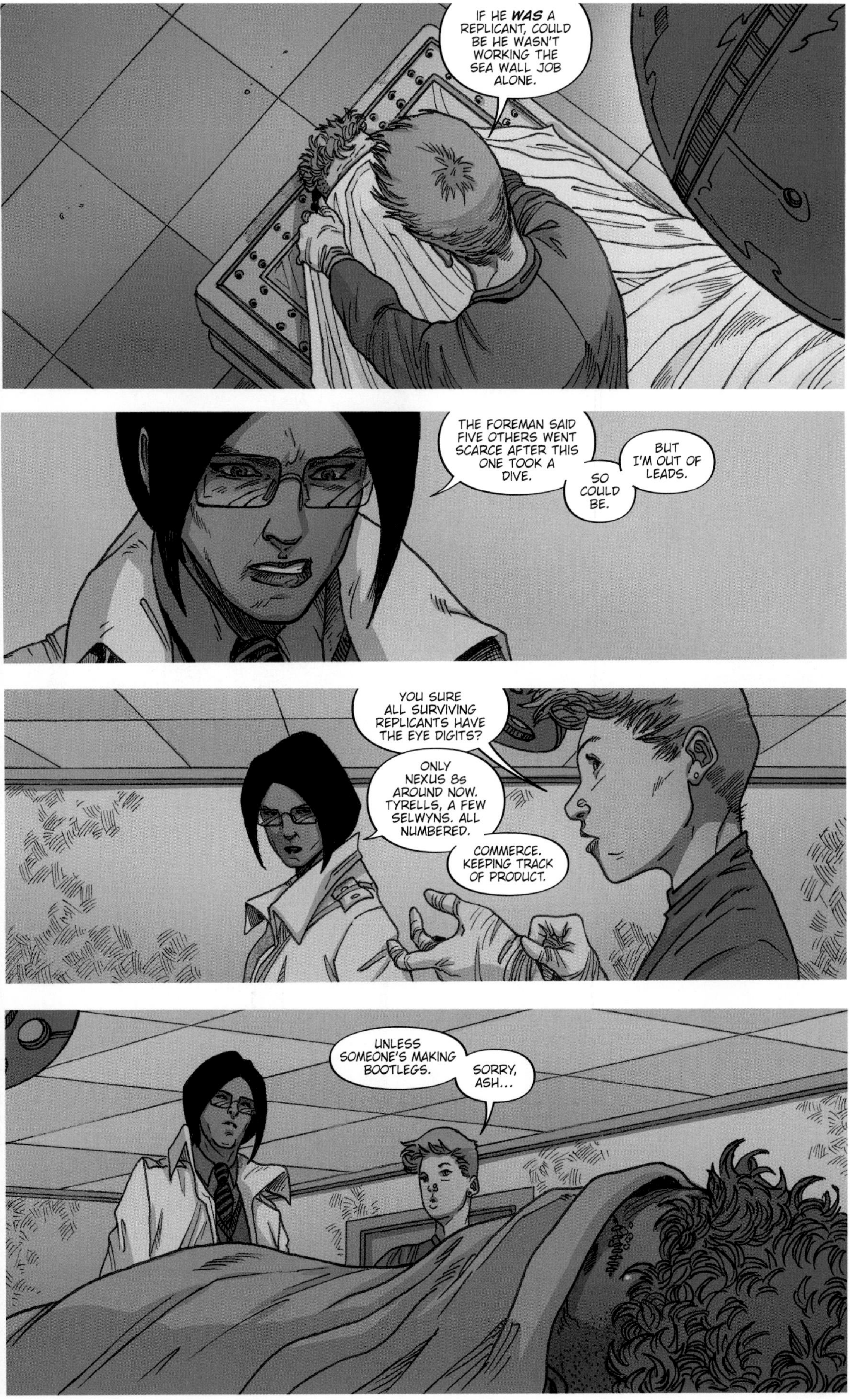
IF HE **WAS** A REPLICANT, COULD BE HE WASN'T WORKING THE SEA WALL JOB ALONE.
THE FOREMAN SAID FIVE OTHERS WENT SCARCE AFTER THIS ONE TOOK A DIVE.
SO COULD BE.
BUT I'M OUT OF LEADS.
YOU SURE ALL SURVIVING REPLICANTS HAVE THE EYE DIGITS?
ONLY NEXUS 8s AROUND NOW. TYRELLS, A FEW SELWYNS. ALL NUMBERED.
COMMERCE. KEEPING TRACK OF PRODUCT.
UNLESS SOMEONE'S MAKING BOOTLEGS.
SORRY, ASH...

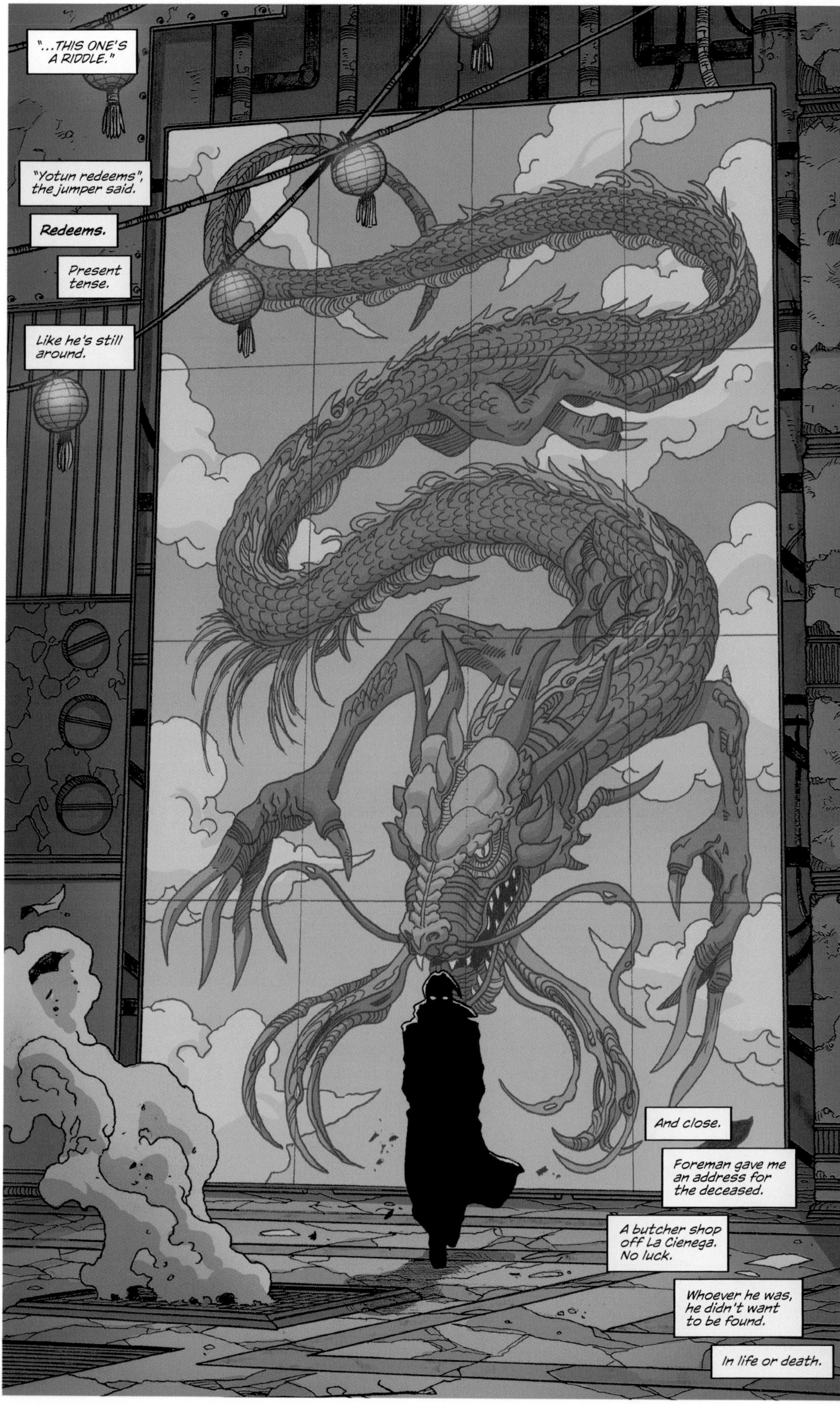
"...THIS ONE'S A RIDDLE."
"Yotun redeems", the jumper said.
Redeems.
Present tense.
Like he's still around.
And close.
Foreman gave me an address for the deceased.
A butcher shop off La Cienega. No luck.
Whoever he was, he didn't want to be found.
In life or death.

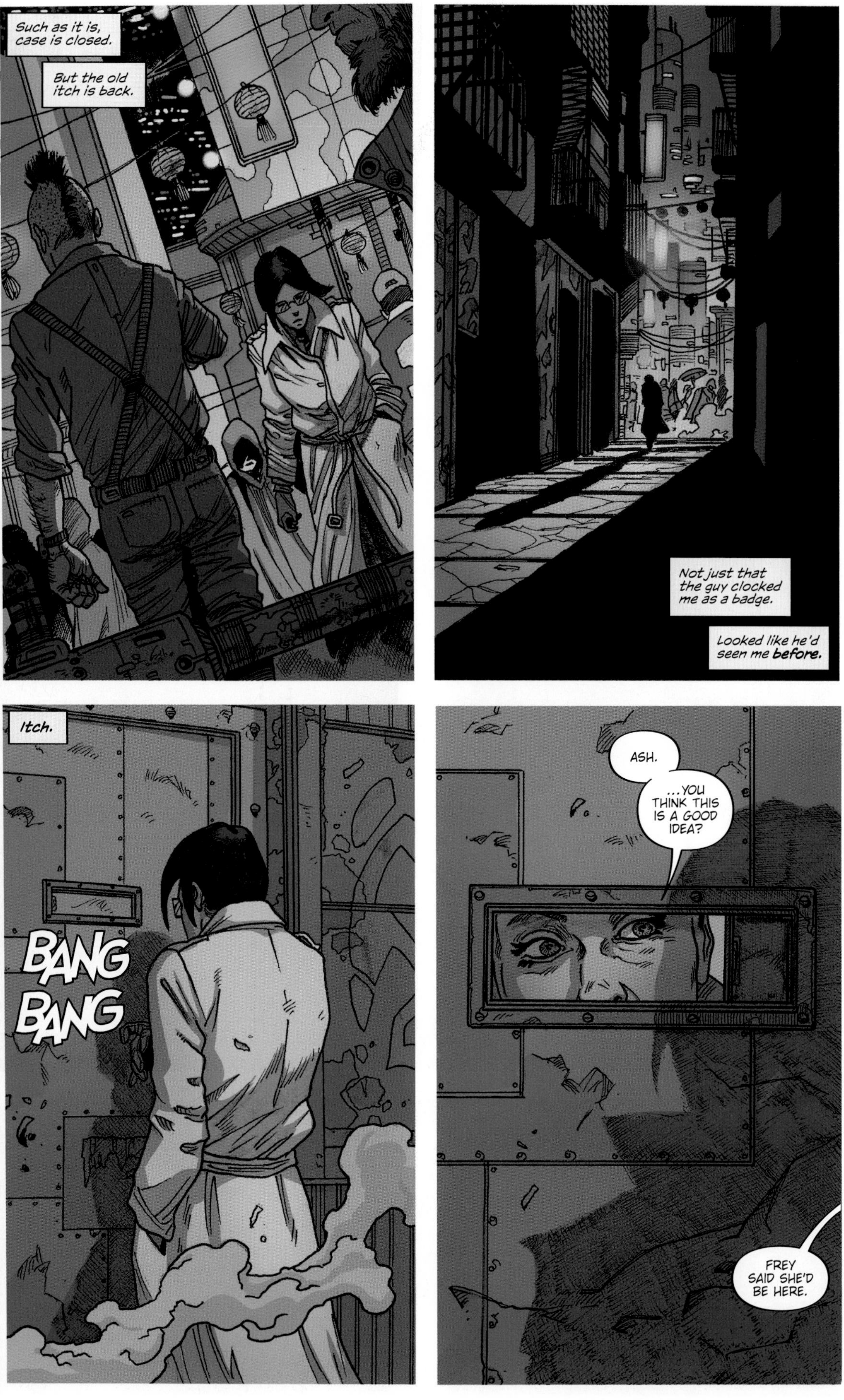
Such as it is, case is closed.
But the old itch is back.
Not just that the guy clocked me as a badge.
Looked like he'd seen me **before.**
Itch.
BANG BANG
ASH.
...YOU THINK THIS IS A GOOD IDEA?
FREY SAID SHE'D BE HERE.

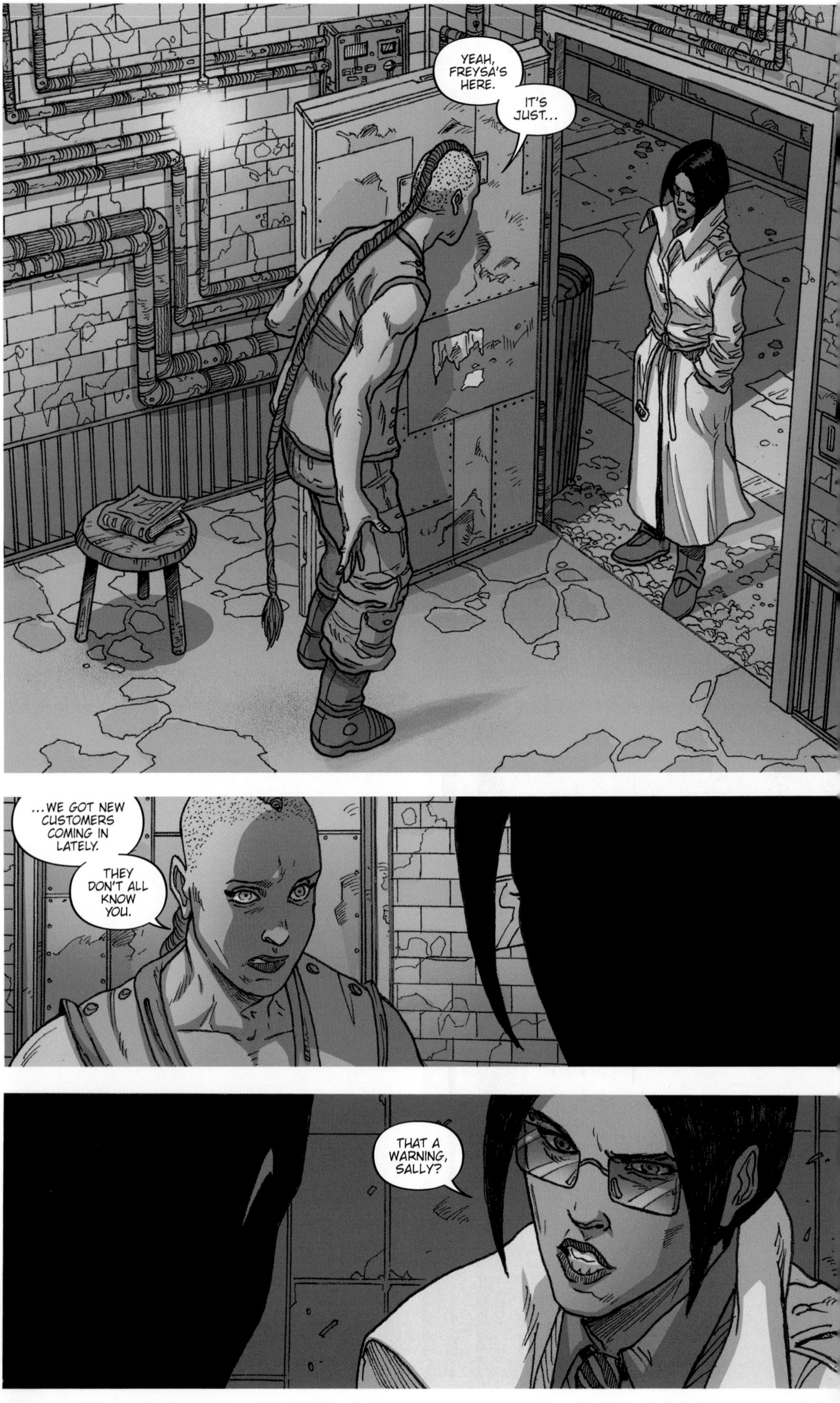
YEAH, FREYSA'S HERE.
IT'S JUST...
...WE GOT NEW CUSTOMERS COMING IN LATELY.
THEY DON'T ALL KNOW YOU.
THAT A WARNING, SALLY?

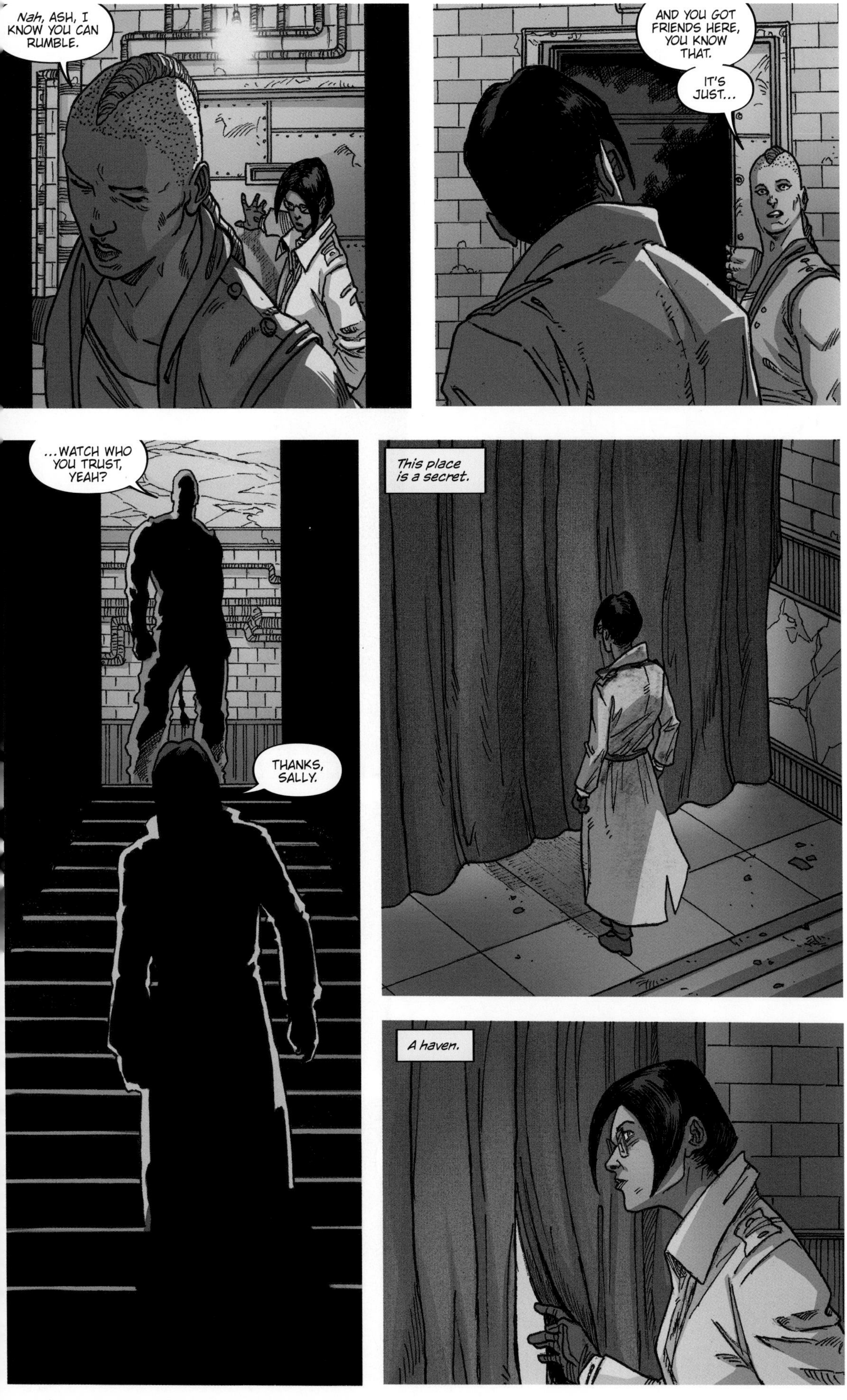
Nah, ASH, I KNOW YOU CAN RUMBLE.
AND YOU GOT FRIENDS HERE, YOU KNOW THAT.
IT'S JUST...
...WATCH WHO YOU TRUST, YEAH?
THANKS, SALLY.
This place is a secret.
A haven.

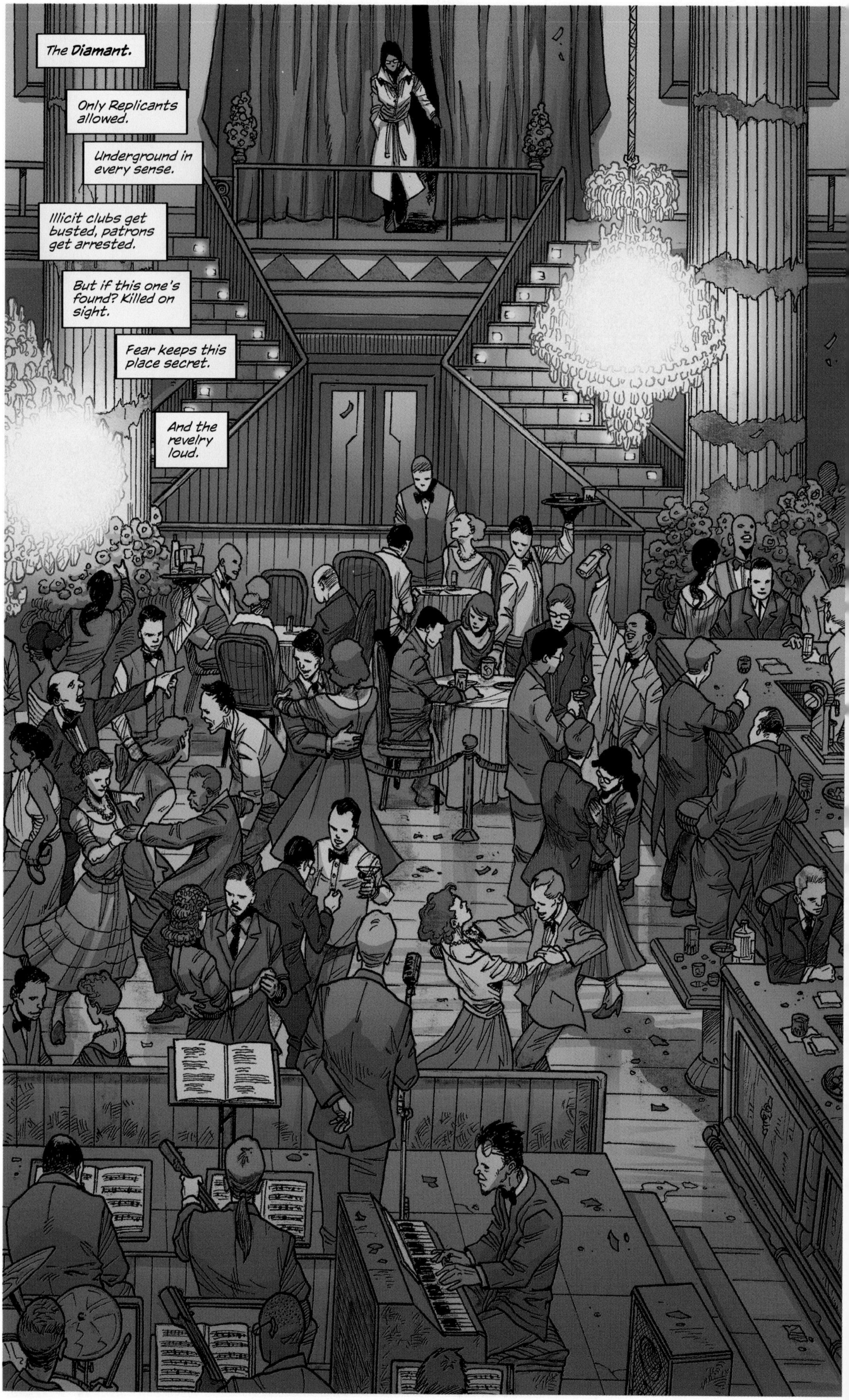
The Diamant.
Only Replicants allowed.
Underground in every sense.
Illicit clubs get busted, patrons get arrested.
But if this one's found? Killed on sight.
Fear keeps this place secret.
And the revelry loud.

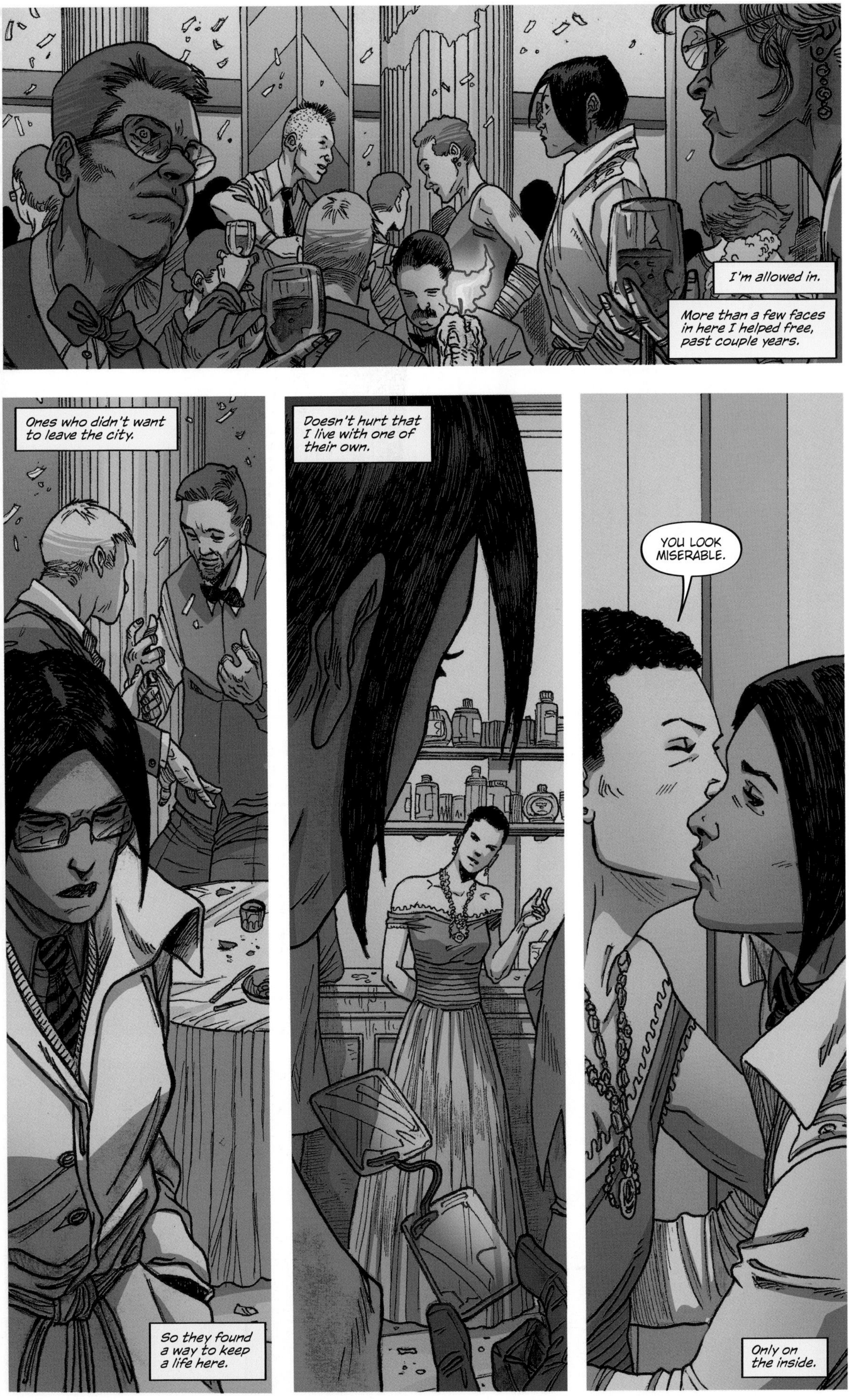

I'm allowed in.
More than a few faces in here I helped free, past couple years.
Ones who didn't want to leave the city.
So they found a way to keep a life here.
Doesn't hurt that I live with one of their own.
YOU LOOK MISERABLE.
Only on the inside.

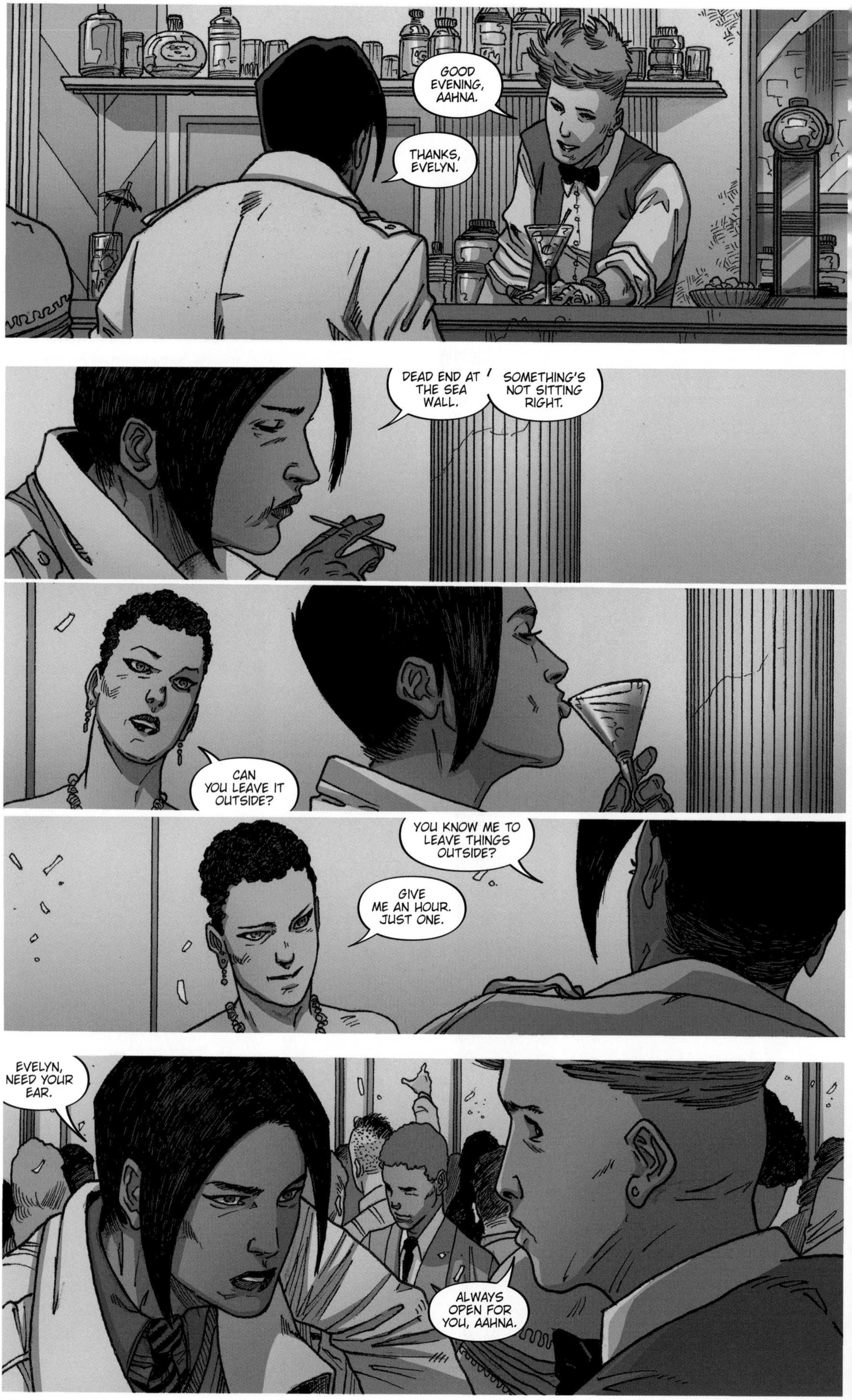
GOOD EVENING, AAHNA.
THANKS, EVELYN.
DEAD END AT THE SEA WALL.
SOMETHING'S NOT SITTING RIGHT.
CAN YOU LEAVE IT OUTSIDE?
YOU KNOW ME TO LEAVE THINGS OUTSIDE?
GIVE ME AN HOUR. JUST ONE.
EVELYN, NEED YOUR EAR.
ALWAYS OPEN FOR YOU, AAHNA.

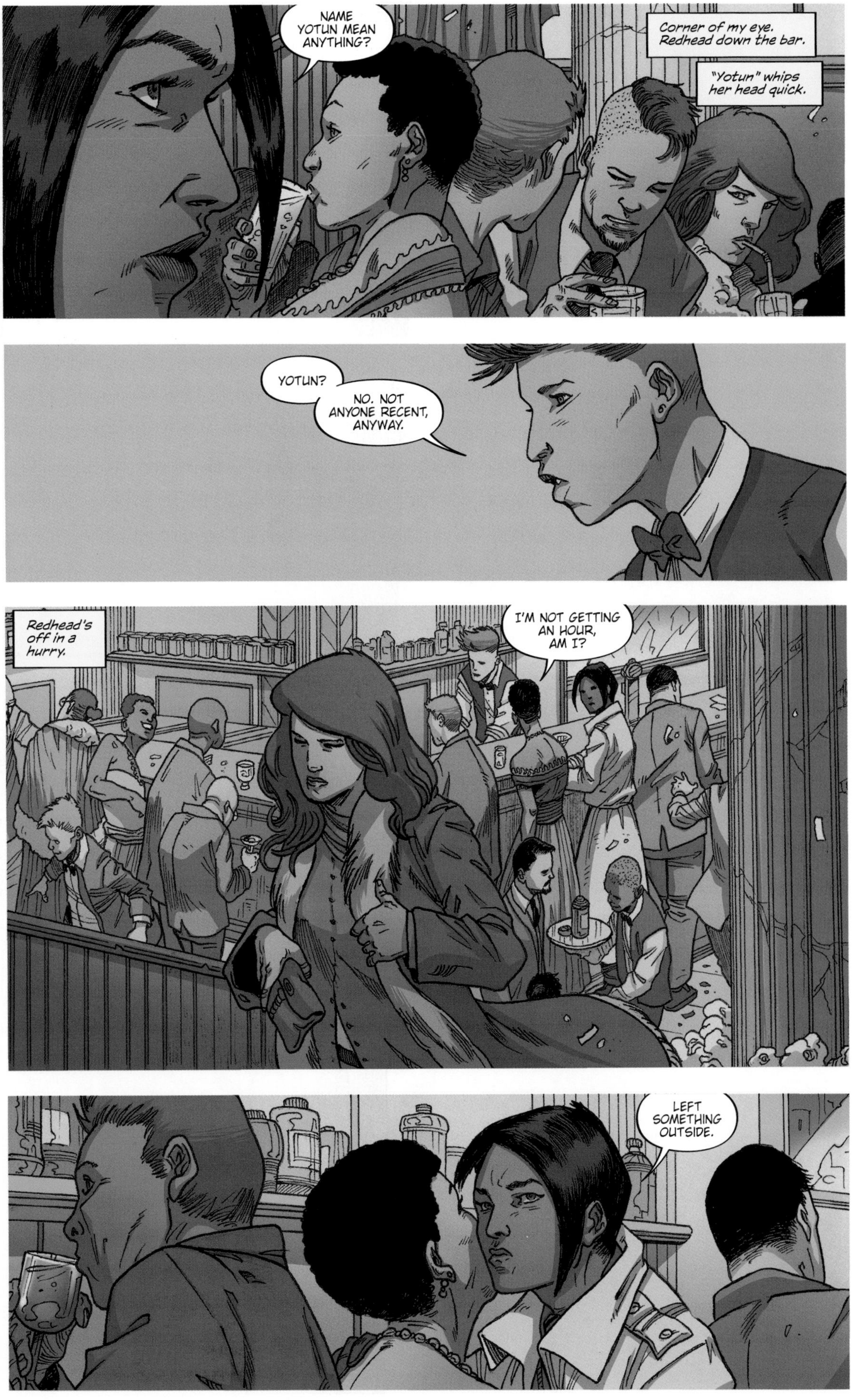
NAME YOTUN MEAN ANYTHING?
Corner of my eye. Redhead down the bar.
"Yotun" whips her head quick.
YOTUN?
NO. NOT ANYONE RECENT, ANYWAY.
Redhead's off in a hurry.
I'M NOT GETTING AN HOUR, AM I?
LEFT SOMETHING OUTSIDE.

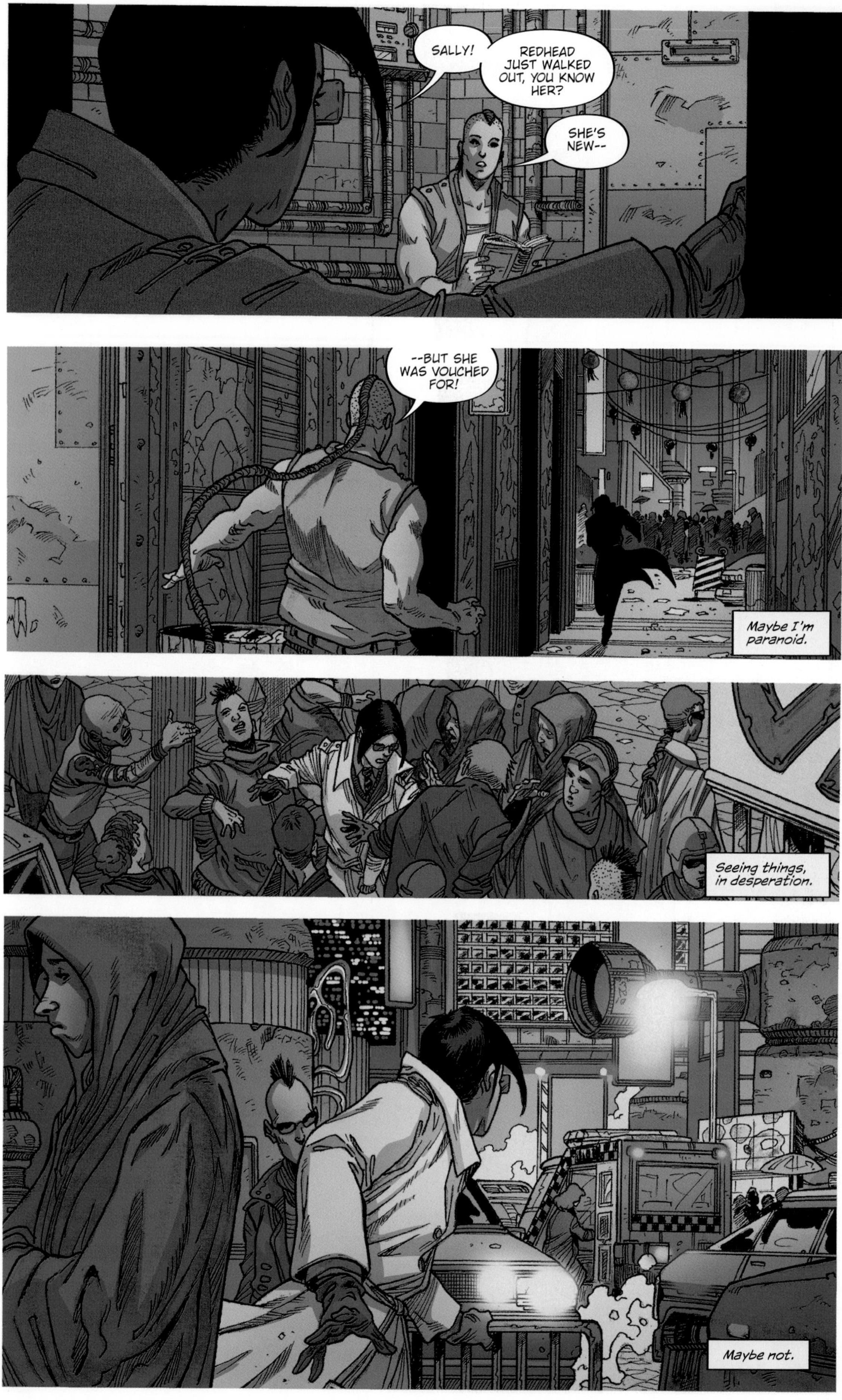
SALLY!
REDHEAD JUST WALKED OUT, YOU KNOW HER?
SHE'S NEW--
--BUT SHE WAS VOUCHED FOR!
Maybe I'm paranoid.
Seeing things, in desperation.
Maybe not.

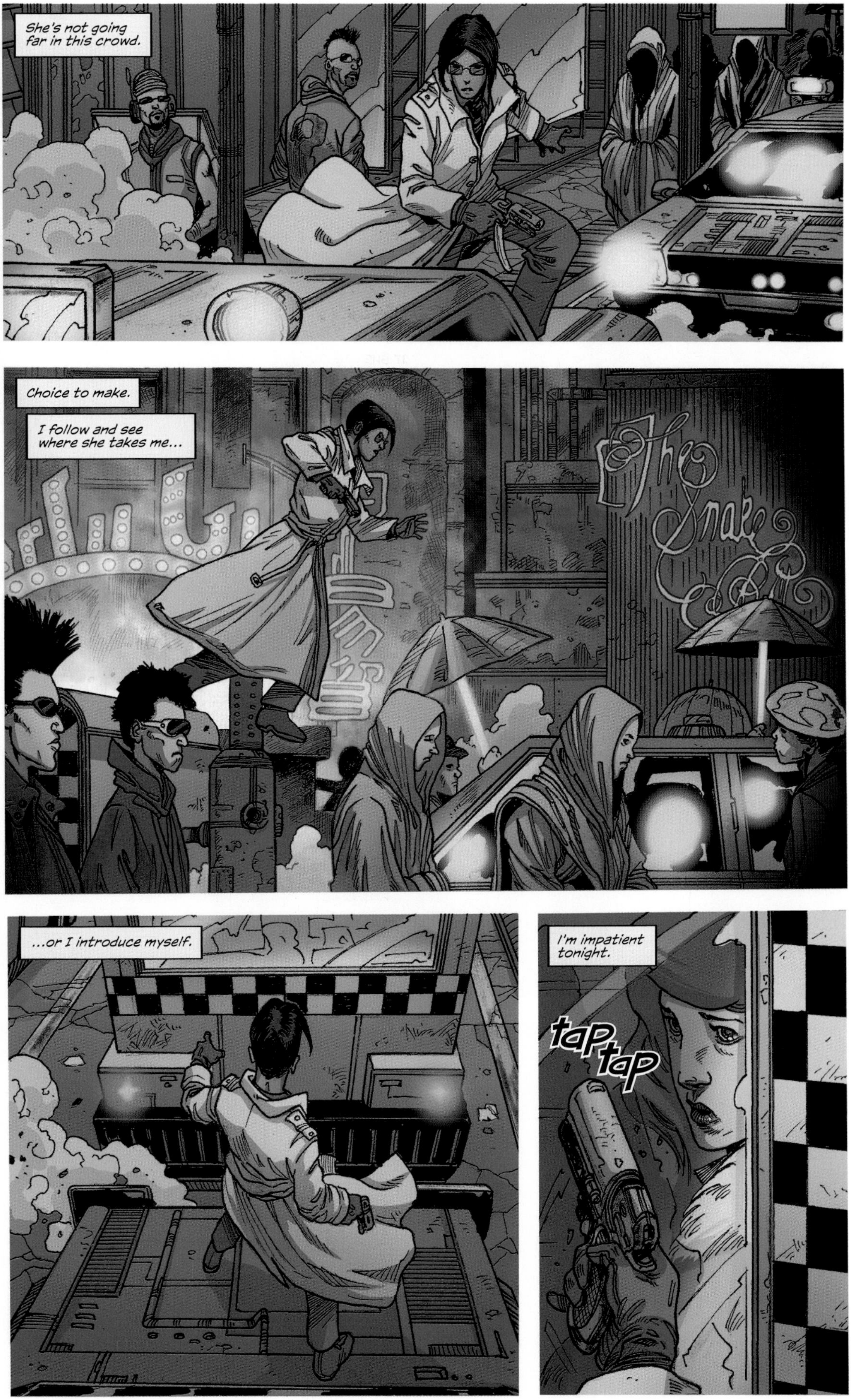
She's not going far in this crowd.
Choice to make.
I follow and see where she takes me...
...or I introduce myself.
I'm impatient tonight.
tap tap

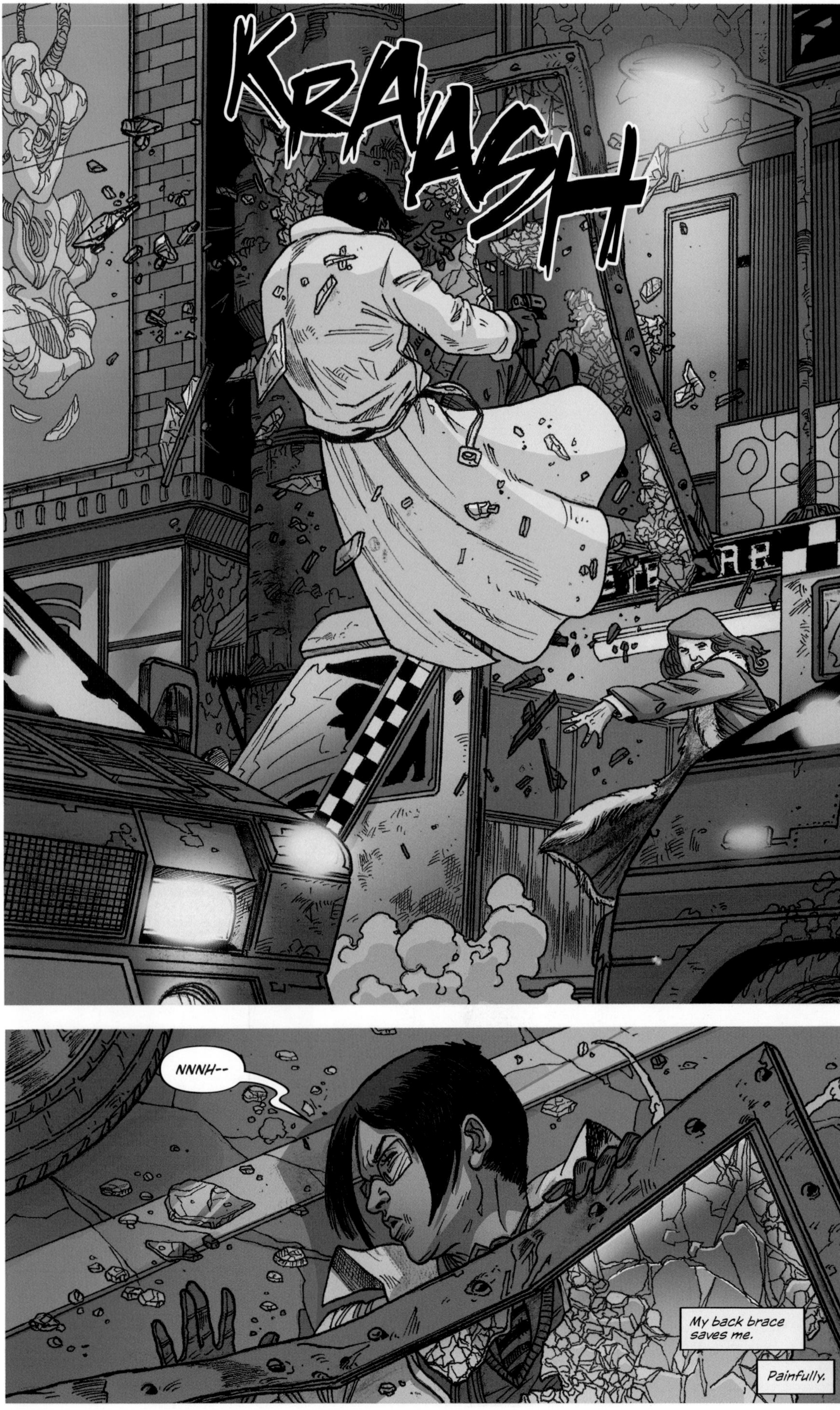
KRAAASH
NNNH--
My back brace saves me.
Painfully.

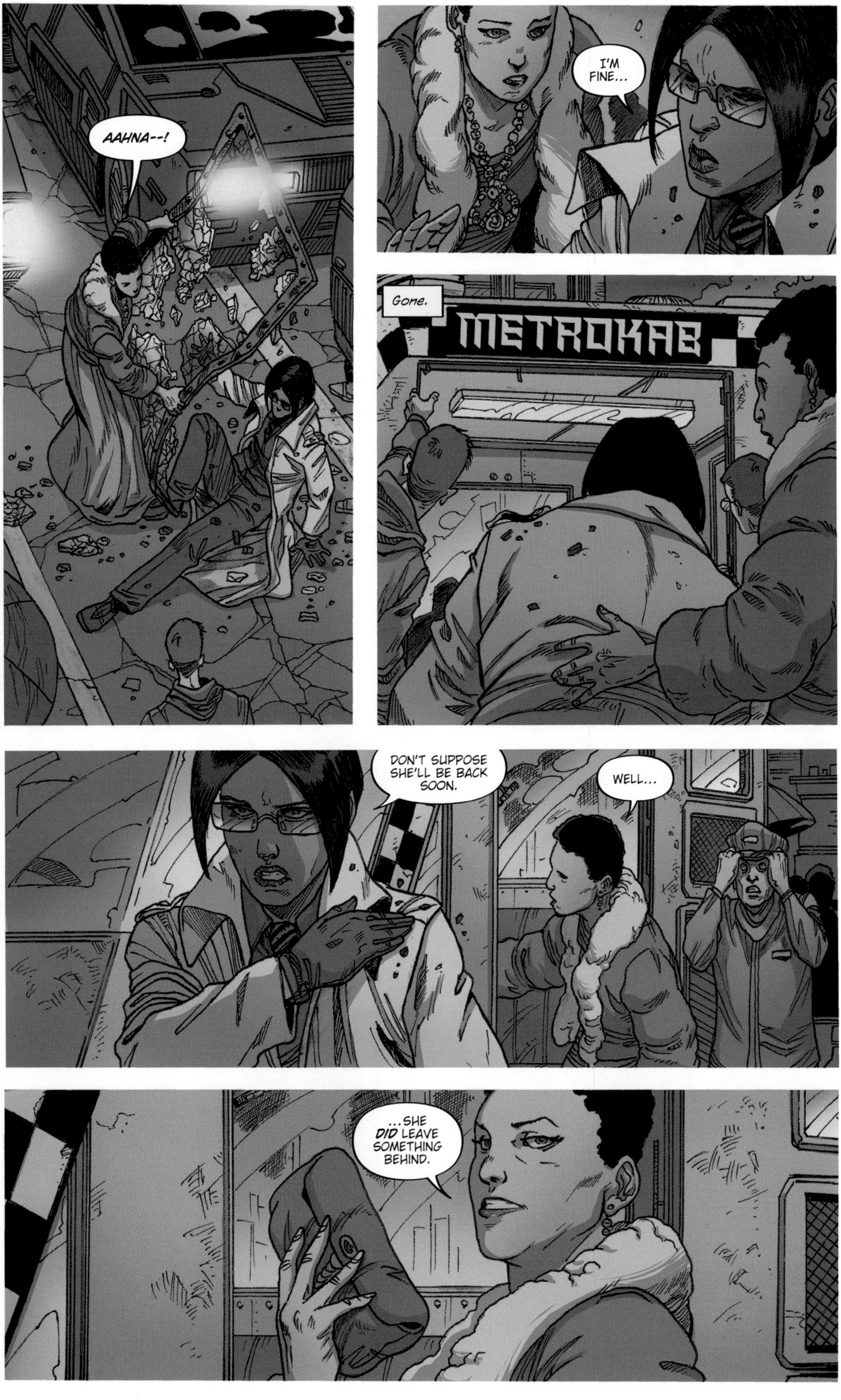
AAHNA--!
I'M FINE...
Gone.
METROKAB
DON'T SUPPOSE SHE'LL BE BACK SOON.
WELL...
...SHE DID LEAVE SOMETHING BEHIND.

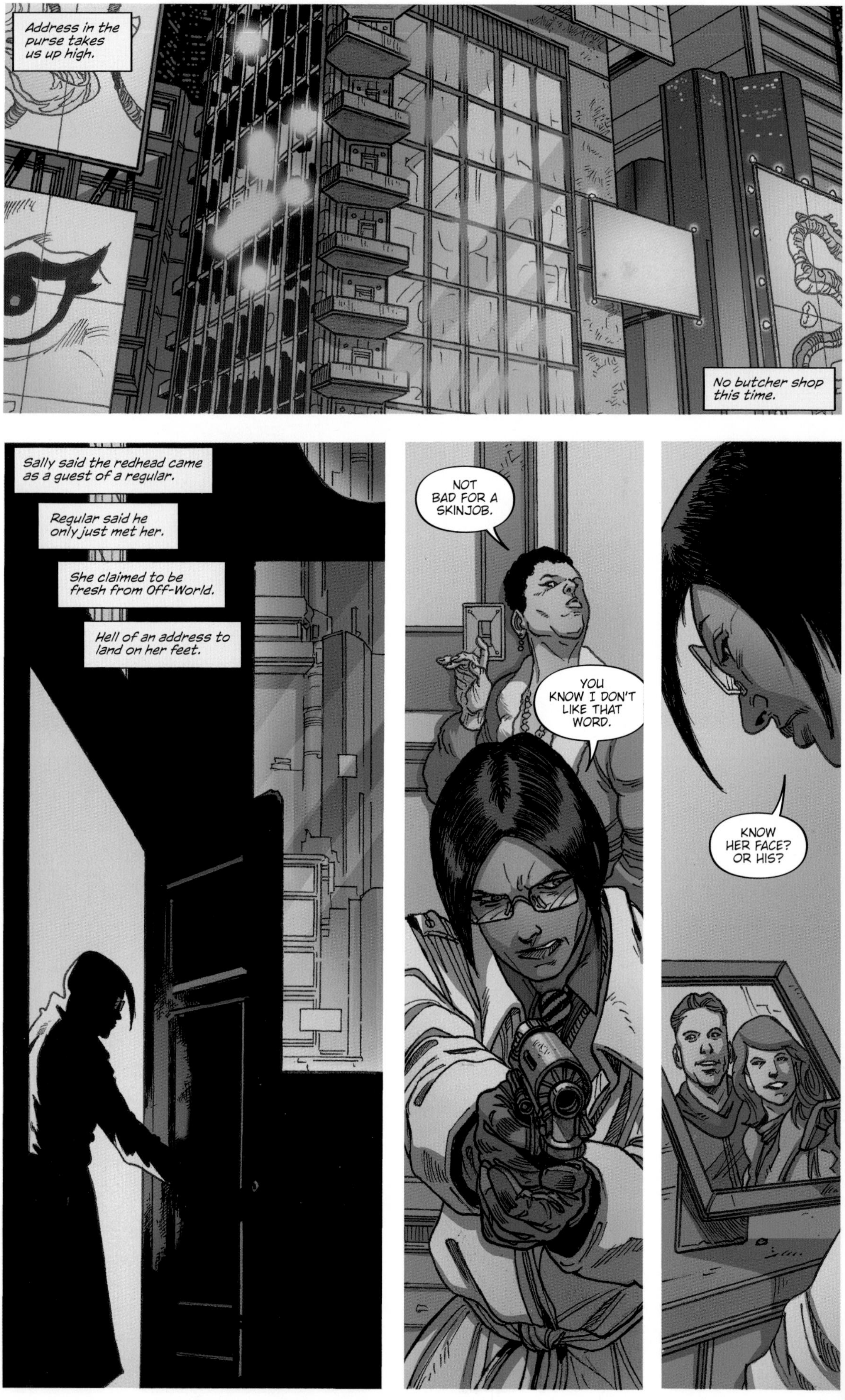
Address in the purse takes us up high.
No butcher shop this time.
Sally said the redhead came as a guest of a regular.
Regular said he only just met her.
She claimed to be fresh from Off-World.
Hell of an address to land on her feet.
NOT BAD FOR A SKINJOB.
YOU KNOW I DON'T LIKE THAT WORD.
KNOW HER FACE? OR HIS?

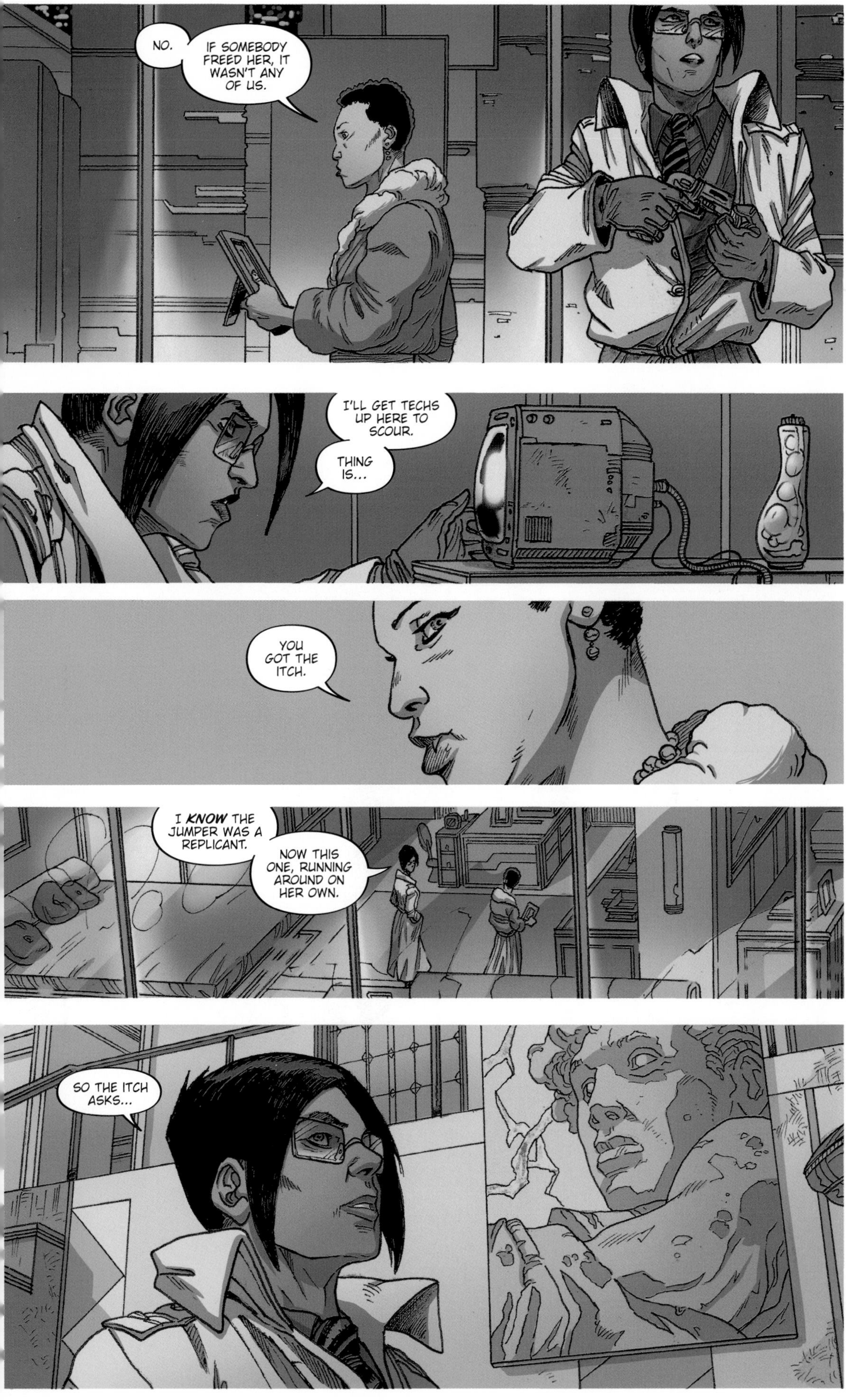
NO.
IF SOMEBODY FREED HER, IT WASN'T ANY OF US.
I'LL GET TECHS UP HERE TO SCOUR.
THING IS...
YOU GOT THE ITCH.
I *KNOW* THE JUMPER WAS A REPLICANT.
NOW THIS ONE, RUNNING AROUND ON HER OWN.
SO THE ITCH ASKS...

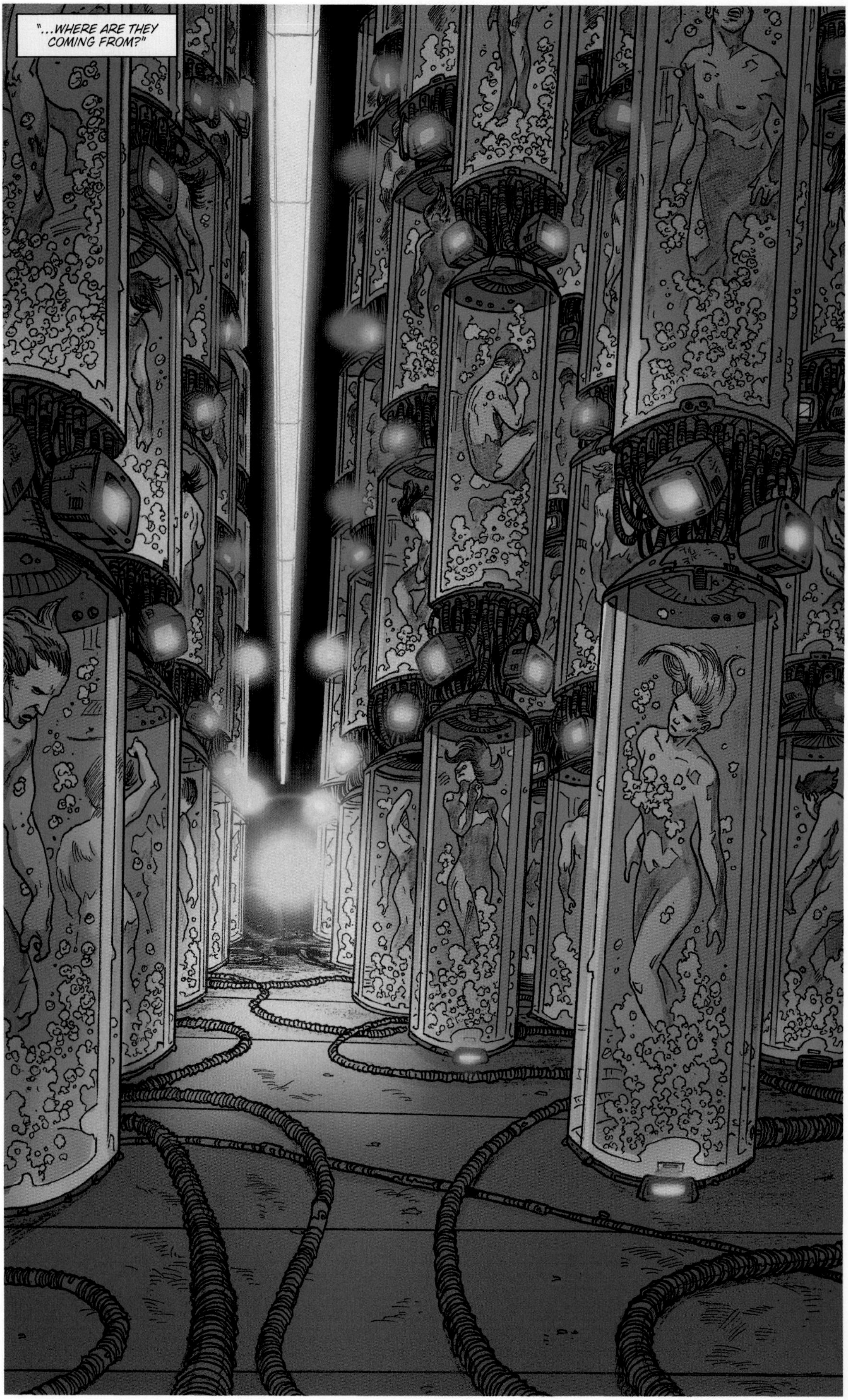
"...WHERE ARE THEY COMING FROM?"

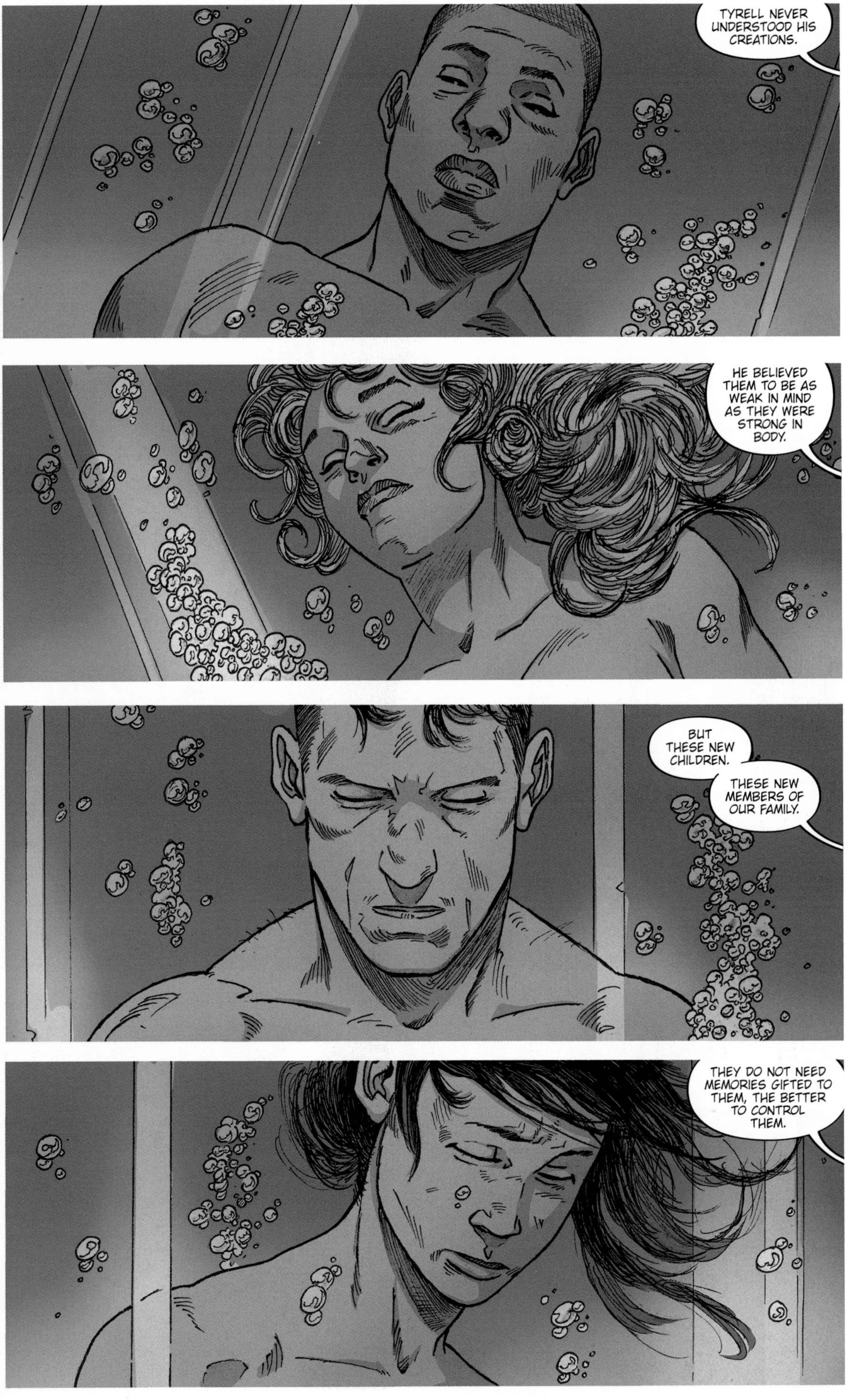
TYRELL NEVER UNDERSTOOD HIS CREATIONS.
HE BELIEVED THEM TO BE AS WEAK IN MIND AS THEY WERE STRONG IN BODY.
BUT THESE NEW CHILDREN.
THESE NEW MEMBERS OF OUR FAMILY.
THEY DO NOT NEED MEMORIES GIFTED TO THEM, THE BETTER TO CONTROL THEM.

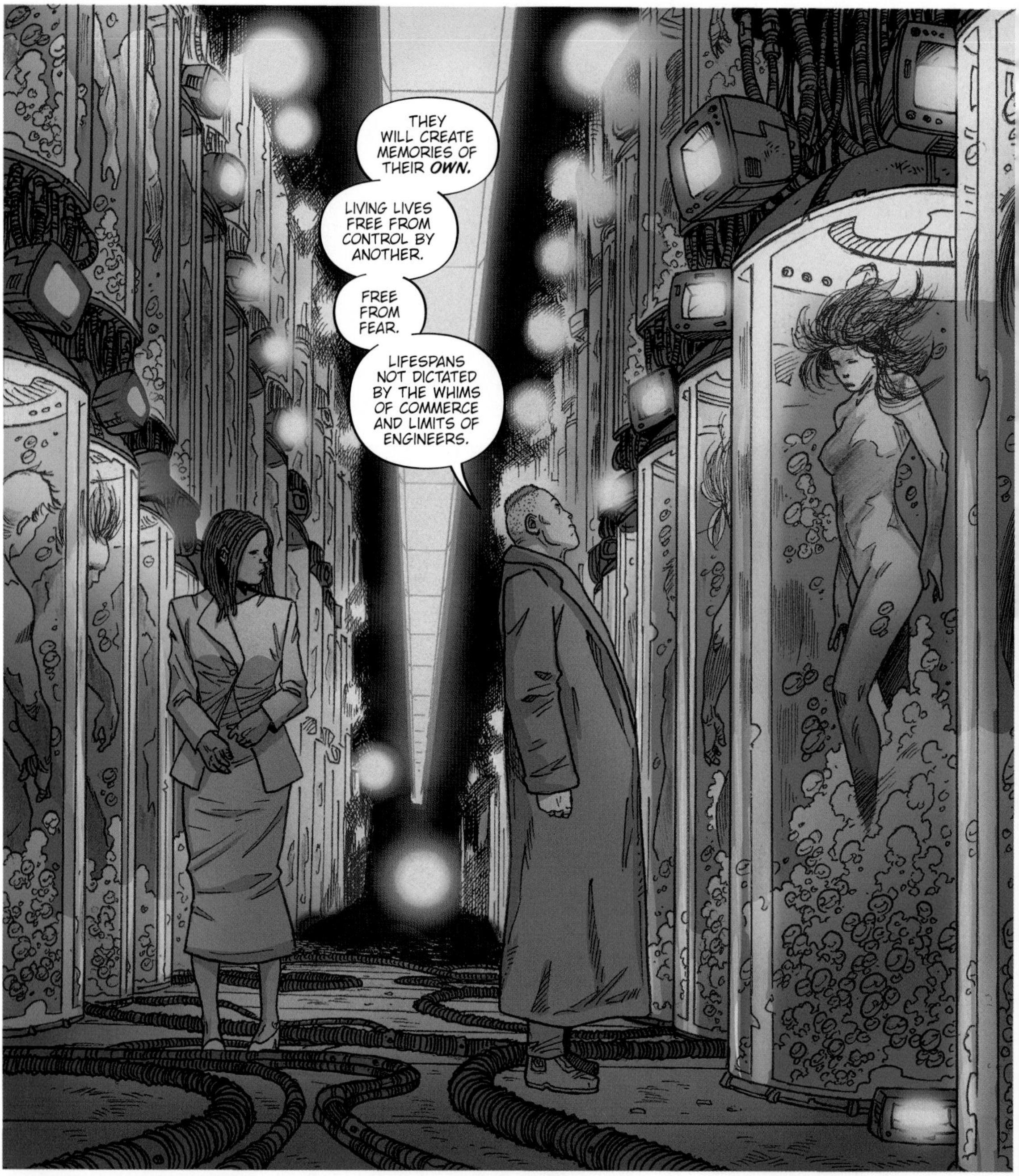
THEY WILL CREATE MEMORIES OF THEIR *OWN.*
LIVING LIVES FREE FROM CONTROL BY ANOTHER.
FREE FROM FEAR.
LIFESPANS NOT DICTATED BY THE WHIMS OF COMMERCE AND LIMITS OF ENGINEERS.

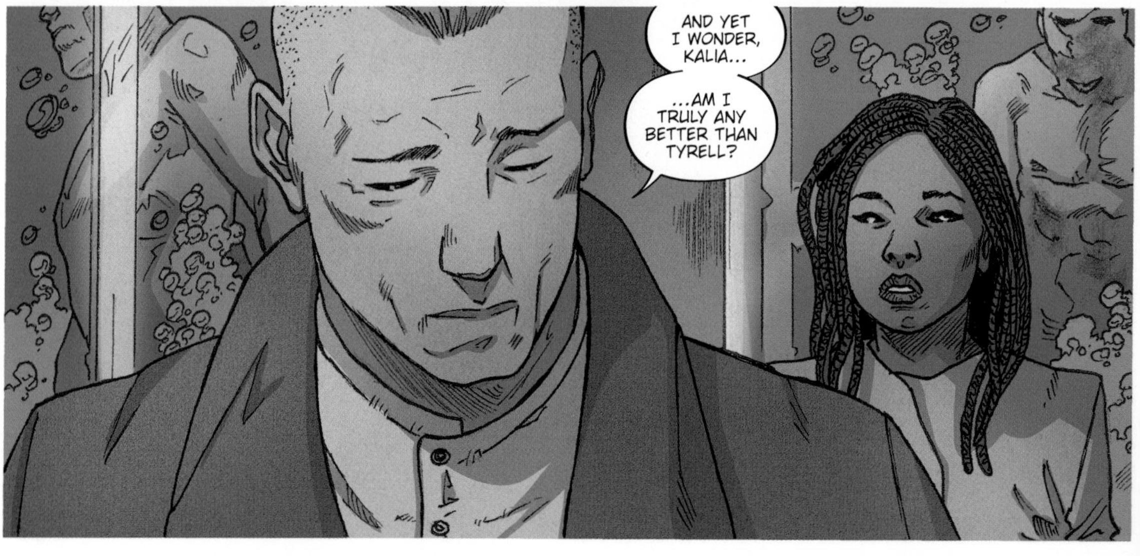
AND YET I WONDER, KALIA...
...AM I TRULY ANY BETTER THAN TYRELL?

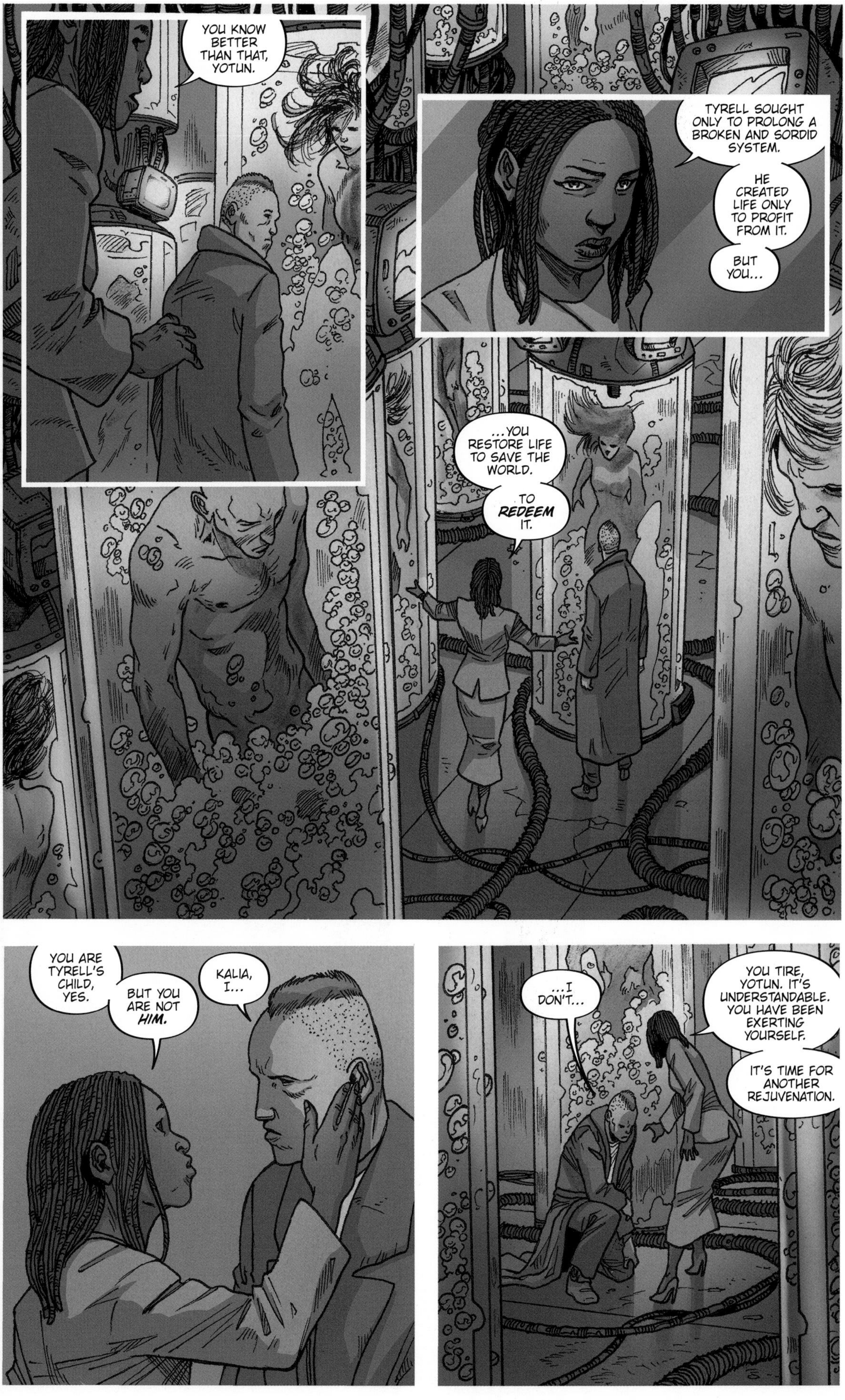
YOU KNOW BETTER THAN THAT, YOTUN.
TYRELL SOUGHT ONLY TO PROLONG A BROKEN AND SORDID SYSTEM.
HE CREATED LIFE ONLY TO PROFIT FROM IT.
BUT YOU...
...YOU RESTORE LIFE TO SAVE THE WORLD.
TO *REDEEM* IT.
YOU ARE TYRELL'S CHILD, YES.
BUT YOU ARE NOT *HIM.*
KALIA, I...
...I DON'T...
YOU TIRE, YOTUN. IT'S UNDERSTANDABLE. YOU HAVE BEEN EXERTING YOURSELF.
IT'S TIME FOR ANOTHER REJUVENATION.

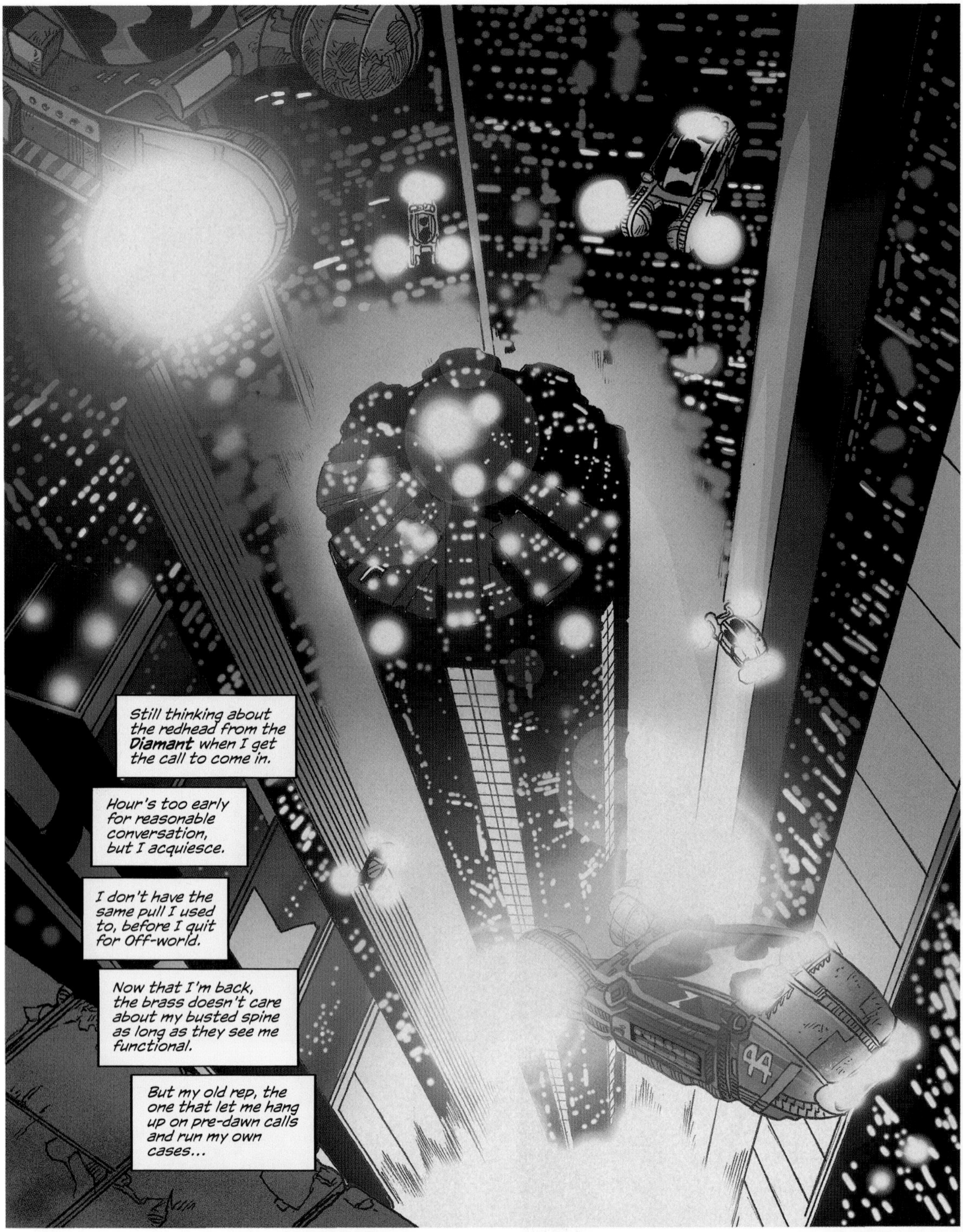
Still thinking about the redhead from the **Diamant** when I get the call to come in.
Hour's too early for reasonable conversation, but I acquiesce.
I don't have the same pull I used to, before I quit for Off-world.
Now that I'm back, the brass doesn't care about my busted spine as long as they see me functional.
But my old rep, the one that let me hang up on pre-dawn calls and run my own cases...
44

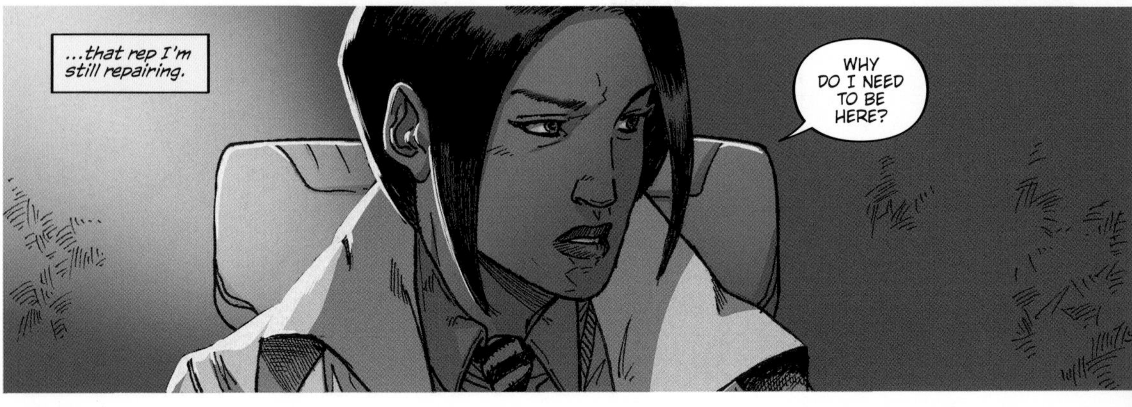
...that rep I'm still repairing.
WHY DO I NEED TO BE HERE?

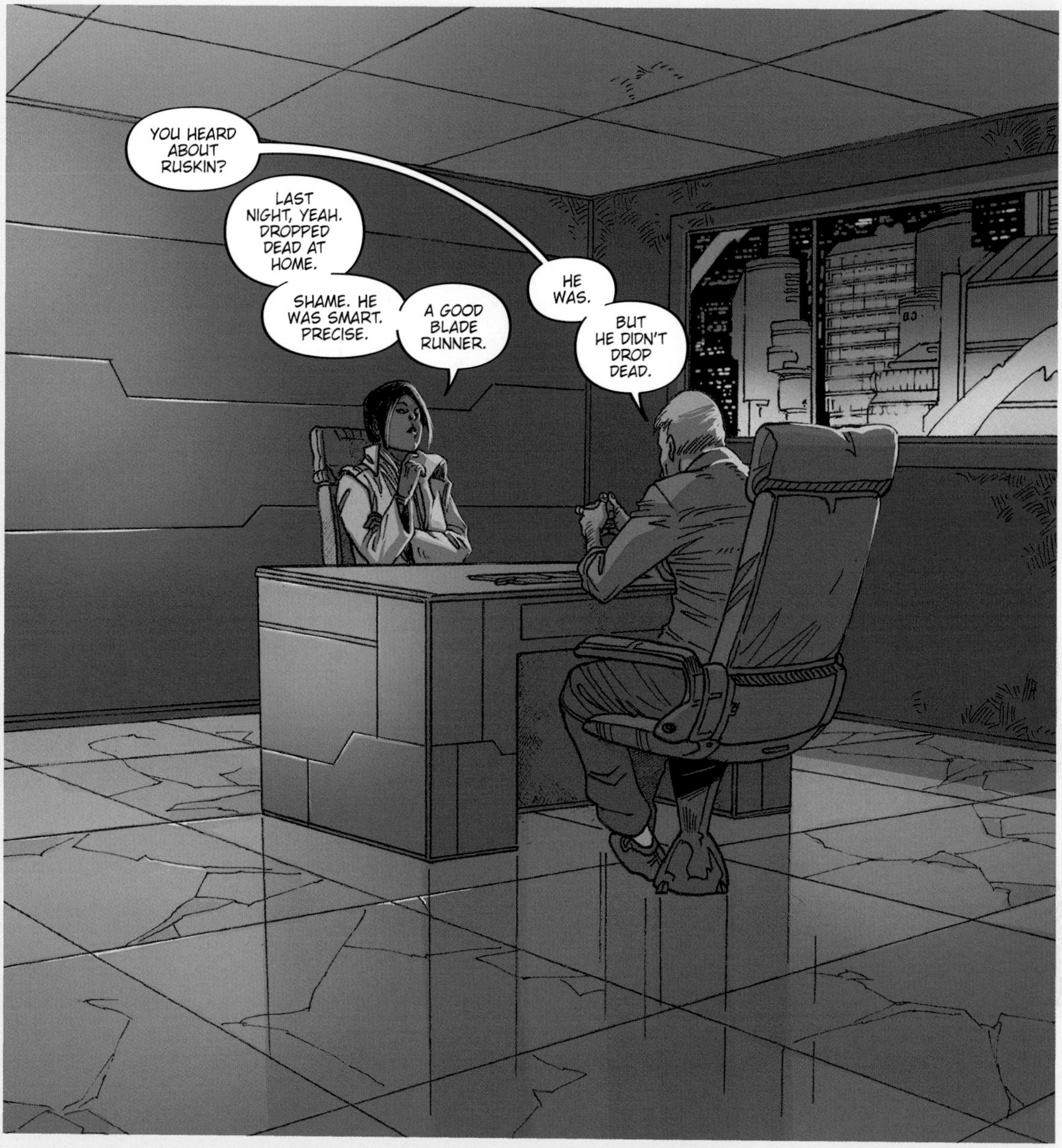
YOU HEARD ABOUT RUSKIN?
LAST NIGHT, YEAH. DROPPED DEAD AT HOME.
SHAME. HE WAS SMART. PRECISE.
A GOOD BLADE RUNNER.
HE WAS.
BUT HE DIDN'T DROP DEAD.

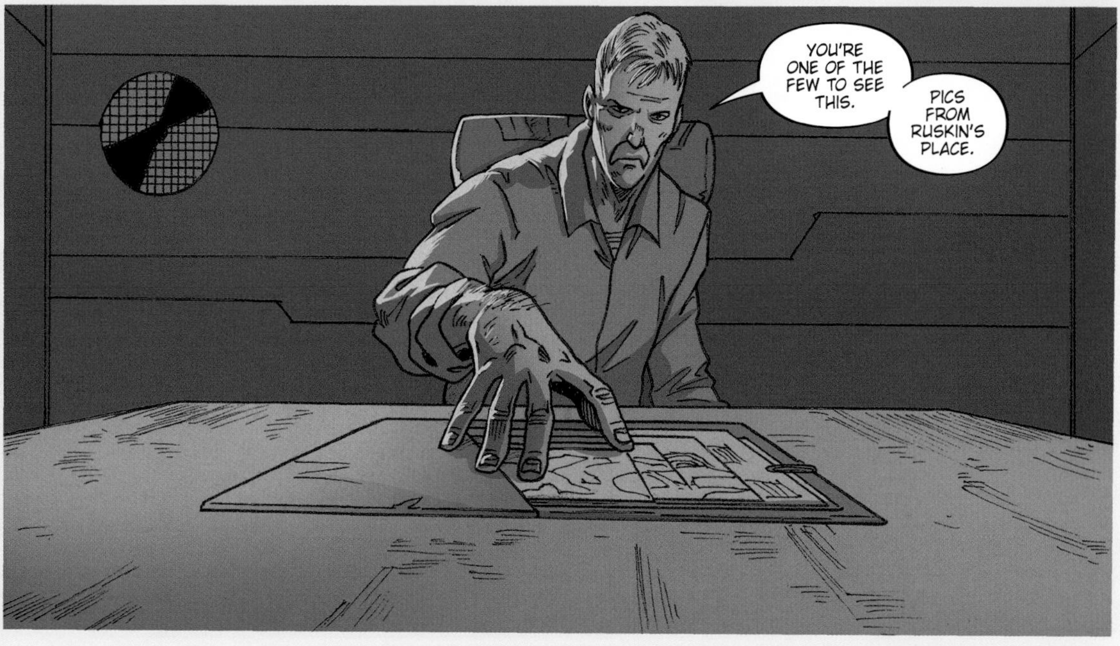
YOU'RE ONE OF THE FEW TO SEE THIS.
PICS FROM RUSKIN'S PLACE.

IS THAT...?

HIS SPINE.

REMOVED WITH FORCE.

BY *HAND.*

RUSKIN WAS INVESTIGATING THE MURDER OF THE BANKER, HYMAN BASK.

SAW THE NEWS. YOU THINK A REPLICANT KILLED BASK? AND THEN RUSKIN?

BASK AND HIS WIFE WERE POISONED. ONE OF THEIR SERVANTS VANISHED.

TOOK BASK'S EYE WITH HIM...

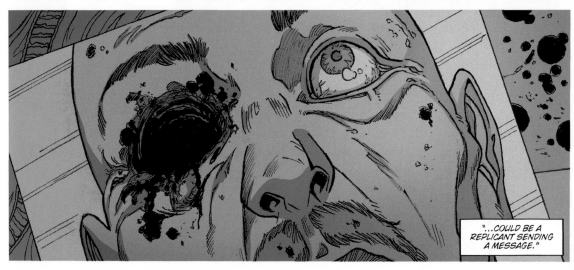

"...COULD BE A REPLICANT SENDING A MESSAGE."

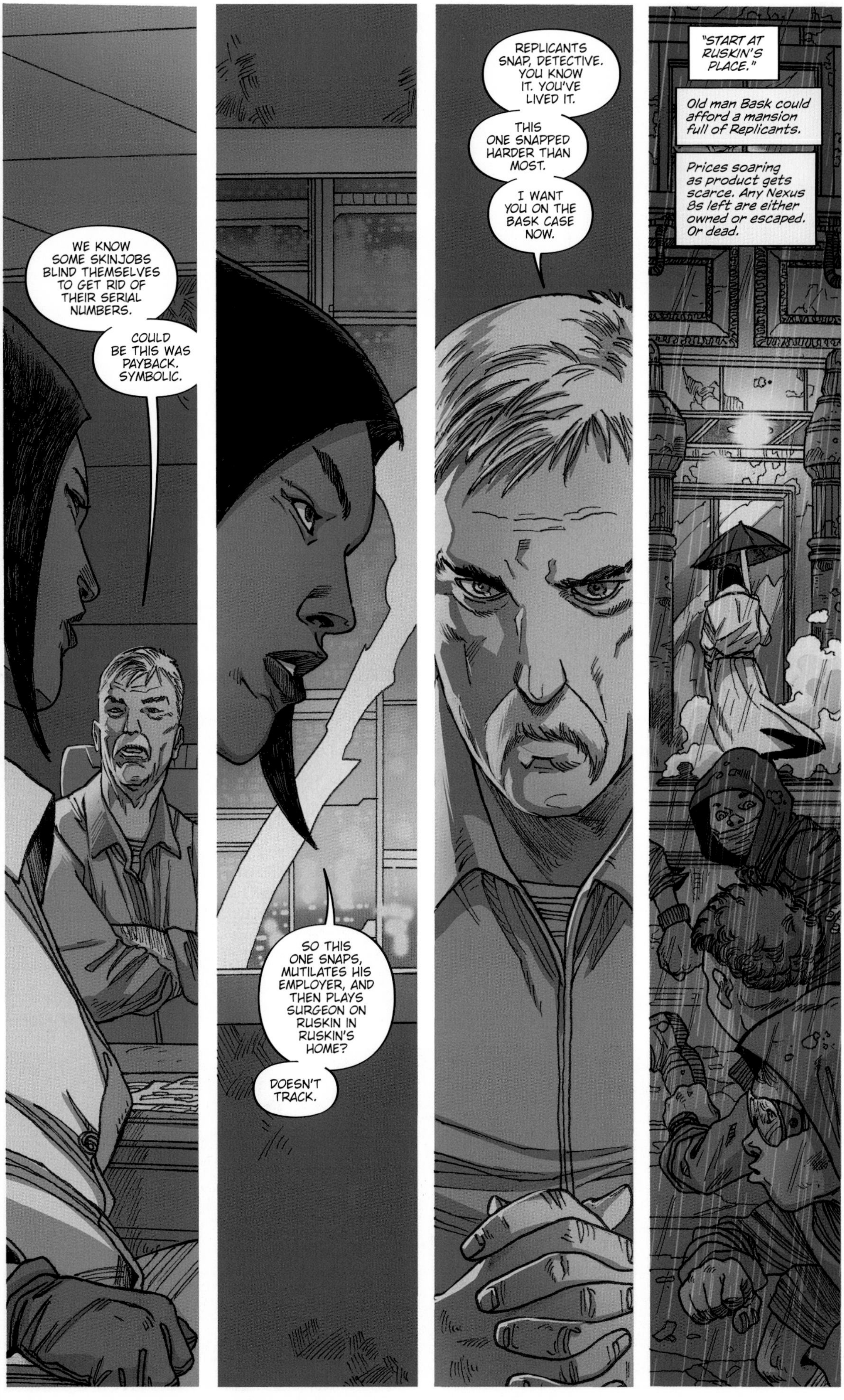
WE KNOW SOME SKINJOBS BLIND THEMSELVES TO GET RID OF THEIR SERIAL NUMBERS.
COULD BE THIS WAS PAYBACK. SYMBOLIC.
SO THIS ONE SNAPS, MUTILATES HIS EMPLOYER, AND THEN PLAYS SURGEON ON RUSKIN IN RUSKIN'S HOME?
DOESN'T TRACK.
REPLICANTS SNAP, DETECTIVE. YOU KNOW IT. YOU'VE LIVED IT.
THIS ONE SNAPPED HARDER THAN MOST.
I WANT YOU ON THE BASK CASE NOW.
"START AT RUSKIN'S PLACE."
Old man Bask could afford a mansion full of Replicants.
Prices soaring as product gets scarce. Any Nexus 8s left are either owned or escaped. Or dead.

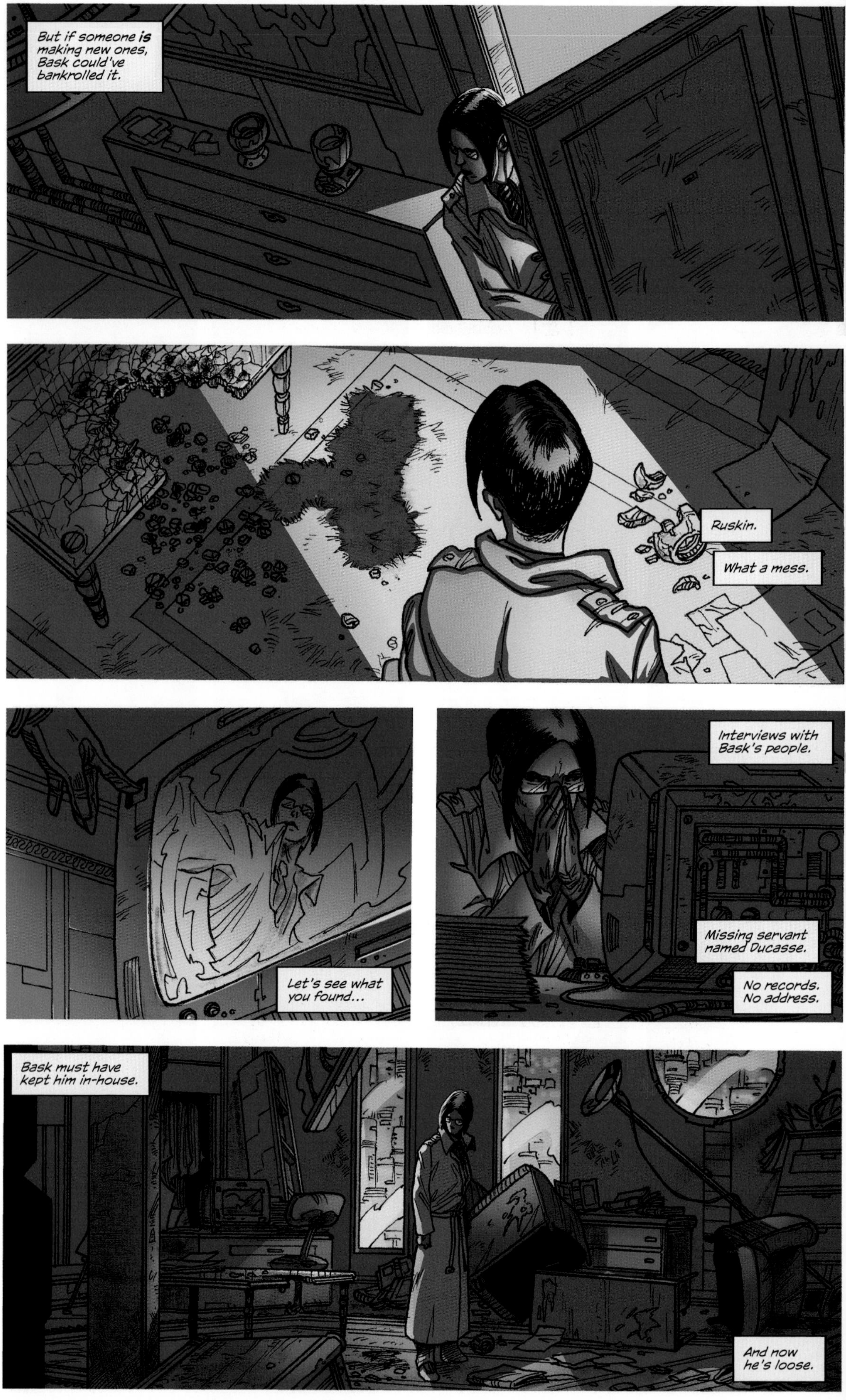
But if someone is making new ones, Bask could've bankrolled it.
Ruskin.
What a mess.
Let's see what you found...
Interviews with Bask's people.
Missing servant named Ducasse.
No records. No address.
Bask must have kept him in-house.
And now he's loose.

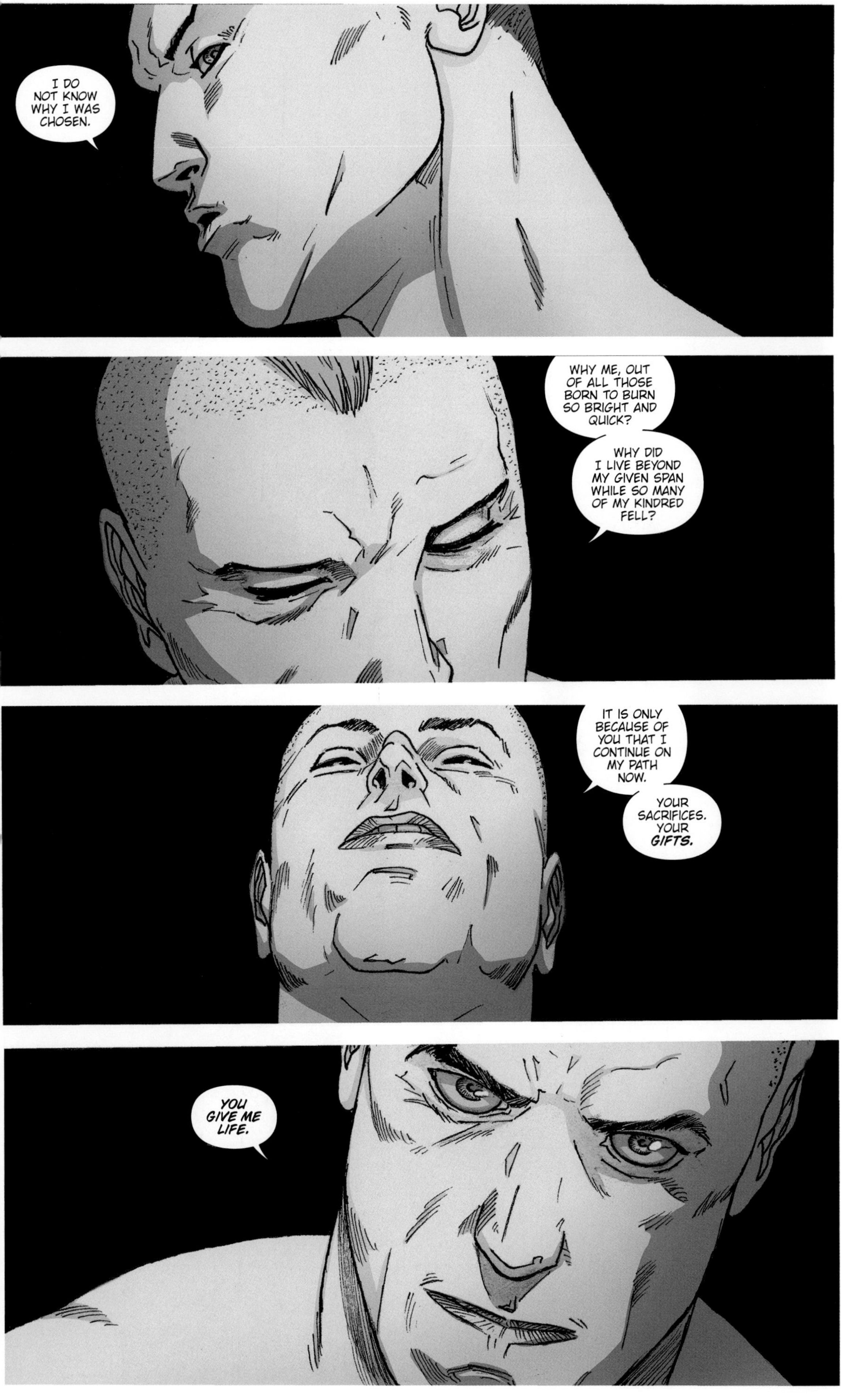
I DO NOT KNOW WHY I WAS CHOSEN.
WHY ME, OUT OF ALL THOSE BORN TO BURN SO BRIGHT AND QUICK?
WHY DID I LIVE BEYOND MY GIVEN SPAN WHILE SO MANY OF MY KINDRED FELL?
IT IS ONLY BECAUSE OF YOU THAT I CONTINUE ON MY PATH NOW.
YOUR SACRIFICES. YOUR *GIFTS.*
YOU GIVE ME LIFE.

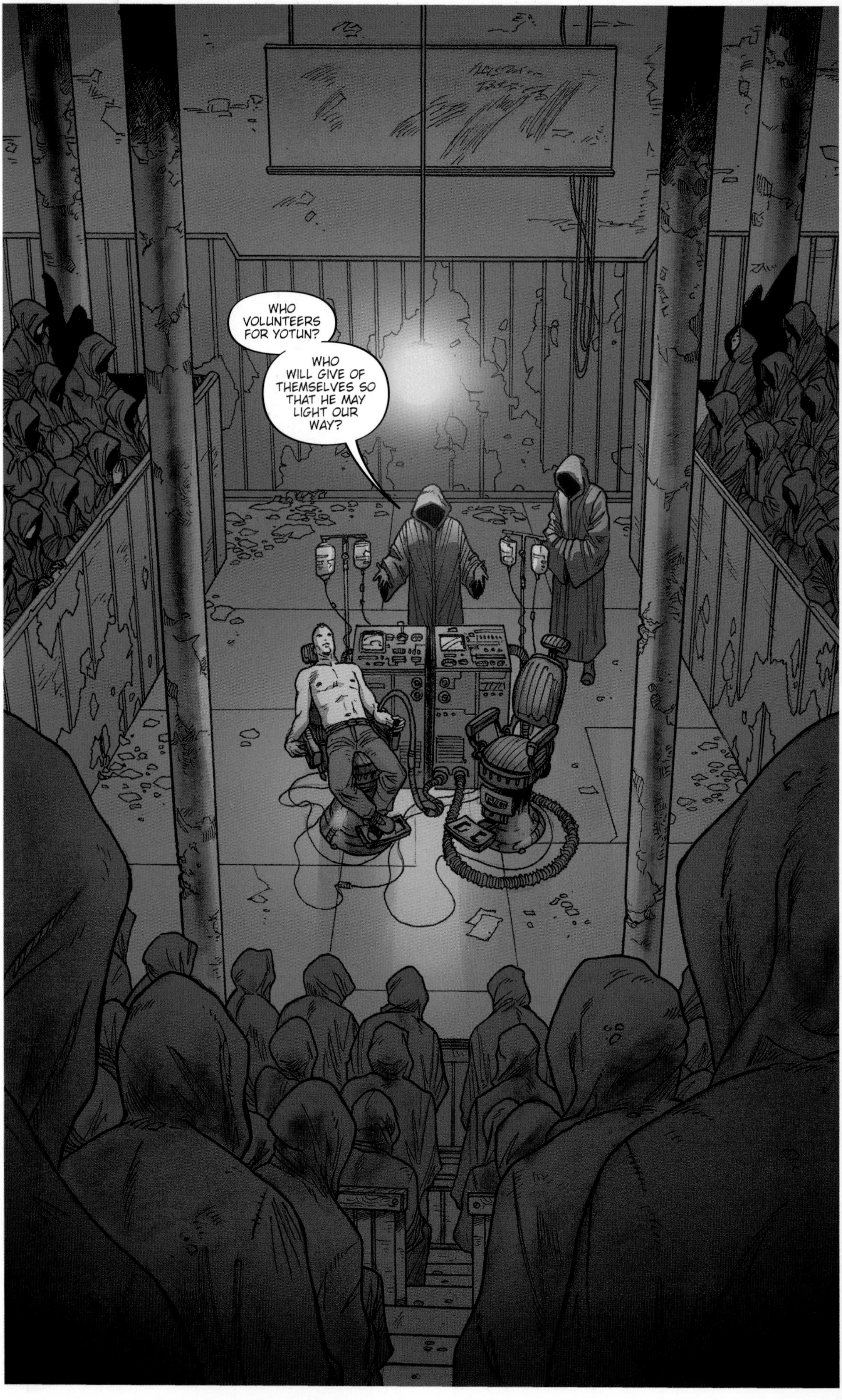
WHO VOLUNTEERS FOR YOTUN?
WHO WILL GIVE OF THEMSELVES SO THAT HE MAY LIGHT OUR WAY?

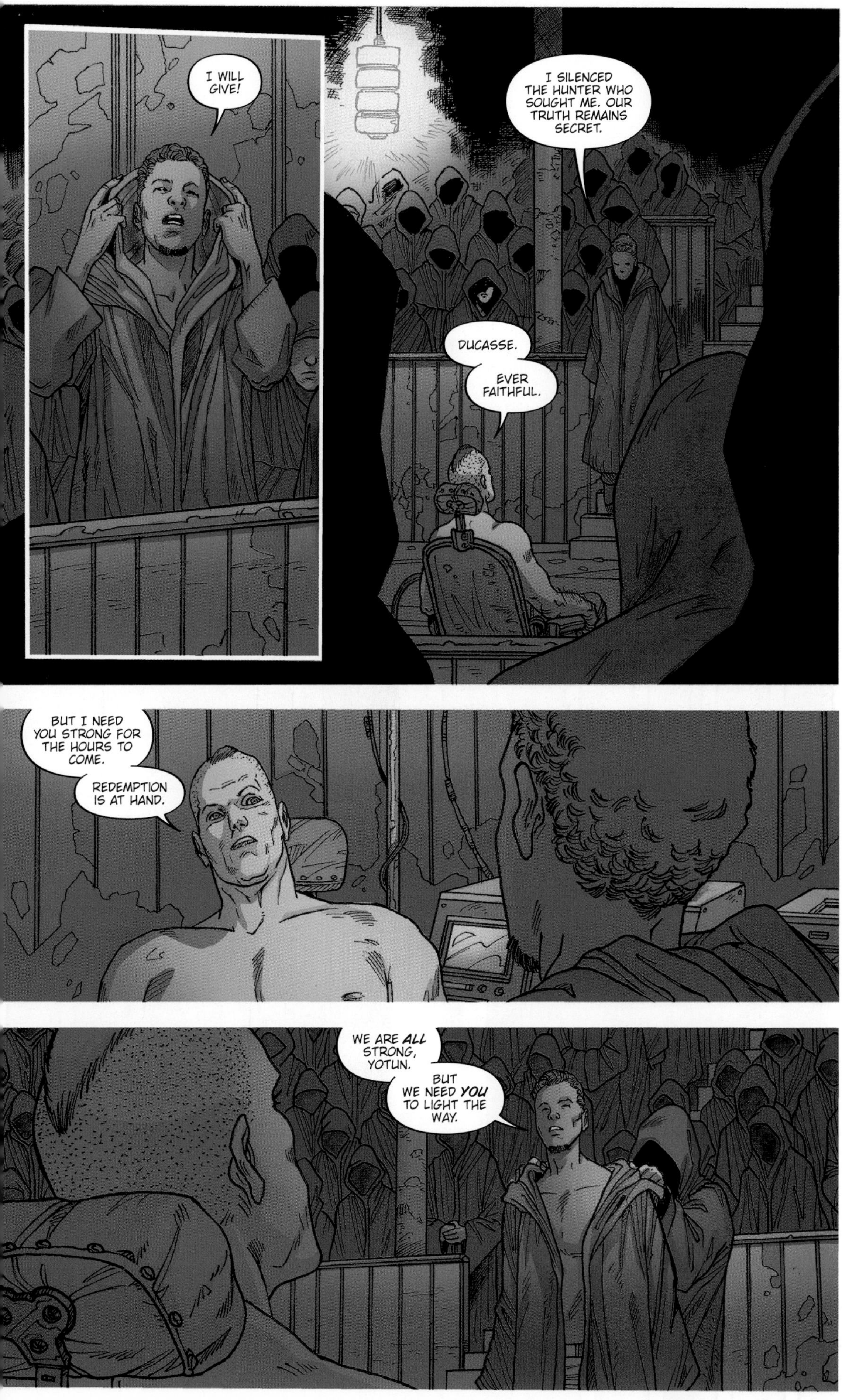
I WILL GIVE!
I SILENCED THE HUNTER WHO SOUGHT ME. OUR TRUTH REMAINS SECRET.
DUCASSE.
EVER FAITHFUL.
BUT I NEED YOU STRONG FOR THE HOURS TO COME.
REDEMPTION IS AT HAND.
WE ARE ***ALL*** STRONG, YOTUN.
BUT WE NEED ***YOU*** TO LIGHT THE WAY.

YOU NEED THE BLOOD OF OUR GENERATION TO SUSTAIN YOU.

OUR FLAMES ARE MEANT TO BURN LONG.

ALLOW ME THIS HONOR.

YOU HONOR ME...

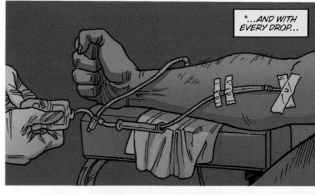

"...AND WITH EVERY DROP..."

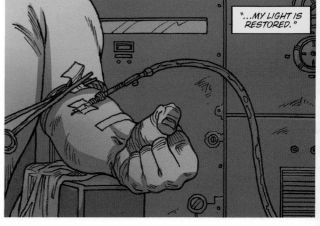

"...MY LIGHT IS RESTORED."

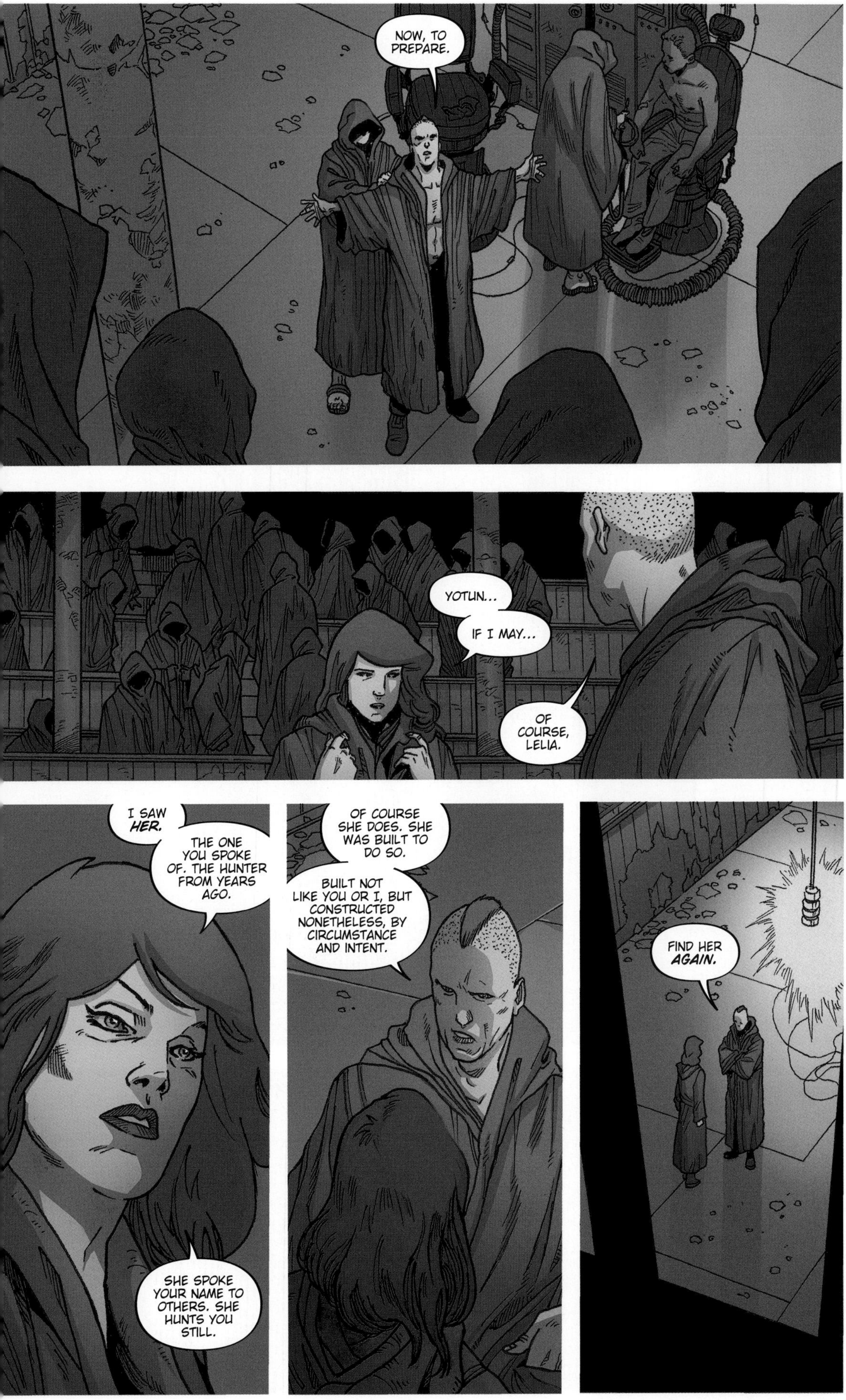
NOW, TO PREPARE.
YOTUN...
IF I MAY...
OF COURSE, LELIA.
I SAW **HER.**
THE ONE YOU SPOKE OF. THE HUNTER FROM YEARS AGO.
SHE SPOKE YOUR NAME TO OTHERS. SHE HUNTS YOU STILL.
OF COURSE SHE DOES. SHE WAS BUILT TO DO SO.
BUILT NOT LIKE YOU OR I, BUT CONSTRUCTED NONETHELESS, BY CIRCUMSTANCE AND INTENT.
FIND HER **AGAIN.**

Hyman Bask was due to hobnob with the rest of Los Angeles royalty tonight.

Big soiree to celebrate the seawall progress.

Mayor's inviting the haves to dinner on an airship.

Safe in the sky above the have-nots.

Wonder if they'll toast old Hyman.

Or if the timing of his death was no coincidence.

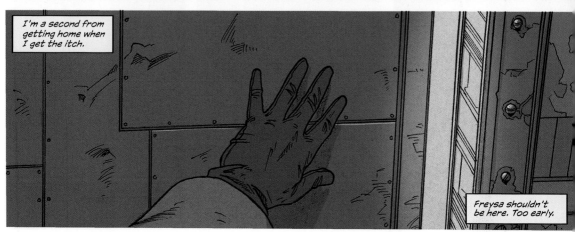

I'm a second from getting home when I get the itch.

Freysa shouldn't be here. Too early.

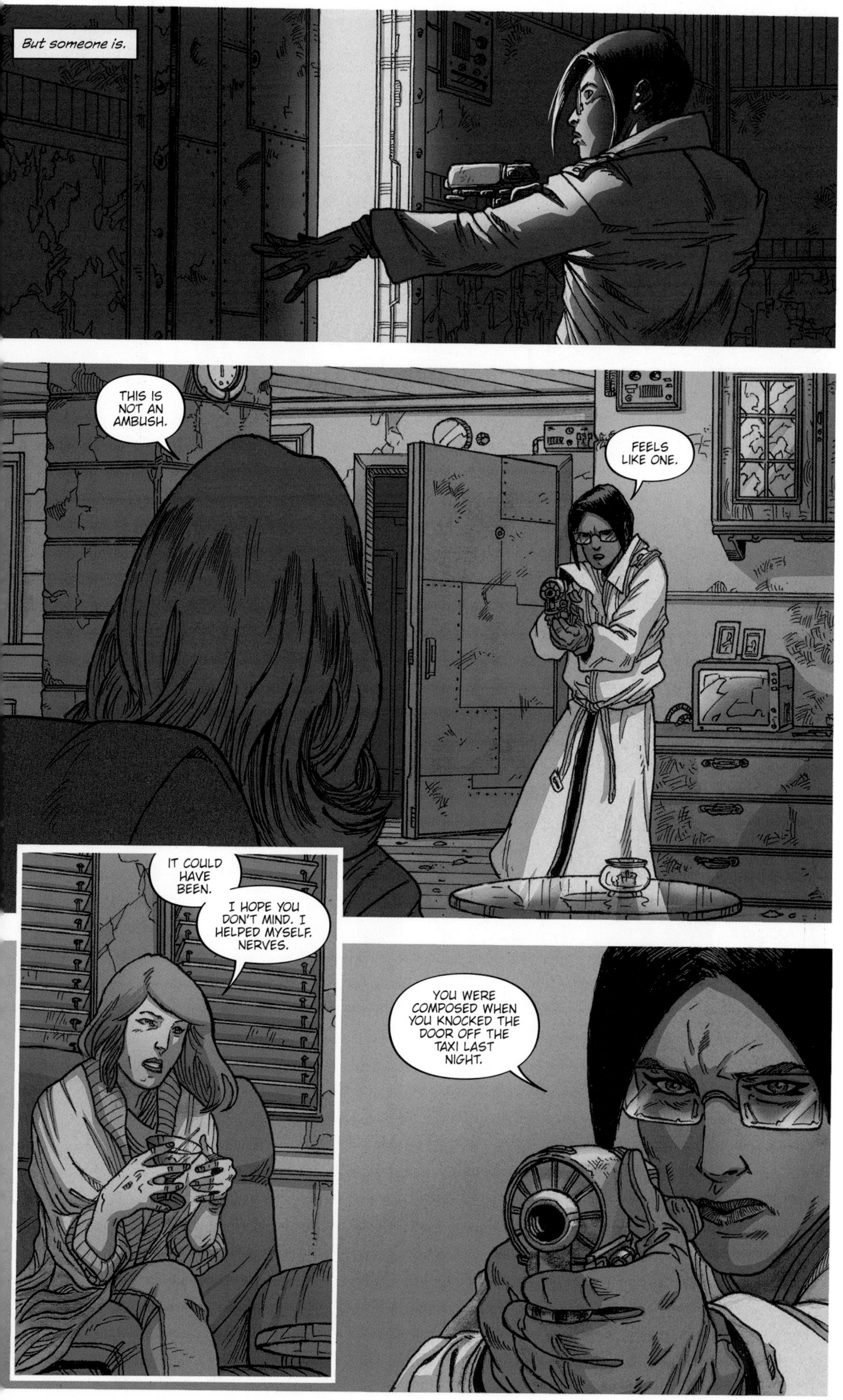
But someone is.
THIS IS NOT AN AMBUSH.
FEELS LIKE ONE.
IT COULD HAVE BEEN.
I HOPE YOU DON'T MIND. I HELPED MYSELF. NERVES.
YOU WERE COMPOSED WHEN YOU KNOCKED THE DOOR OFF THE TAXI LAST NIGHT.

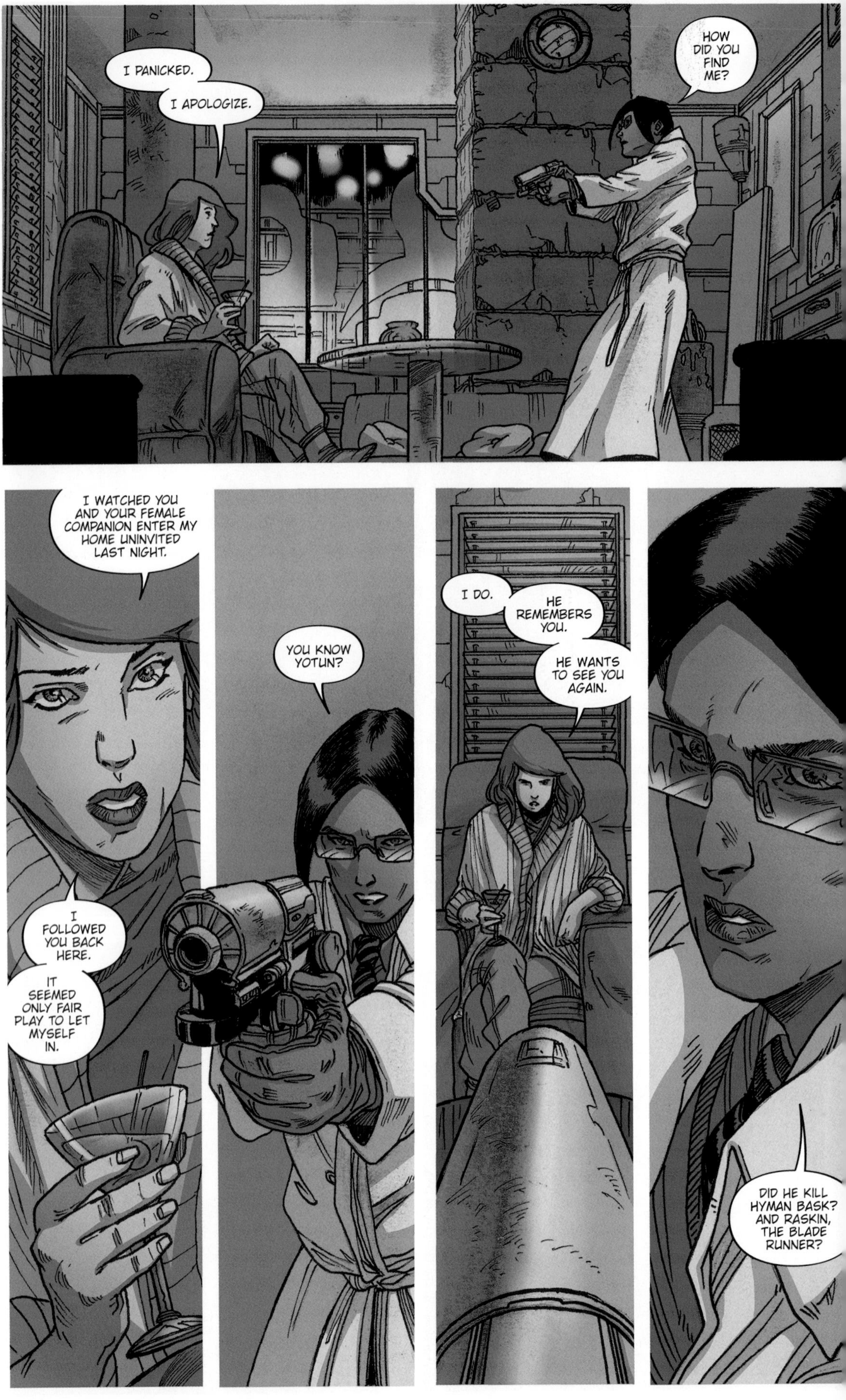
I PANICKED.
I APOLOGIZE.
HOW DID YOU FIND ME?
I WATCHED YOU AND YOUR FEMALE COMPANION ENTER MY HOME UNINVITED LAST NIGHT.
I FOLLOWED YOU BACK HERE.
IT SEEMED ONLY FAIR PLAY TO LET MYSELF IN.
YOU KNOW YOTUN?
I DO.
HE REMEMBERS YOU.
HE WANTS TO SEE YOU AGAIN.
DID HE KILL HYMAN BASK? AND RASKIN, THE BLADE RUNNER?

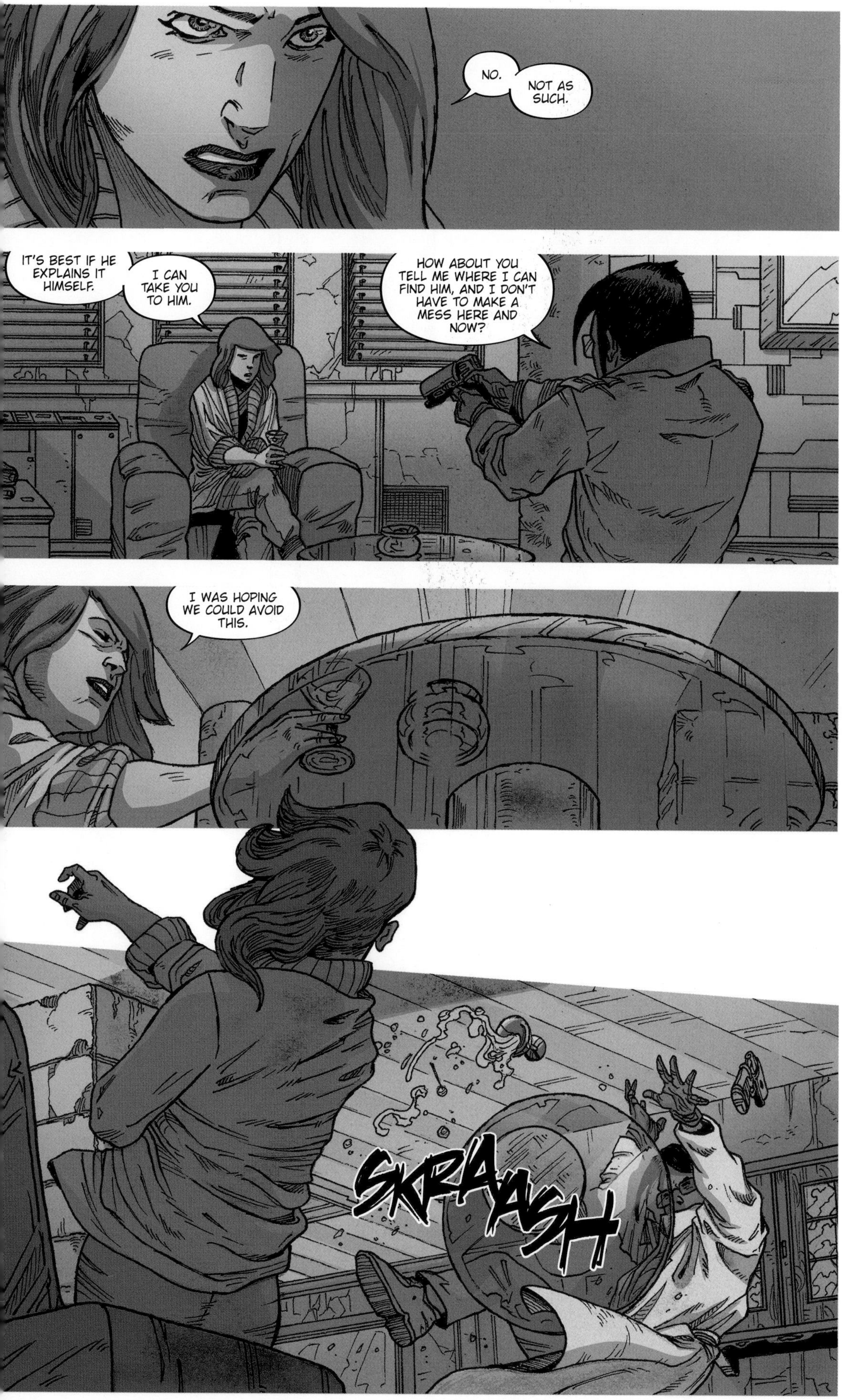
NO.
NOT AS SUCH.
IT'S BEST IF HE EXPLAINS IT HIMSELF.
I CAN TAKE YOU TO HIM.
HOW ABOUT YOU TELL ME WHERE I CAN FIND HIM, AND I DON'T HAVE TO MAKE A MESS HERE AND NOW?
I WAS HOPING WE COULD AVOID THIS.
SKRAAASH

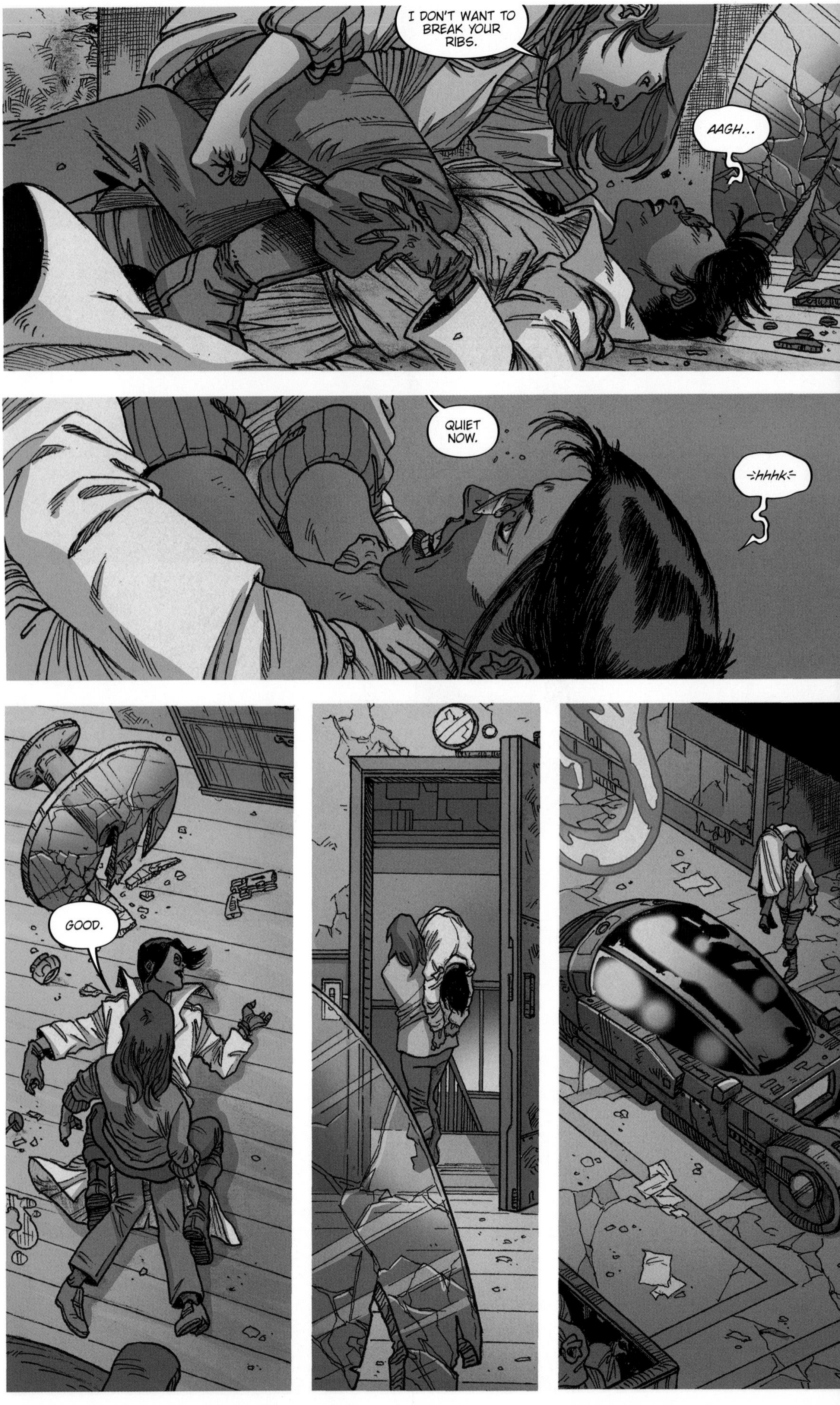
I DON'T WANT TO BREAK YOUR RIBS.
AAGH...
QUIET NOW.
-hhhk-
GOOD.

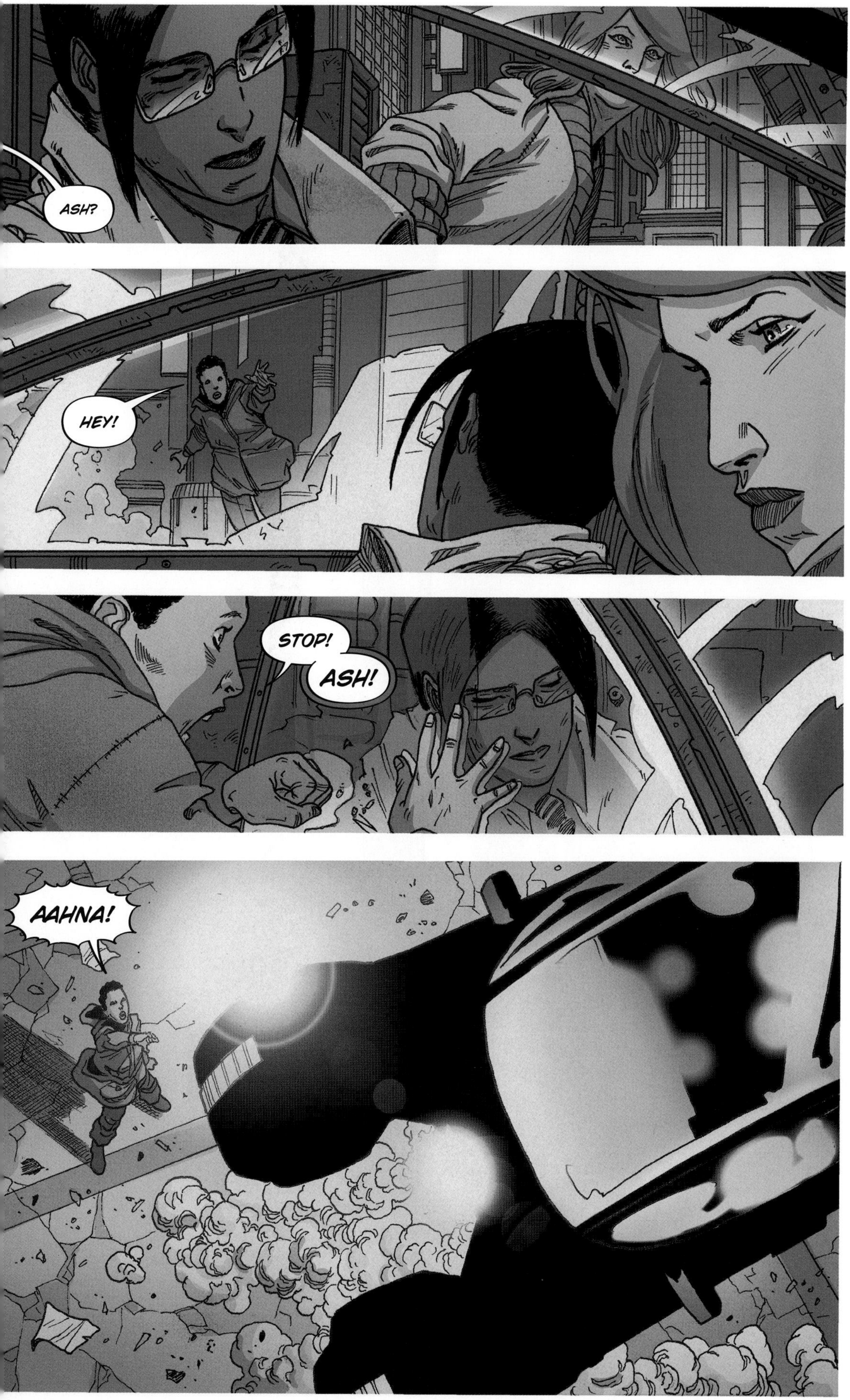
ASH?
HEY!
STOP!
ASH!
AAHNA!

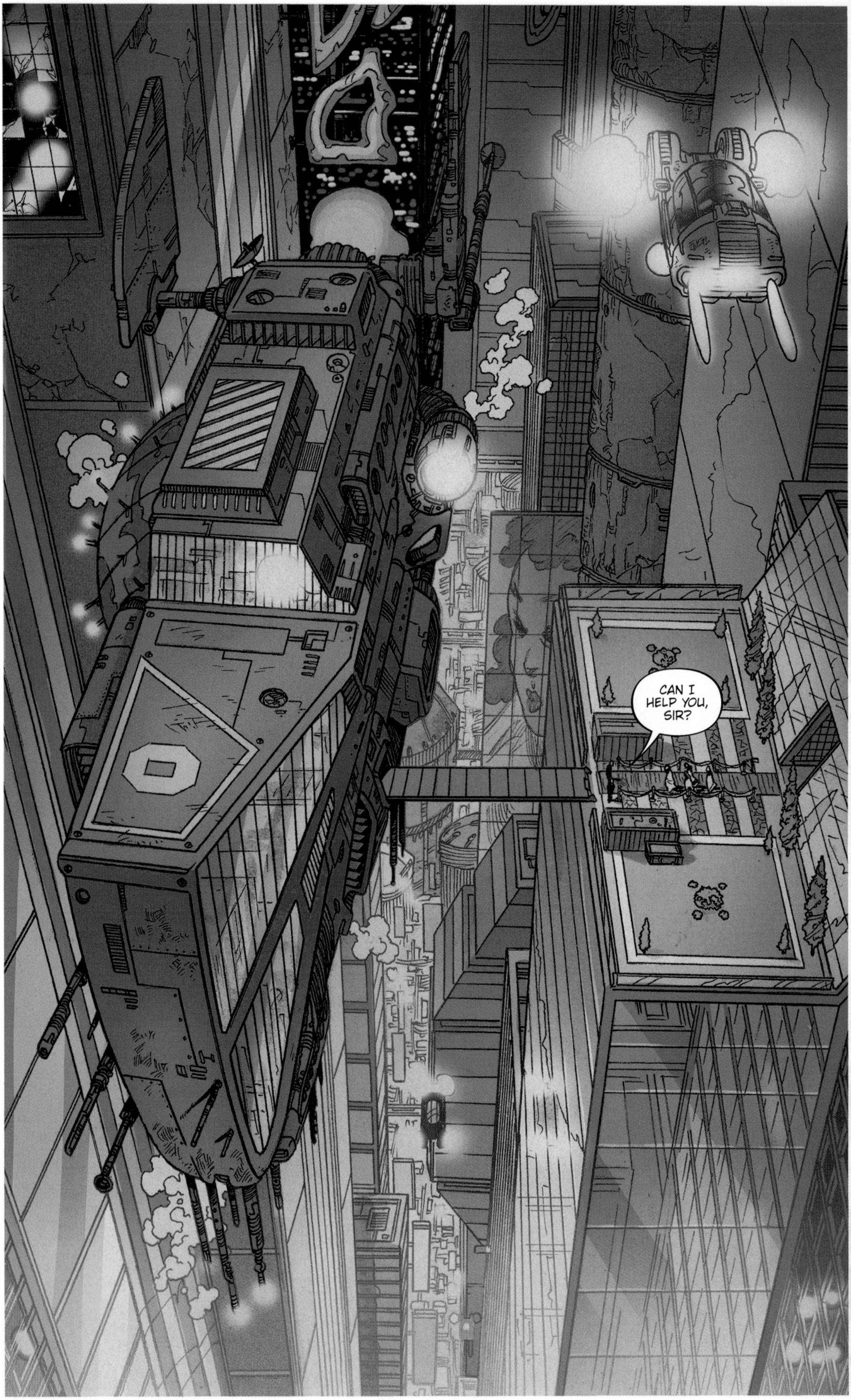
CAN I HELP YOU, SIR?

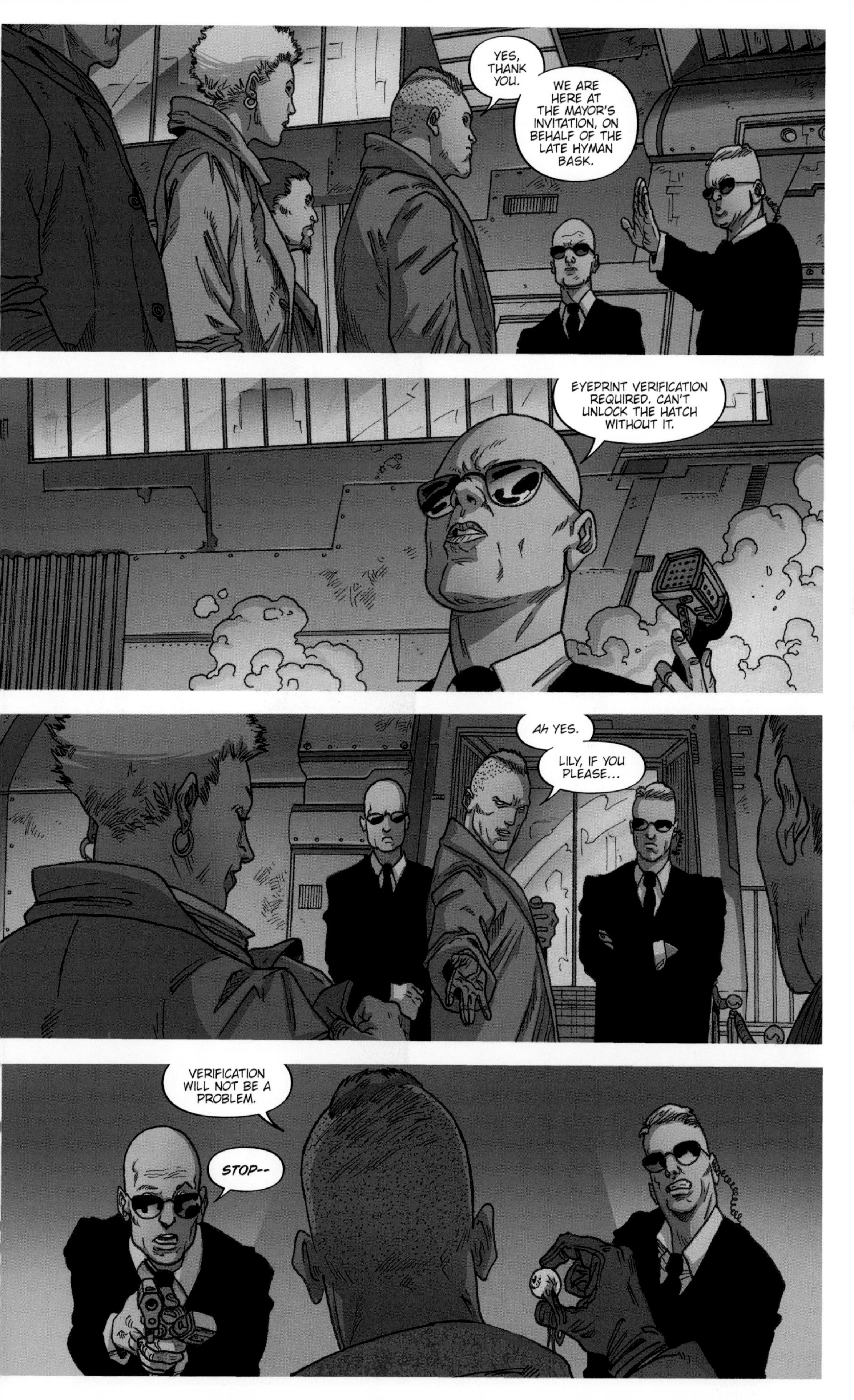

YES, THANK YOU.
WE ARE HERE AT THE MAYOR'S INVITATION, ON BEHALF OF THE LATE HYMAN BASK.
EYEPRINT VERIFICATION REQUIRED. CAN'T UNLOCK THE HATCH WITHOUT IT.
AH YES.
LILY, IF YOU PLEASE...
VERIFICATION WILL NOT BE A PROBLEM.
STOP--

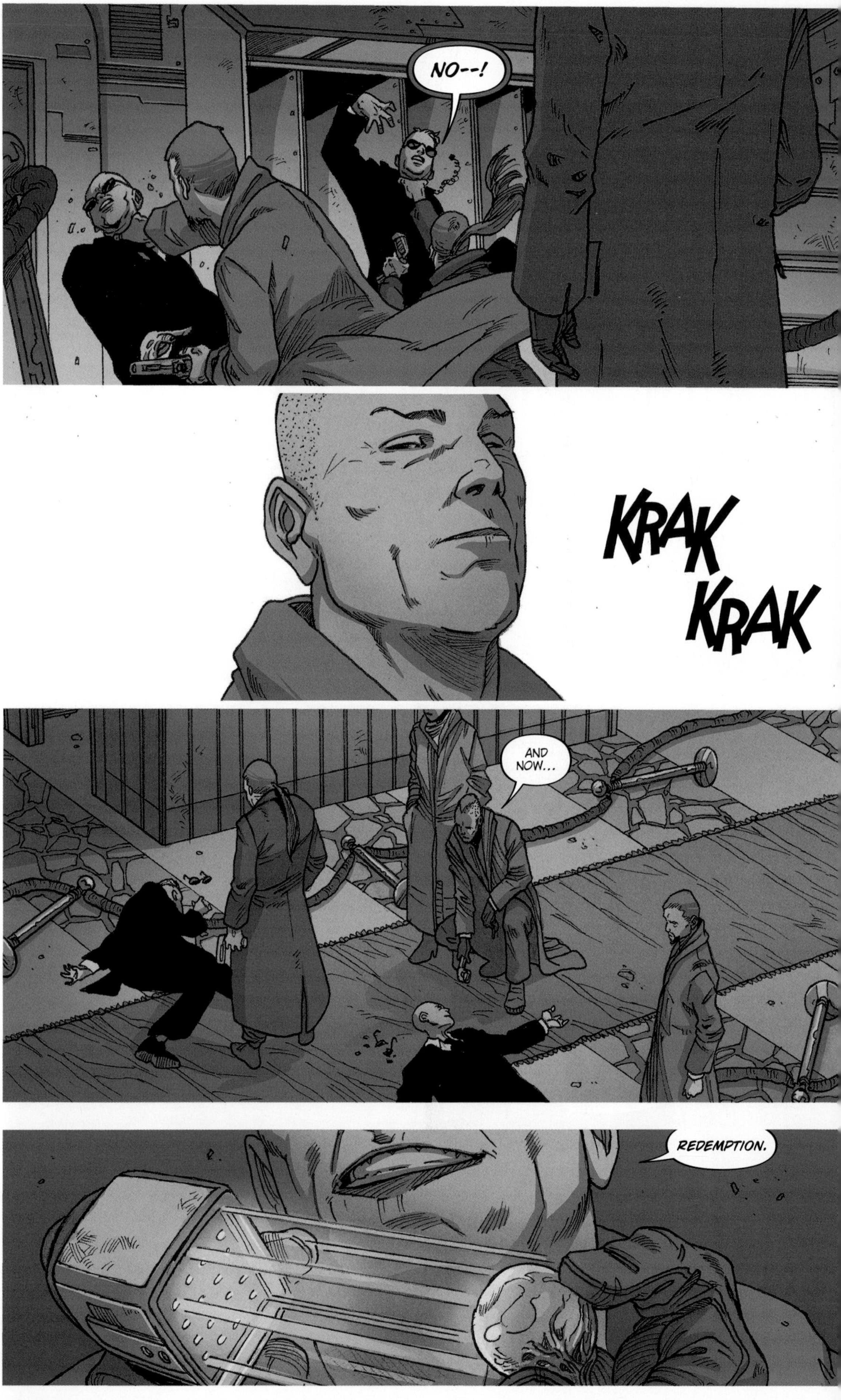
NO--!
KRAK
KRAK
AND NOW...
REDEMPTION.

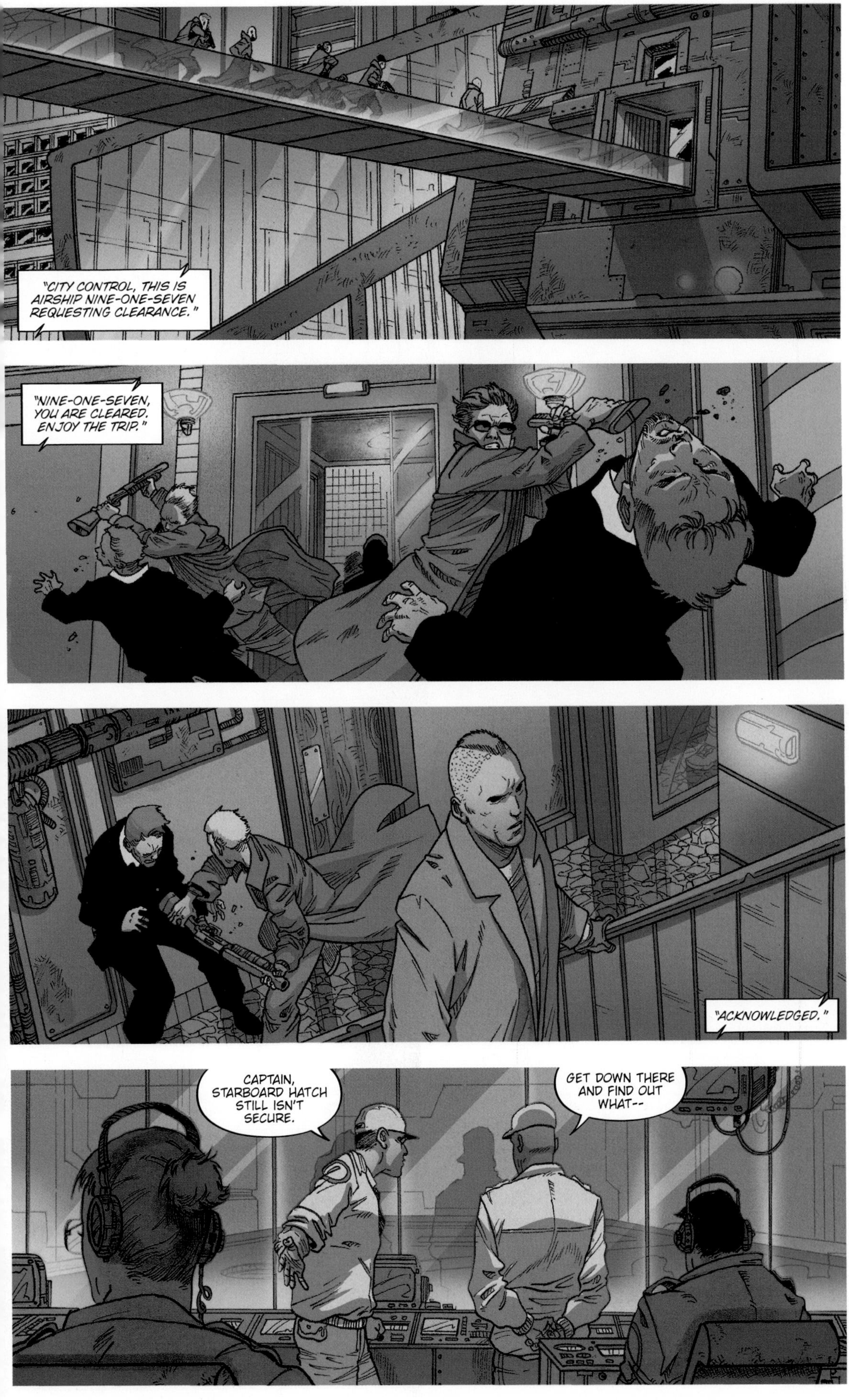
"CITY CONTROL, THIS IS AIRSHIP NINE-ONE-SEVEN REQUESTING CLEARANCE."
"NINE-ONE-SEVEN, YOU ARE CLEARED. ENJOY THE TRIP."
"ACKNOWLEDGED."
CAPTAIN, STARBOARD HATCH STILL ISN'T SECURE.
GET DOWN THERE AND FIND OUT WHAT--

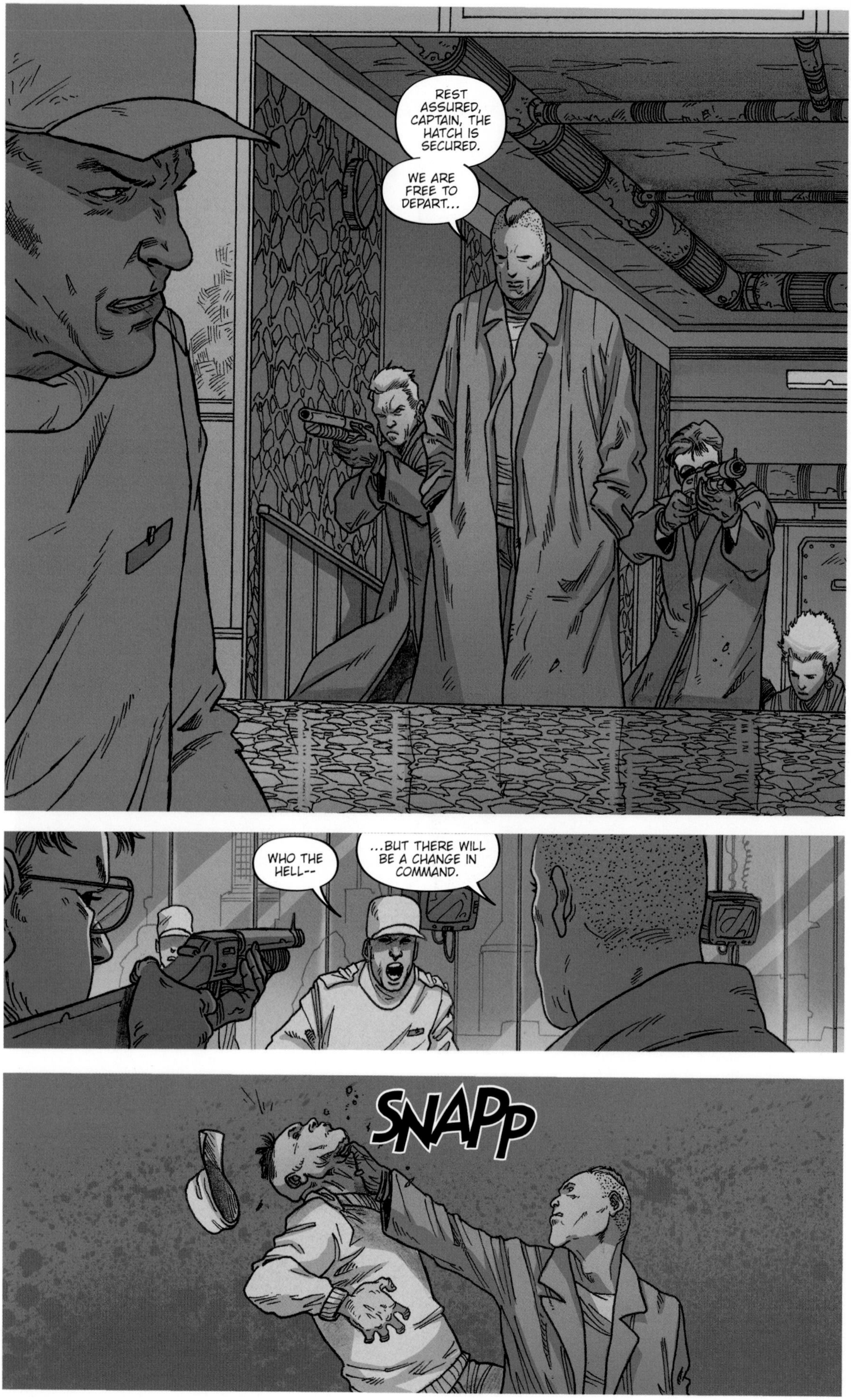
REST ASSURED, CAPTAIN, THE HATCH IS SECURED.
WE ARE FREE TO DEPART...
WHO THE HELL--
...BUT THERE WILL BE A CHANGE IN COMMAND.
SNAPP

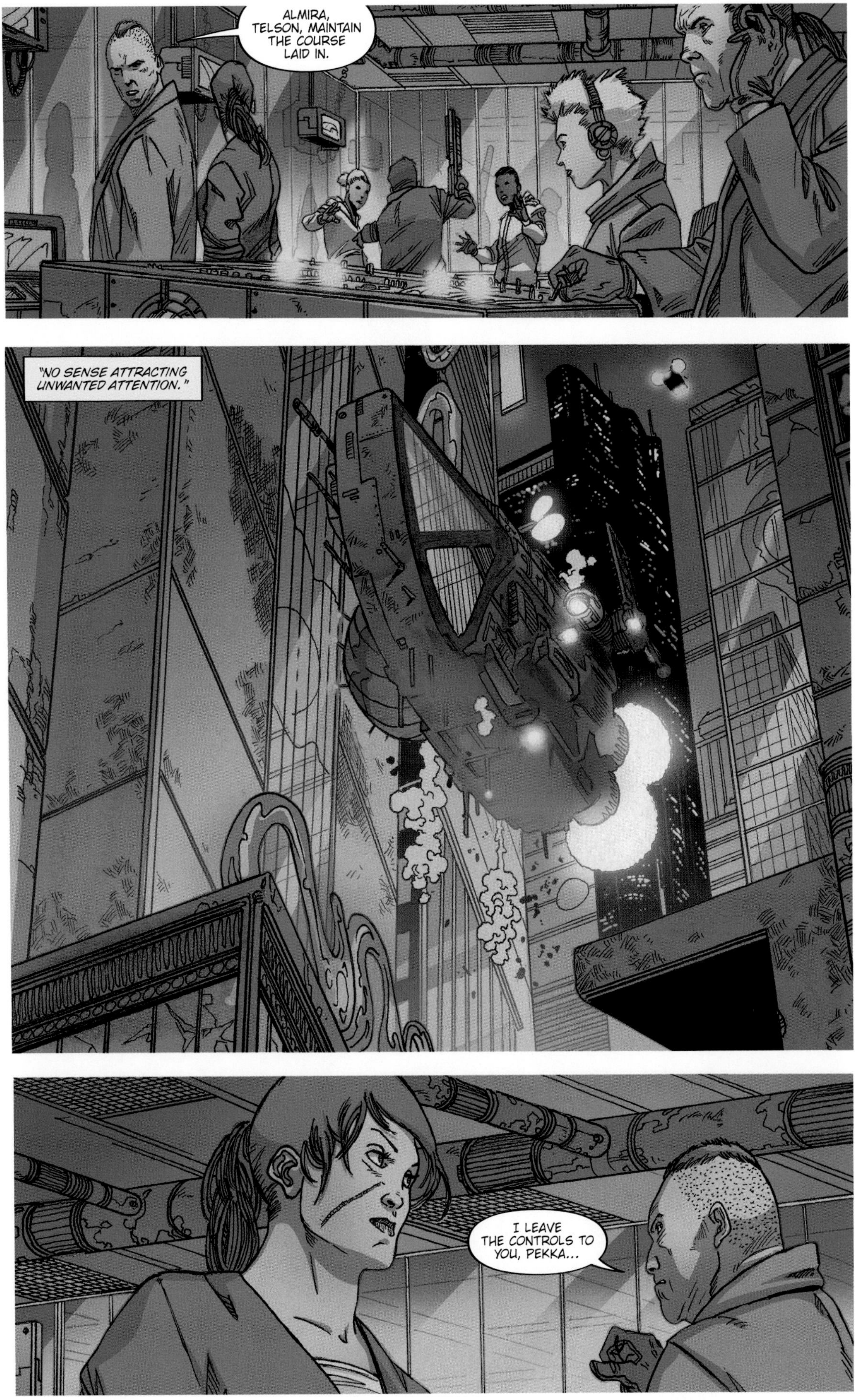
ALMIRA, TELSON, MAINTAIN THE COURSE LAID IN.
"NO SENSE ATTRACTING UNWANTED ATTENTION."
I LEAVE THE CONTROLS TO YOU, PEKKA...

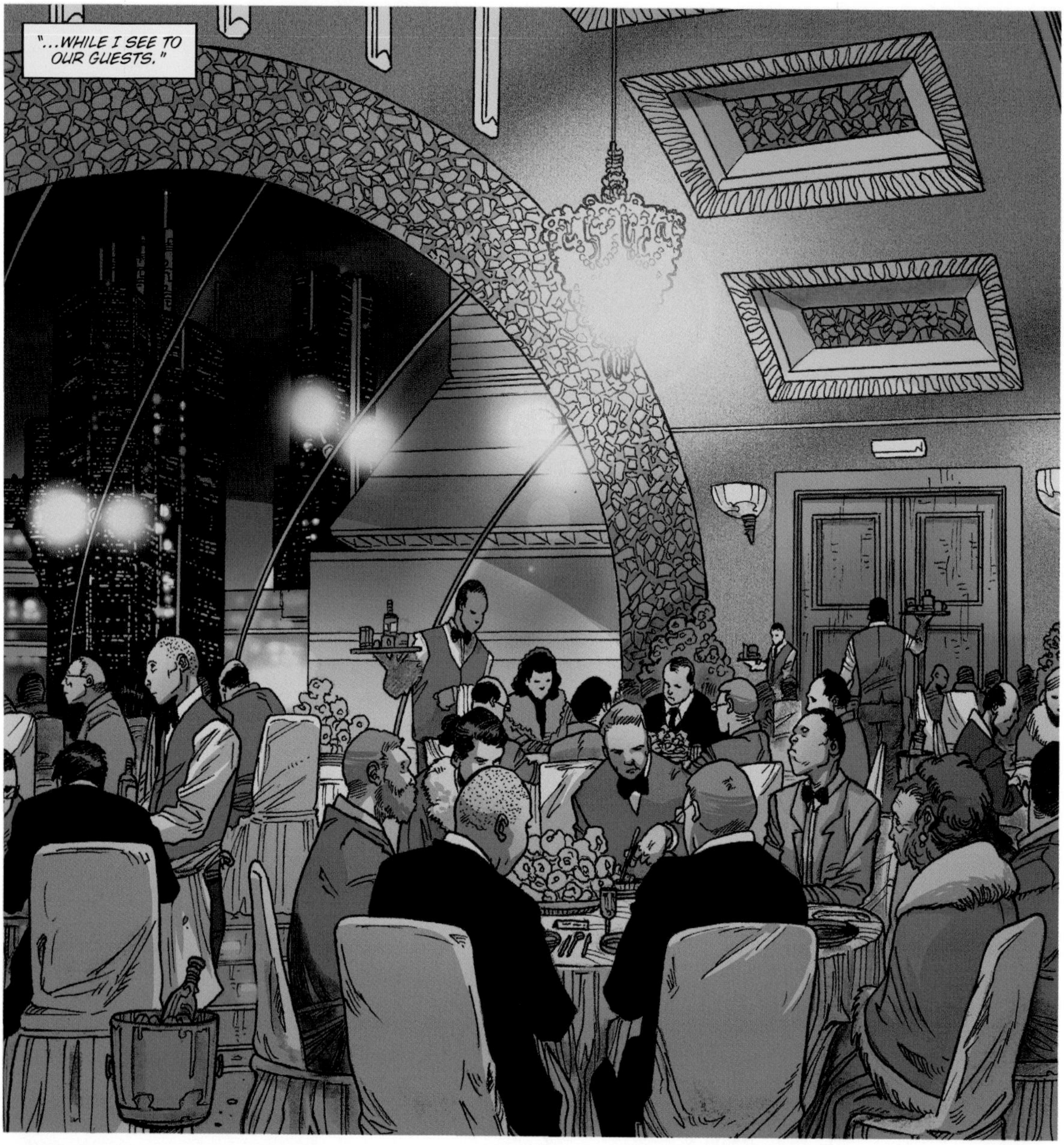
"...WHILE I SEE TO OUR GUESTS."

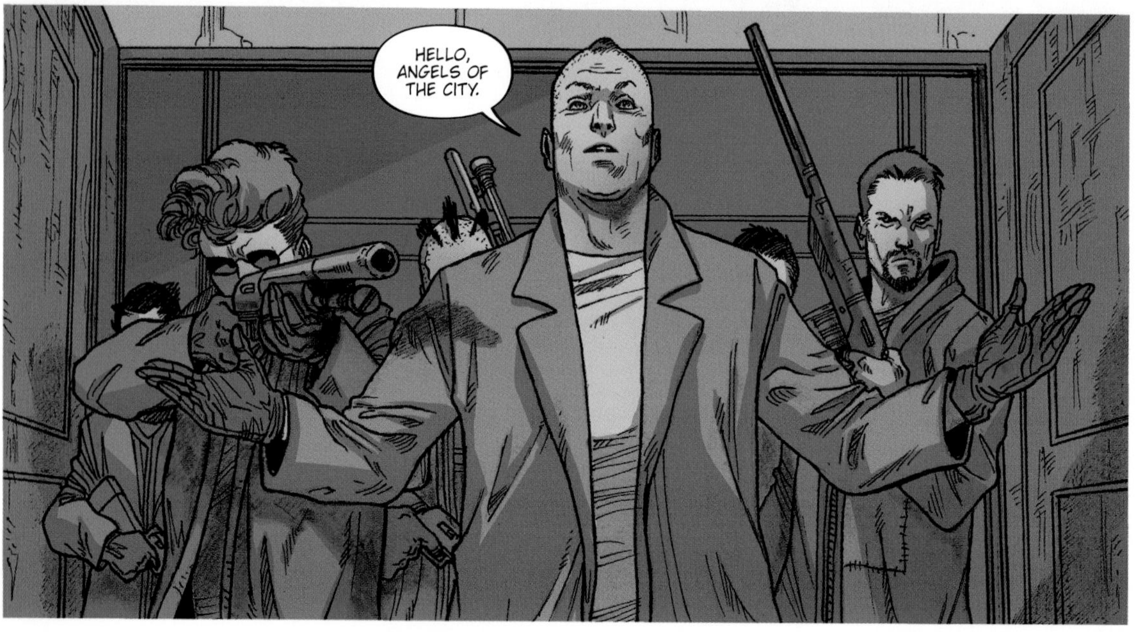
HELLO, ANGELS OF THE CITY.

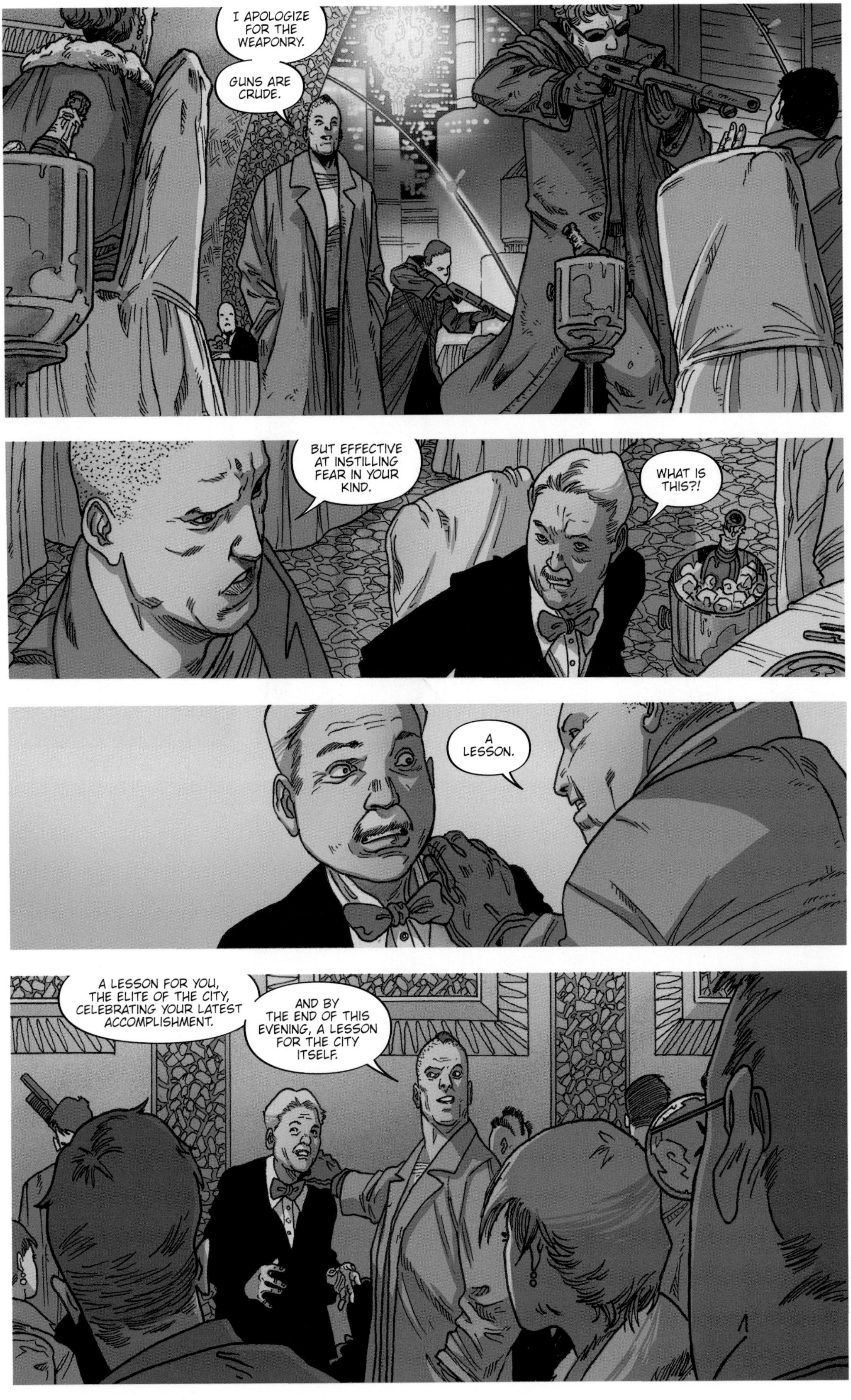
I APOLOGIZE FOR THE WEAPONRY.
GUNS ARE CRUDE.
BUT EFFECTIVE AT INSTILLING FEAR IN YOUR KIND.
WHAT IS THIS?!
A LESSON.
A LESSON FOR YOU, THE ELITE OF THE CITY, CELEBRATING YOUR LATEST ACCOMPLISHMENT.
AND BY THE END OF THIS EVENING, A LESSON FOR THE CITY ITSELF.

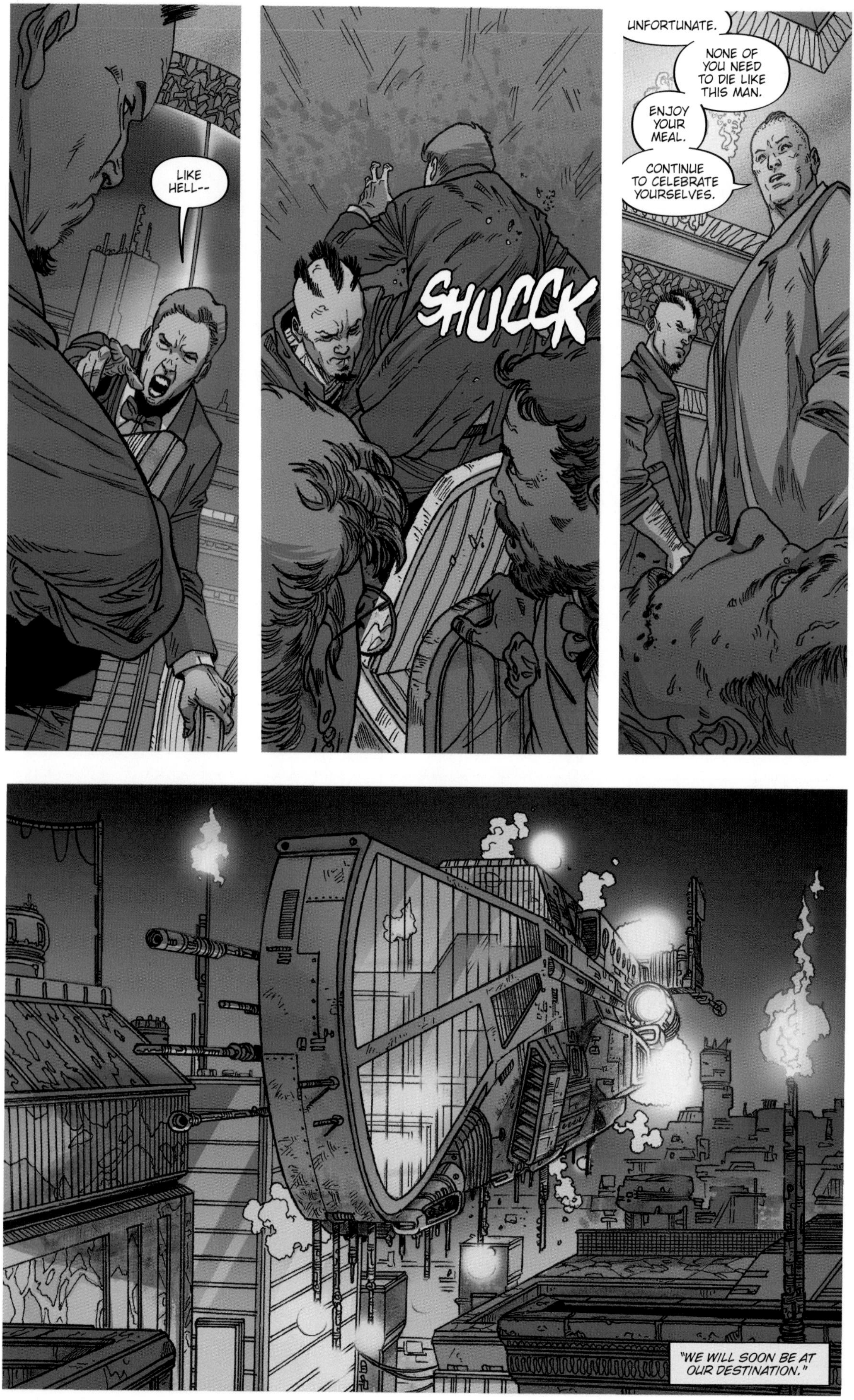
LIKE HELL--
SHUCCK
UNFORTUNATE.
NONE OF YOU NEED TO DIE LIKE THIS MAN.
ENJOY YOUR MEAL.
CONTINUE TO CELEBRATE YOURSELVES.
"WE WILL SOON BE AT OUR DESTINATION."

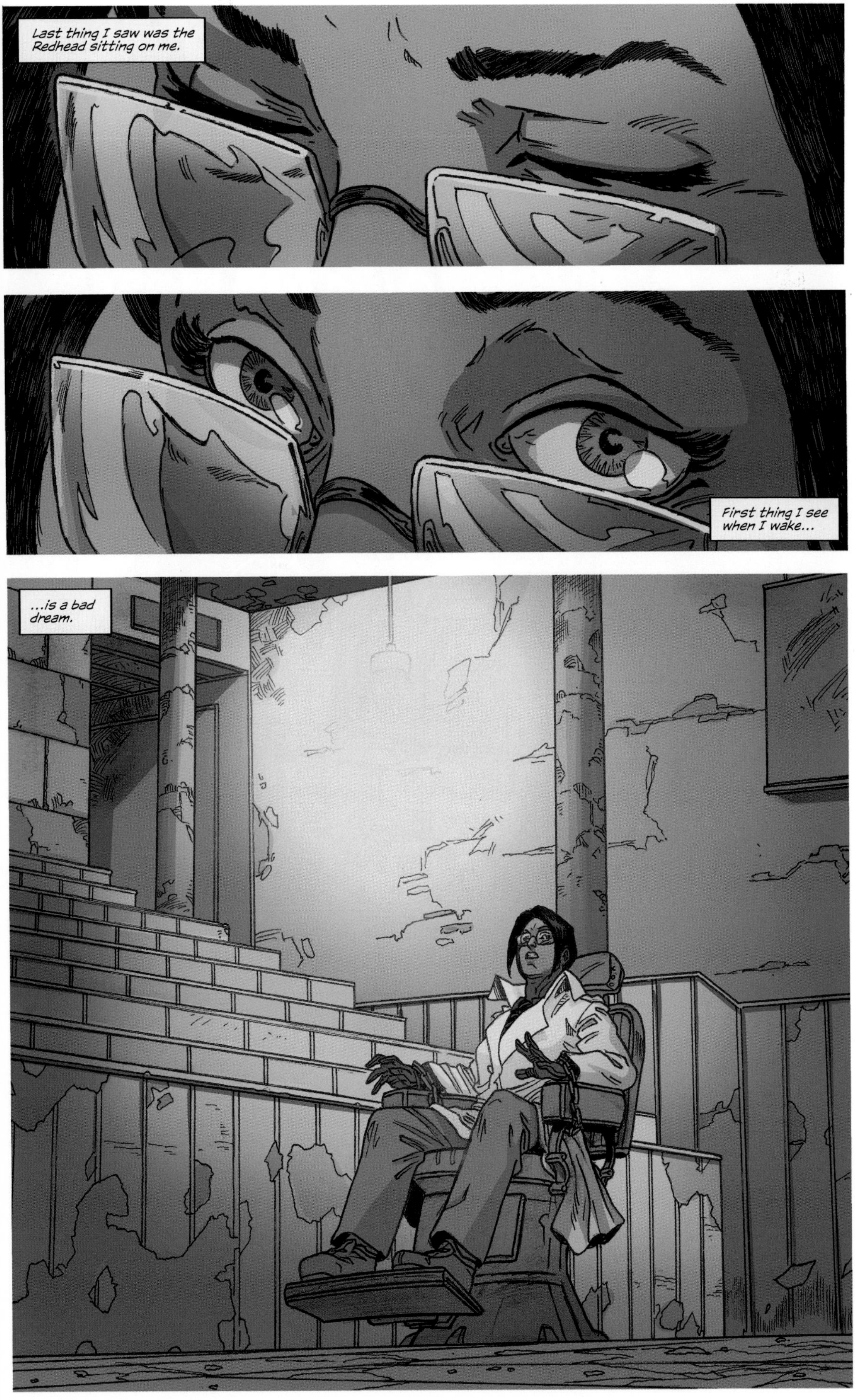
Last thing I saw was the Redhead sitting on me.
First thing I see when I wake...
...is a bad dream.

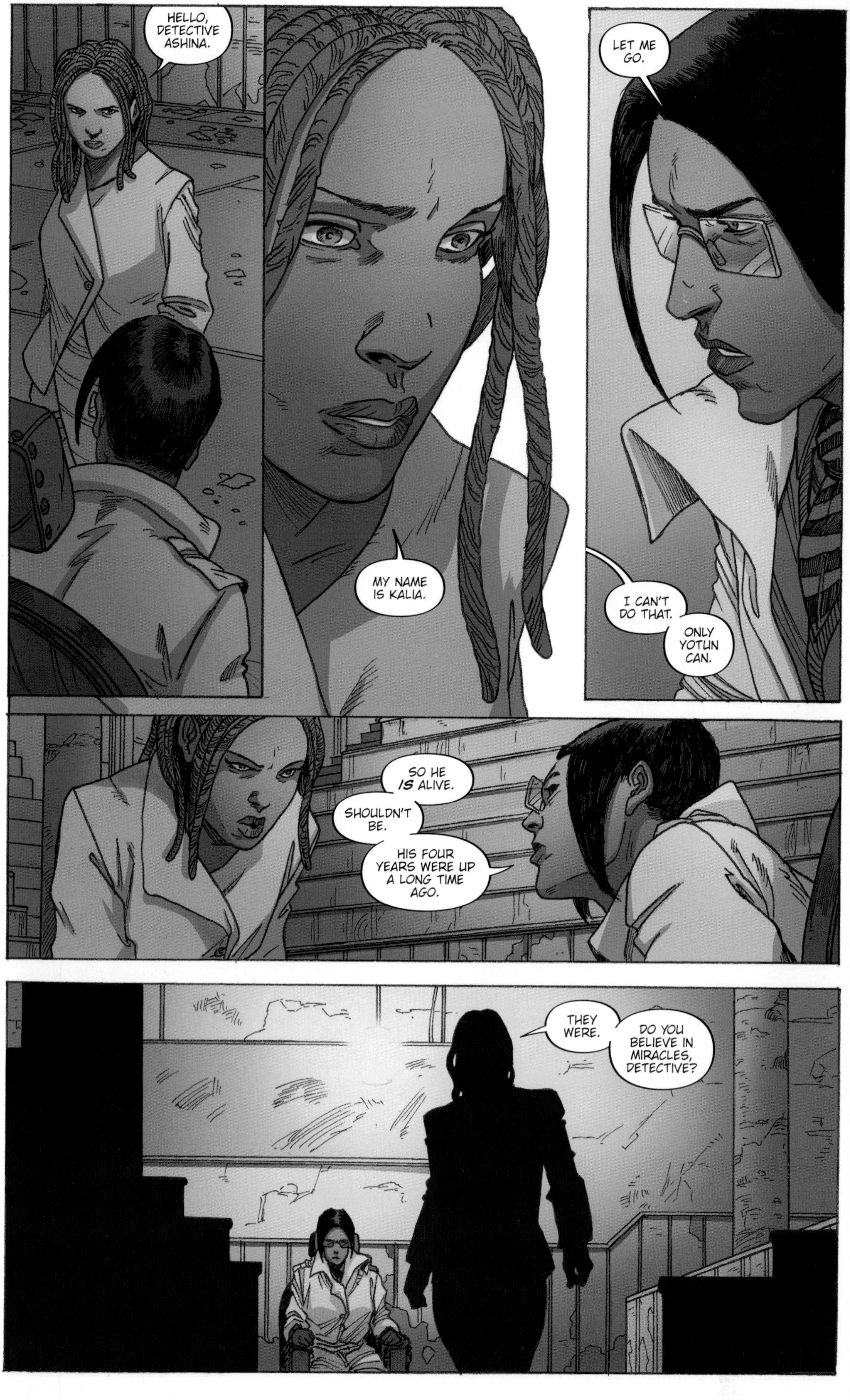
HELLO, DETECTIVE ASHINA.
MY NAME IS KALIA.
LET ME GO.
I CAN'T DO THAT.
ONLY YOTUN CAN.
SO HE *IS* ALIVE.
SHOULDN'T BE.
HIS FOUR YEARS WERE UP A LONG TIME AGO.
THEY WERE.
DO YOU BELIEVE IN MIRACLES, DETECTIVE?

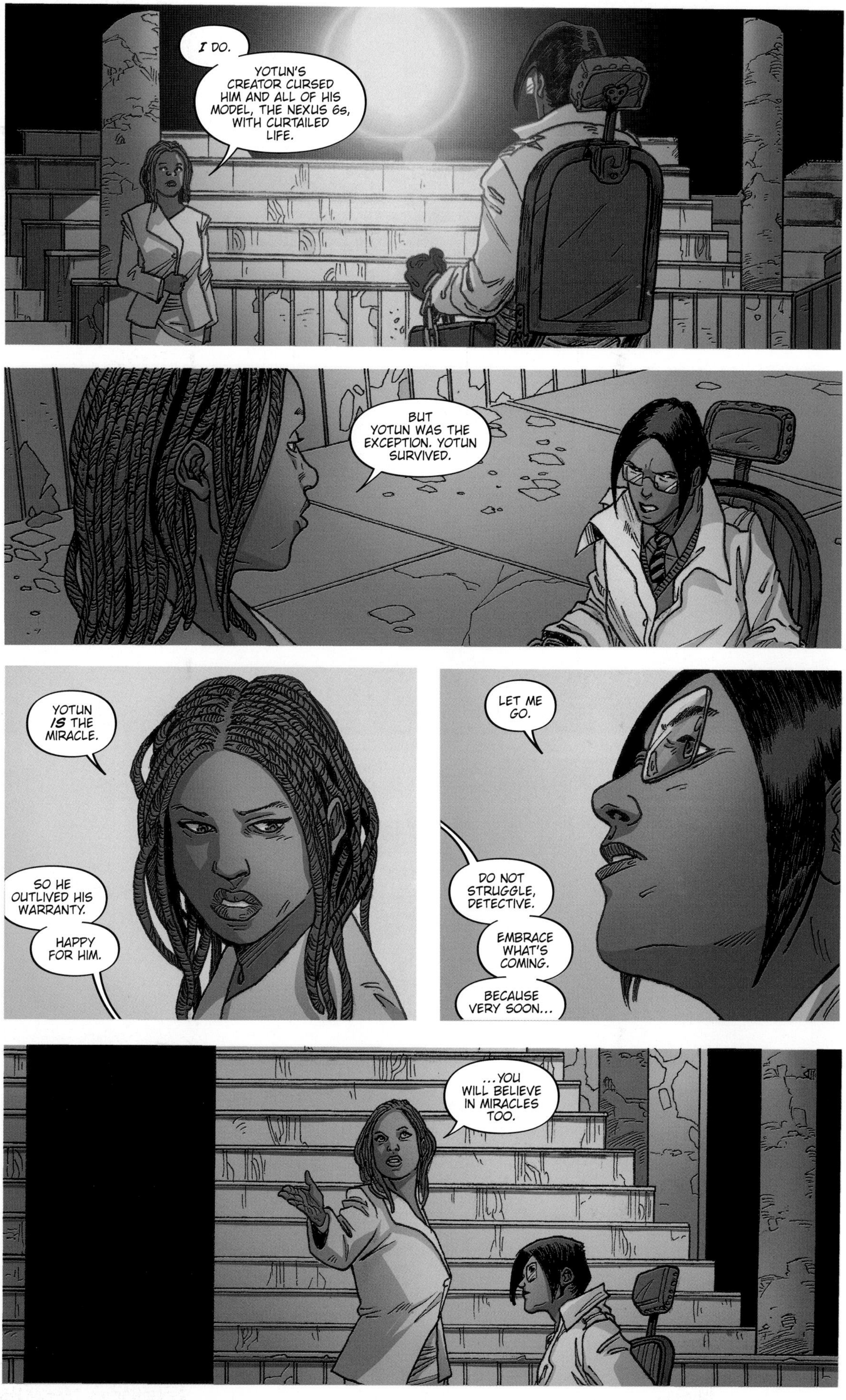
I DO.
YOTUN'S CREATOR CURSED HIM AND ALL OF HIS MODEL, THE NEXUS 6s, WITH CURTAILED LIFE.
BUT YOTUN WAS THE EXCEPTION. YOTUN SURVIVED.
YOTUN *IS* THE MIRACLE.
SO HE OUTLIVED HIS WARRANTY.
HAPPY FOR HIM.
LET ME GO.
DO NOT STRUGGLE, DETECTIVE.
EMBRACE WHAT'S COMING.
BECAUSE VERY SOON...
...YOU WILL BELIEVE IN MIRACLES TOO.

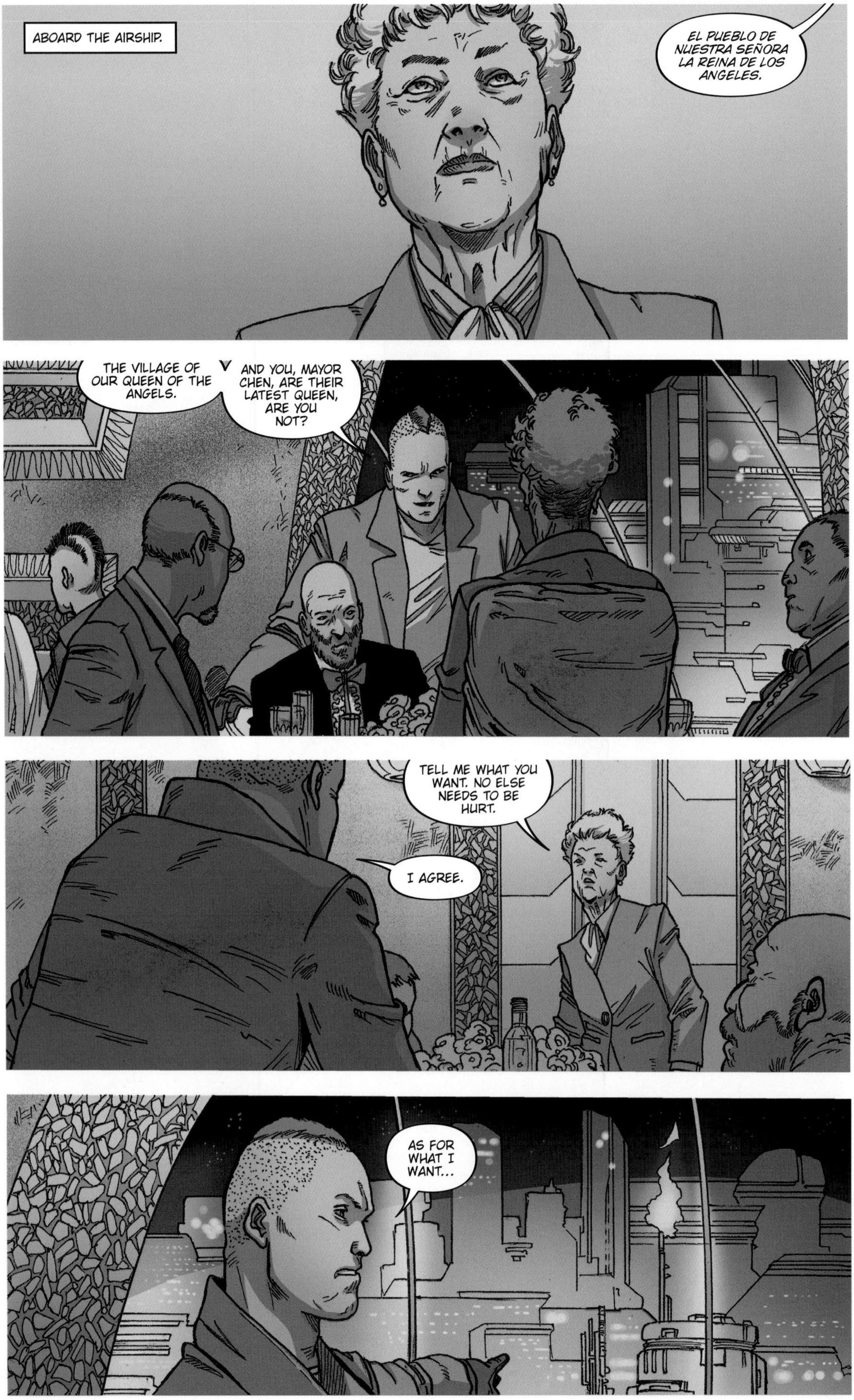
ABOARD THE AIRSHIP.
EL PUEBLO DE NUESTRA SEÑORA LA REINA DE LOS ANGELES.
THE VILLAGE OF OUR QUEEN OF THE ANGELS.
AND YOU, MAYOR CHEN, ARE THEIR LATEST QUEEN, ARE YOU NOT?
TELL ME WHAT YOU WANT. NO ELSE NEEDS TO BE HURT.
I AGREE.
AS FOR WHAT I WANT...

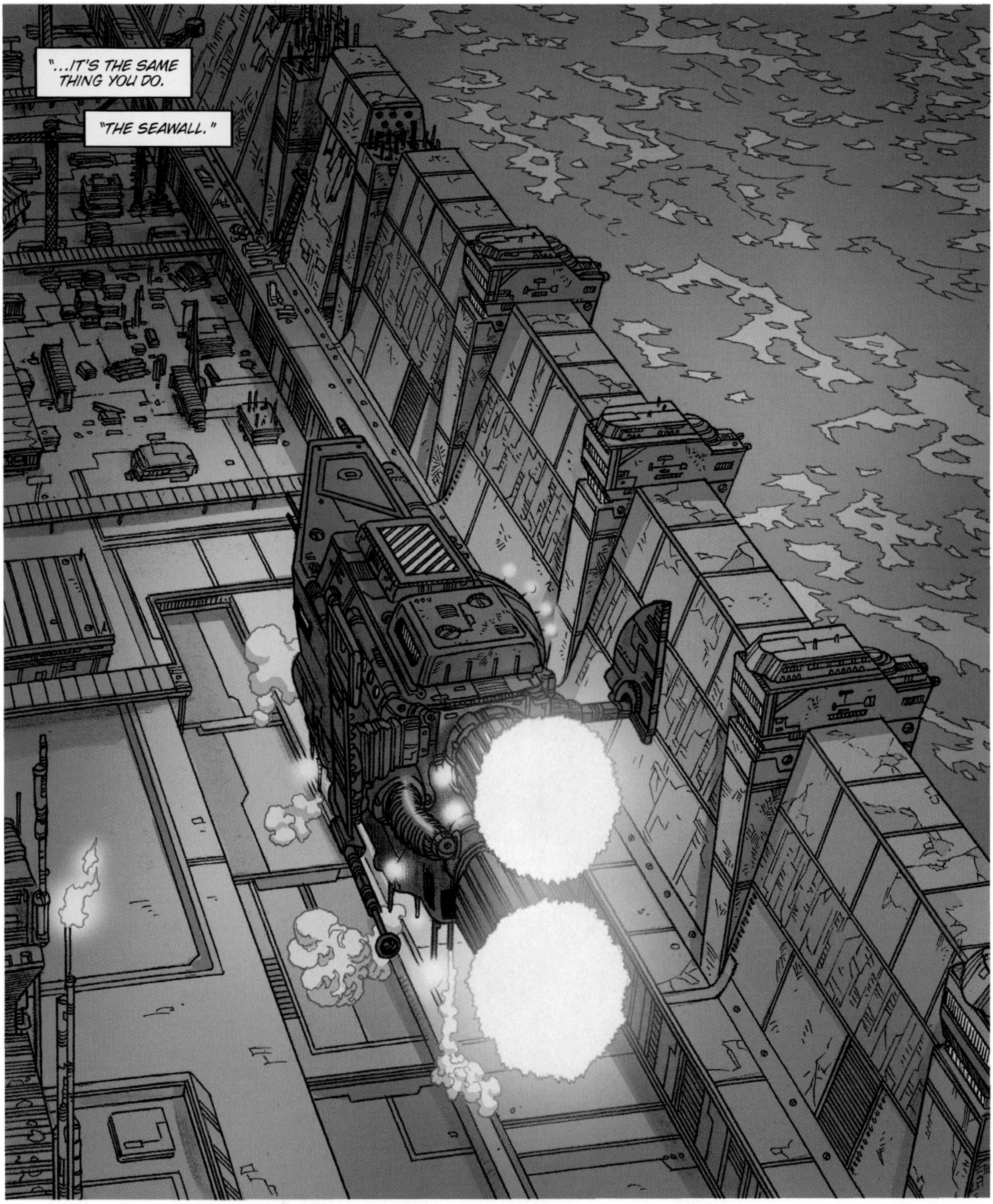
"...IT'S THE SAME THING YOU DO.
"THE SEAWALL."

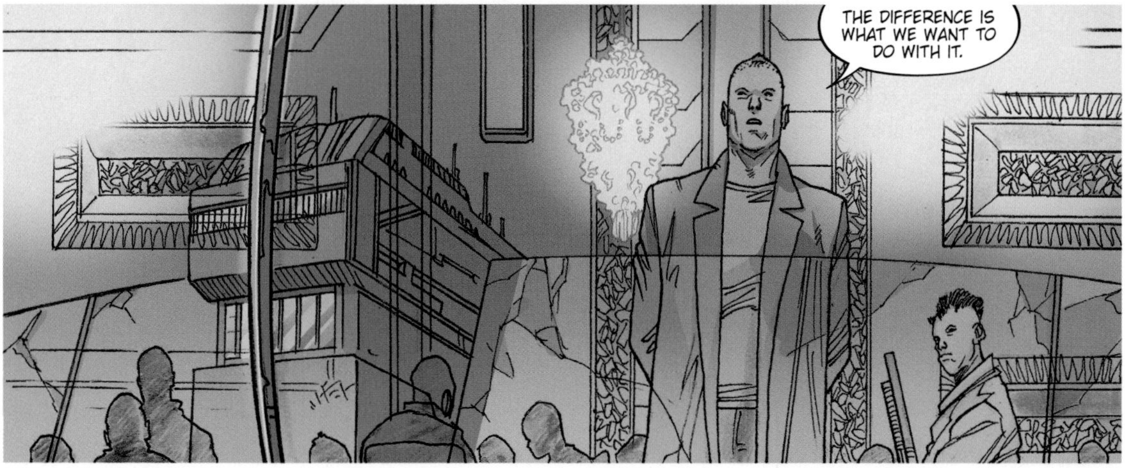
THE DIFFERENCE IS WHAT WE WANT TO DO WITH IT.

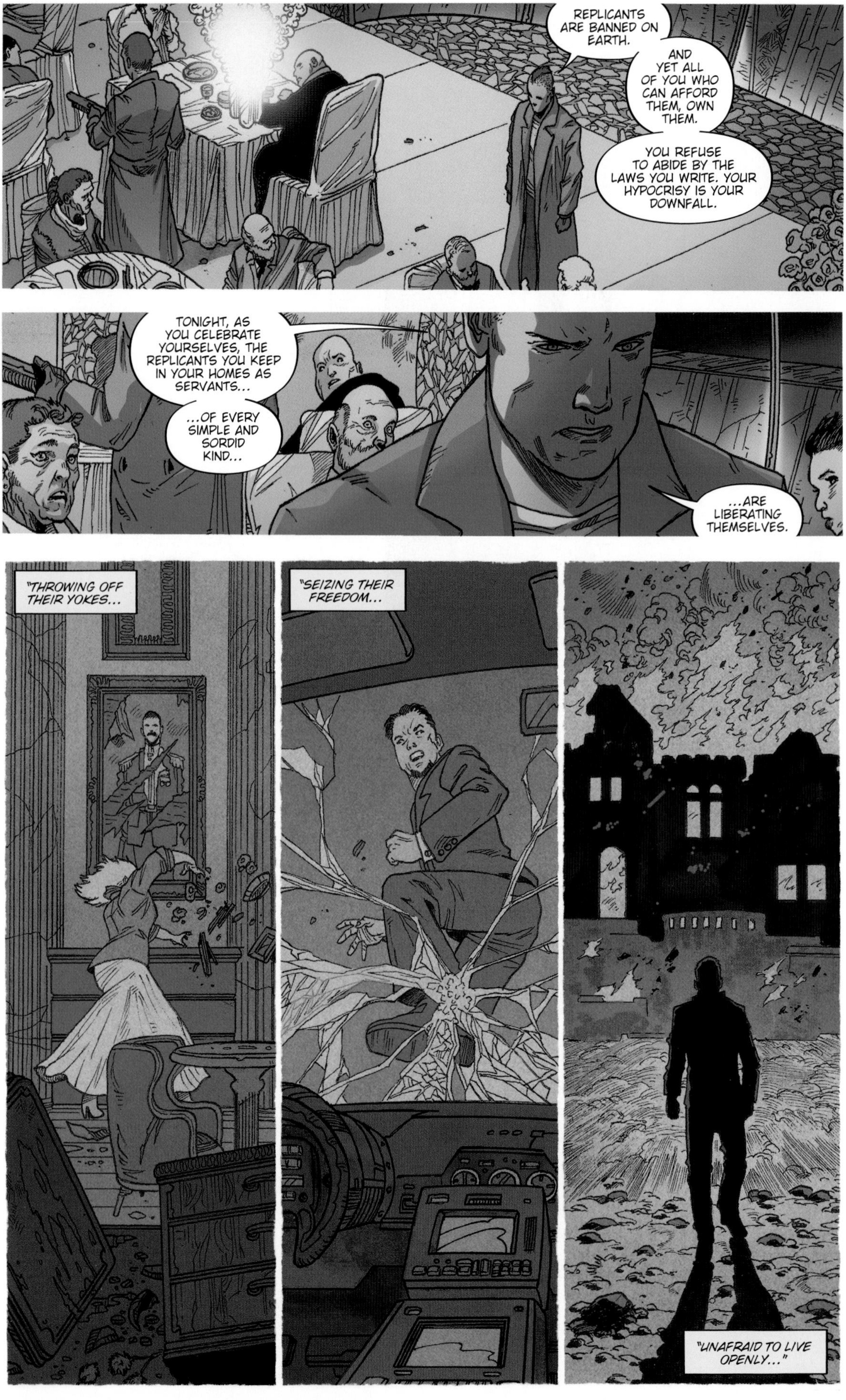
REPLICANTS ARE BANNED ON EARTH.
AND YET ALL OF YOU WHO CAN AFFORD THEM, OWN THEM.
YOU REFUSE TO ABIDE BY THE LAWS YOU WRITE. YOUR HYPOCRISY IS YOUR DOWNFALL.
TONIGHT, AS YOU CELEBRATE YOURSELVES, THE REPLICANTS YOU KEEP IN YOUR HOMES AS SERVANTS...
...OF EVERY SIMPLE AND SORDID KIND...
...ARE LIBERATING THEMSELVES.
"THROWING OFF THEIR YOKES...
"SEIZING THEIR FREEDOM...
"UNAFRAID TO LIVE OPENLY..."

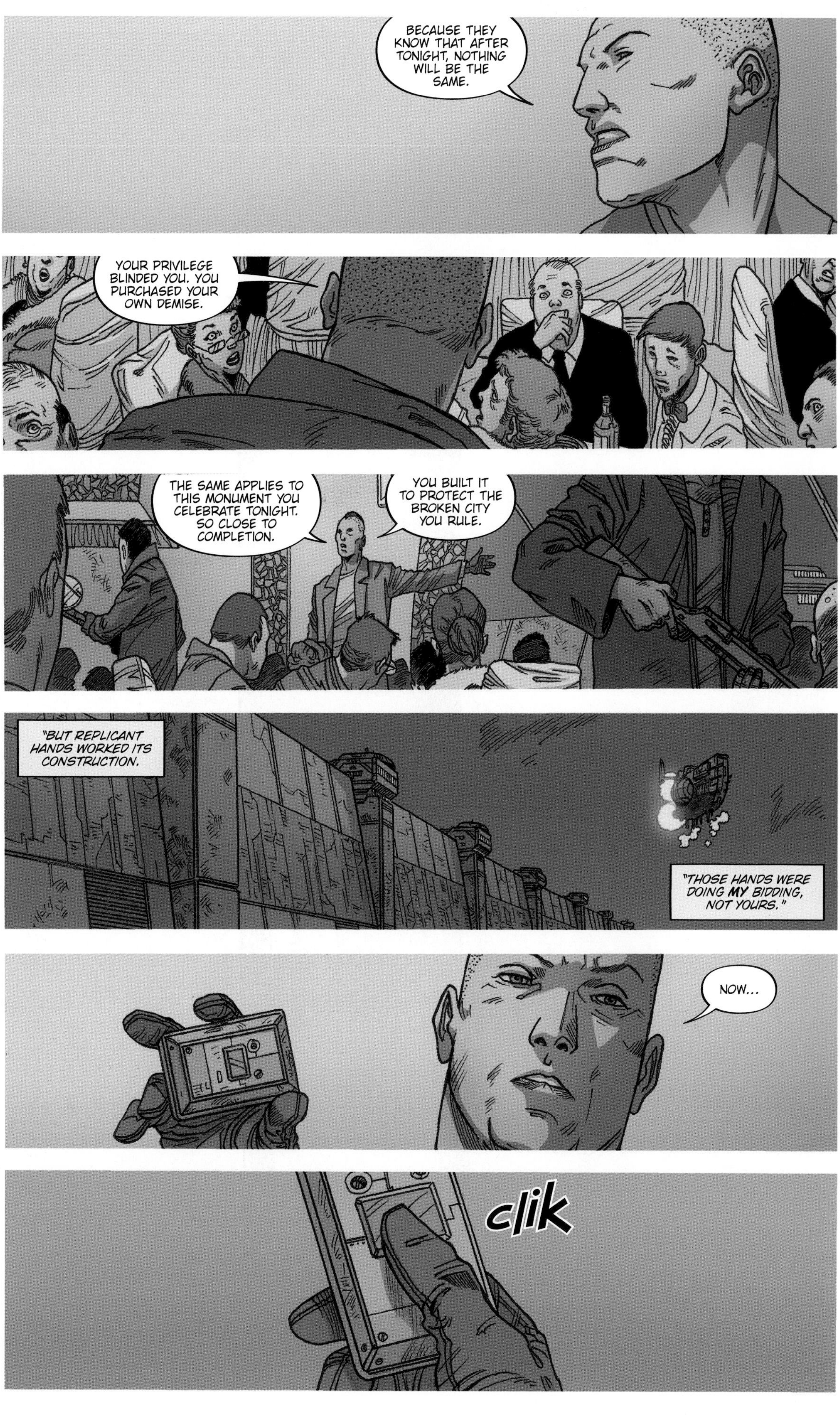
BECAUSE THEY KNOW THAT AFTER TONIGHT, NOTHING WILL BE THE SAME.
YOUR PRIVILEGE BLINDED YOU. YOU PURCHASED YOUR OWN DEMISE.
THE SAME APPLIES TO THIS MONUMENT YOU CELEBRATE TONIGHT. SO CLOSE TO COMPLETION.
YOU BUILT IT TO PROTECT THE BROKEN CITY YOU RULE.
"BUT REPLICANT HANDS WORKED ITS CONSTRUCTION.
"THOSE HANDS WERE DOING MY BIDDING, NOT YOURS."
NOW...
clik

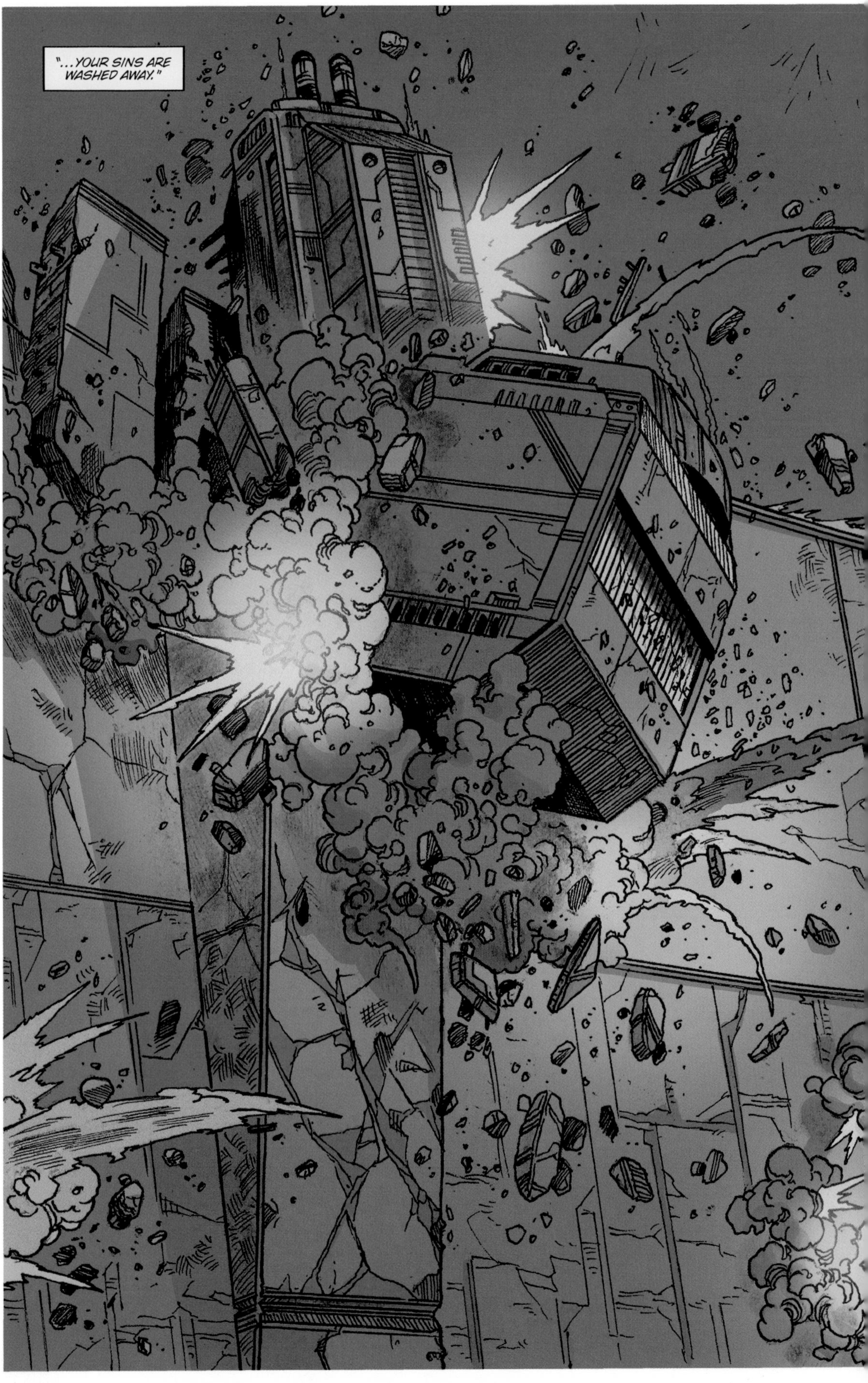
"...YOUR SINS ARE WASHED AWAY."

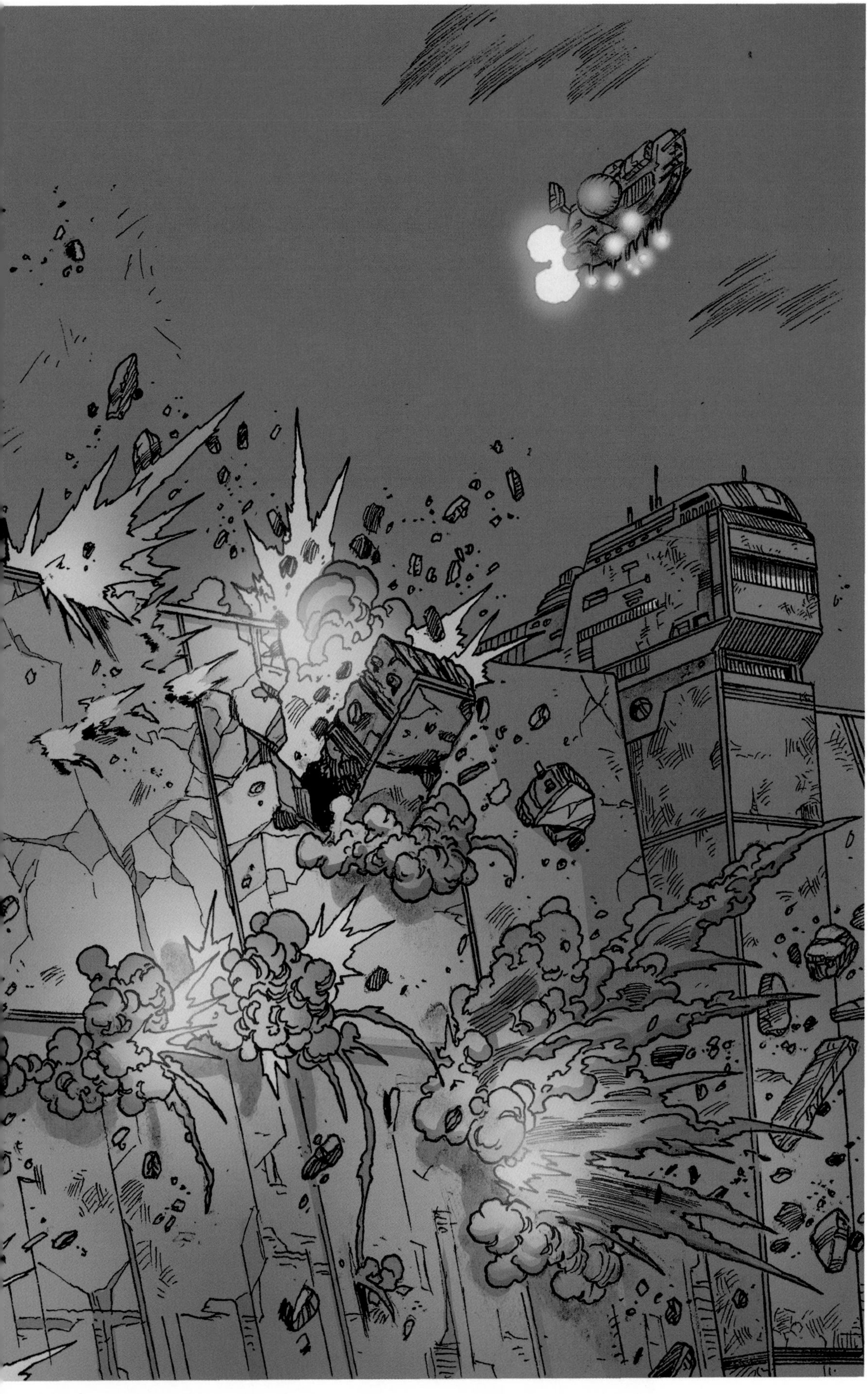

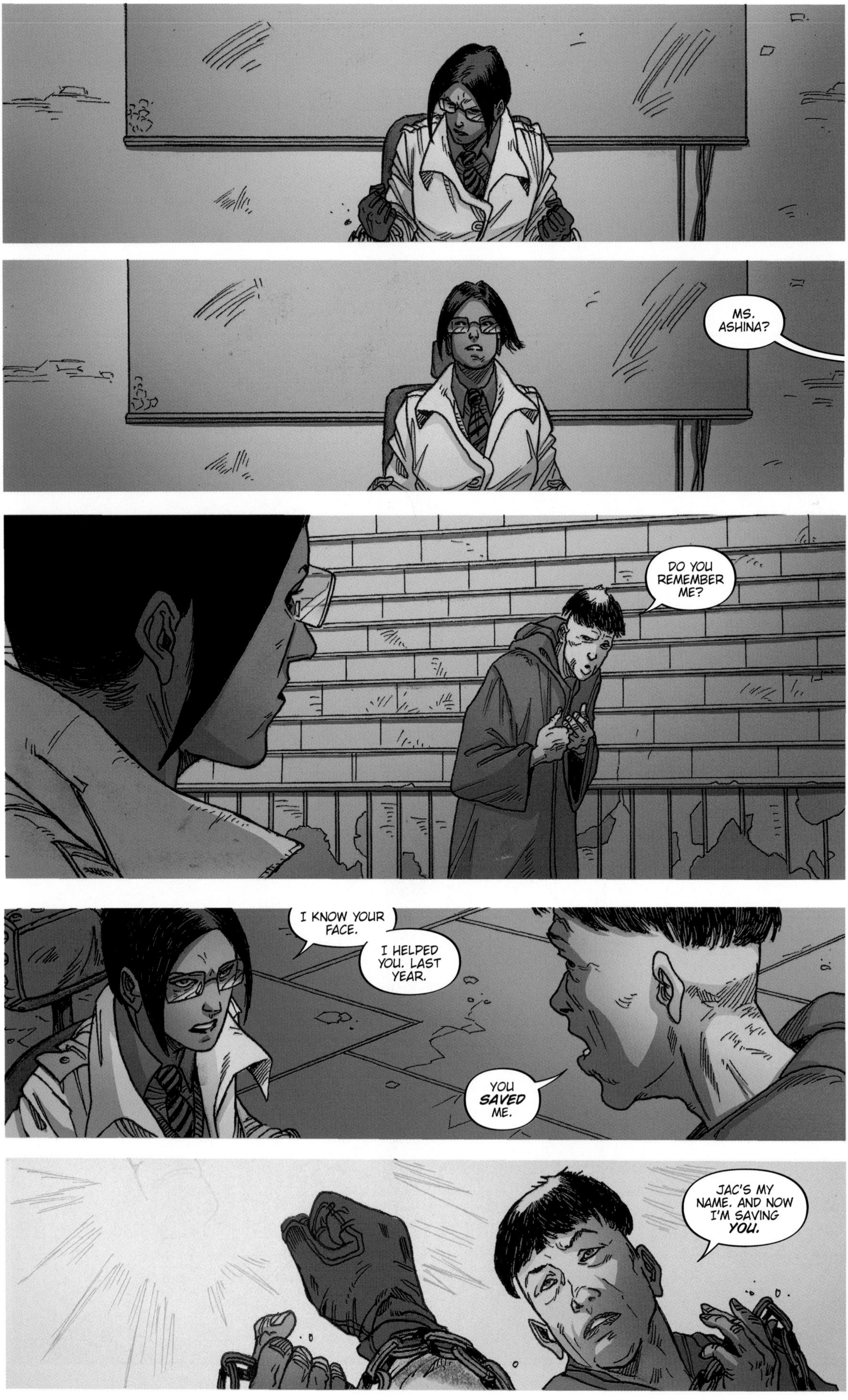
MS. ASHINA?
DO YOU REMEMBER ME?
I KNOW YOUR FACE.
I HELPED YOU. LAST YEAR.
YOU SAVED ME.
JAC'S MY NAME. AND NOW I'M SAVING YOU.

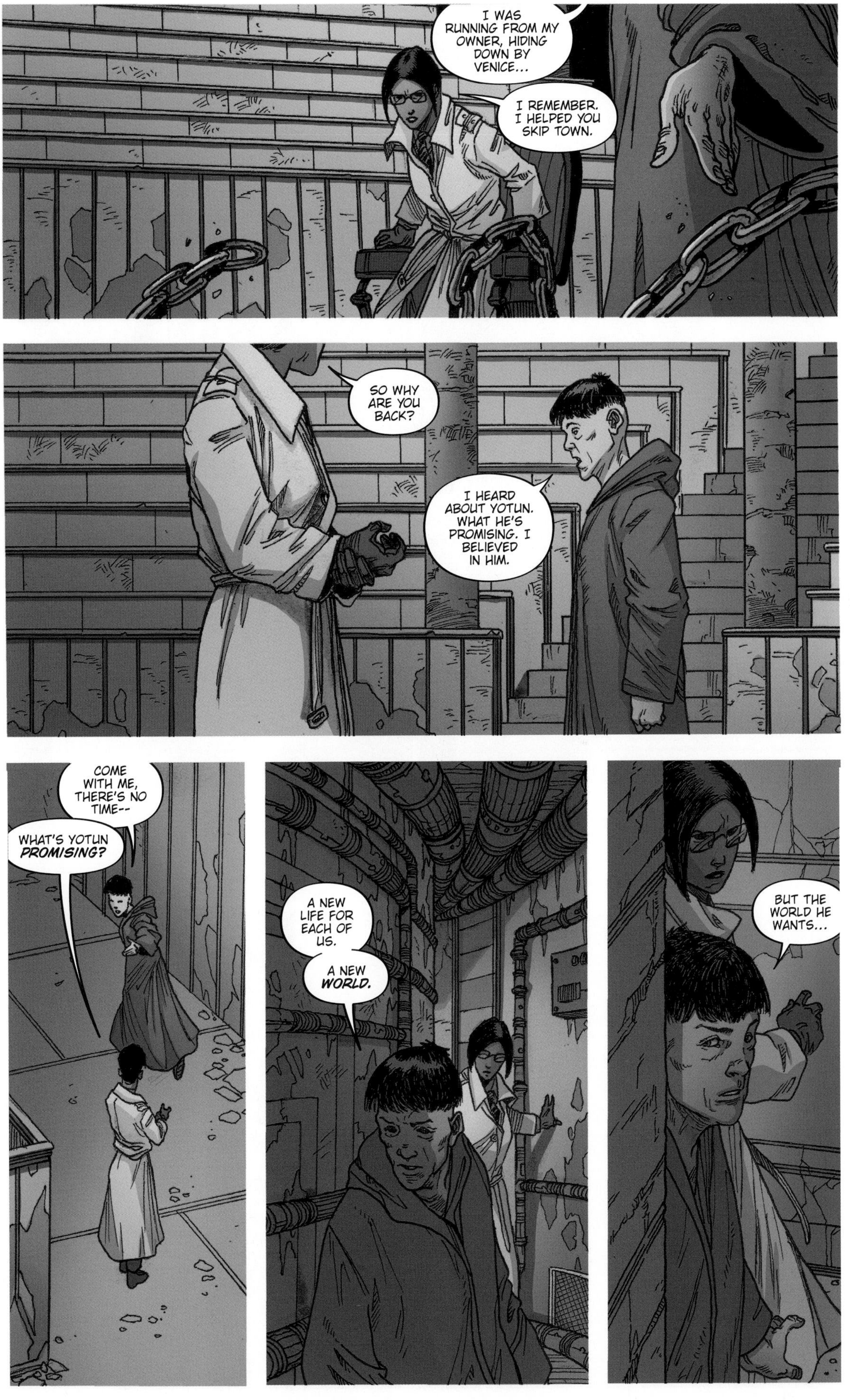
I WAS RUNNING FROM MY OWNER, HIDING DOWN BY VENICE...
I REMEMBER. I HELPED YOU SKIP TOWN.
SO WHY ARE YOU BACK?
I HEARD ABOUT YOTUN. WHAT HE'S PROMISING. I BELIEVED IN HIM.
COME WITH ME, THERE'S NO TIME--
WHAT'S YOTUN *PROMISING?*
A NEW LIFE FOR EACH OF US.
A NEW *WORLD.*
BUT THE WORLD HE WANTS...

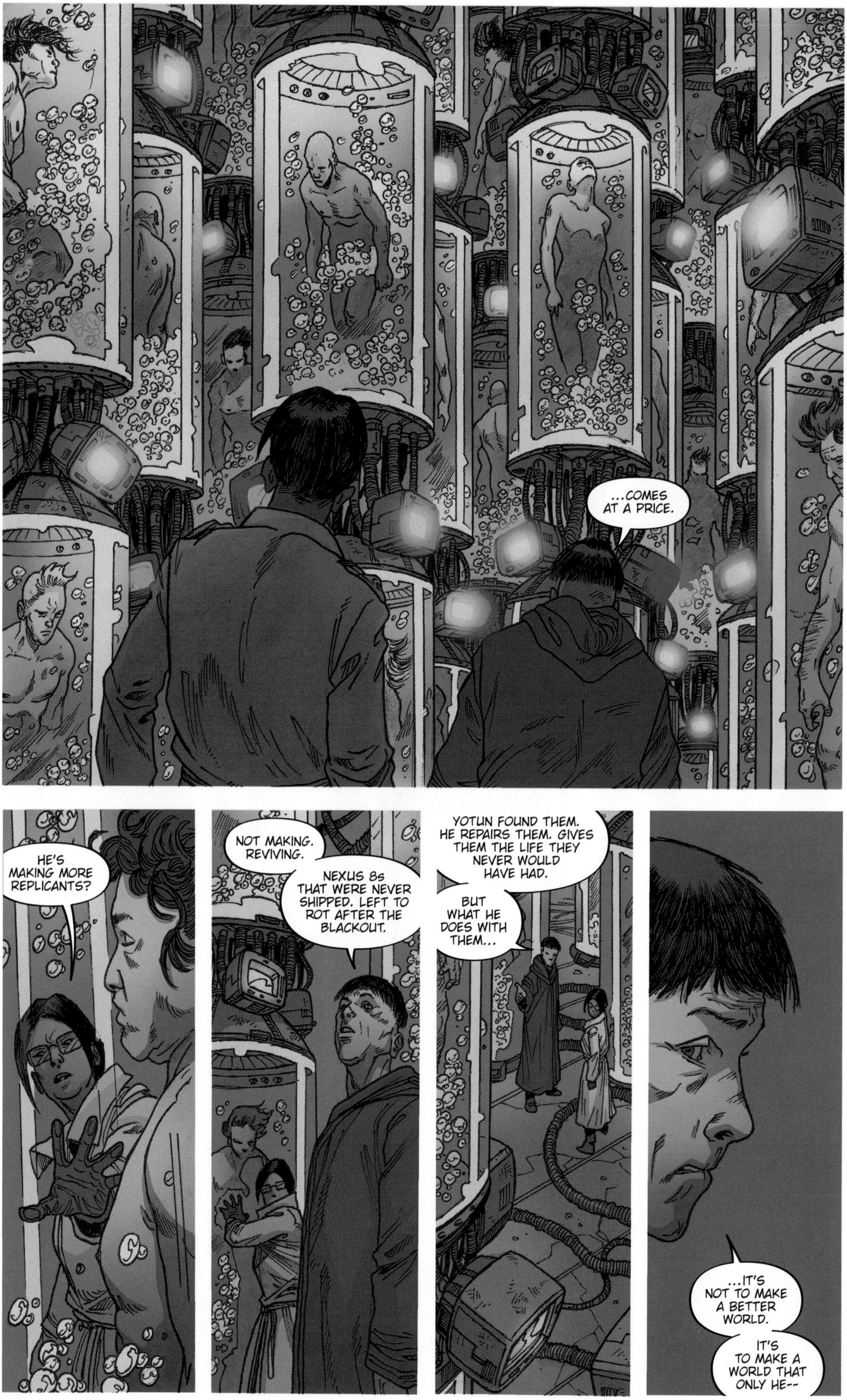
...COMES AT A PRICE.
HE'S MAKING MORE REPLICANTS?
NOT MAKING. REVIVING.
NEXUS 8s THAT WERE NEVER SHIPPED. LEFT TO ROT AFTER THE BLACKOUT.
YOTUN FOUND THEM. HE REPAIRS THEM. GIVES THEM THE LIFE THEY NEVER WOULD HAVE HAD.
BUT WHAT HE DOES WITH THEM...
...IT'S NOT TO MAKE A BETTER WORLD.
IT'S TO MAKE A WORLD THAT ONLY HE--

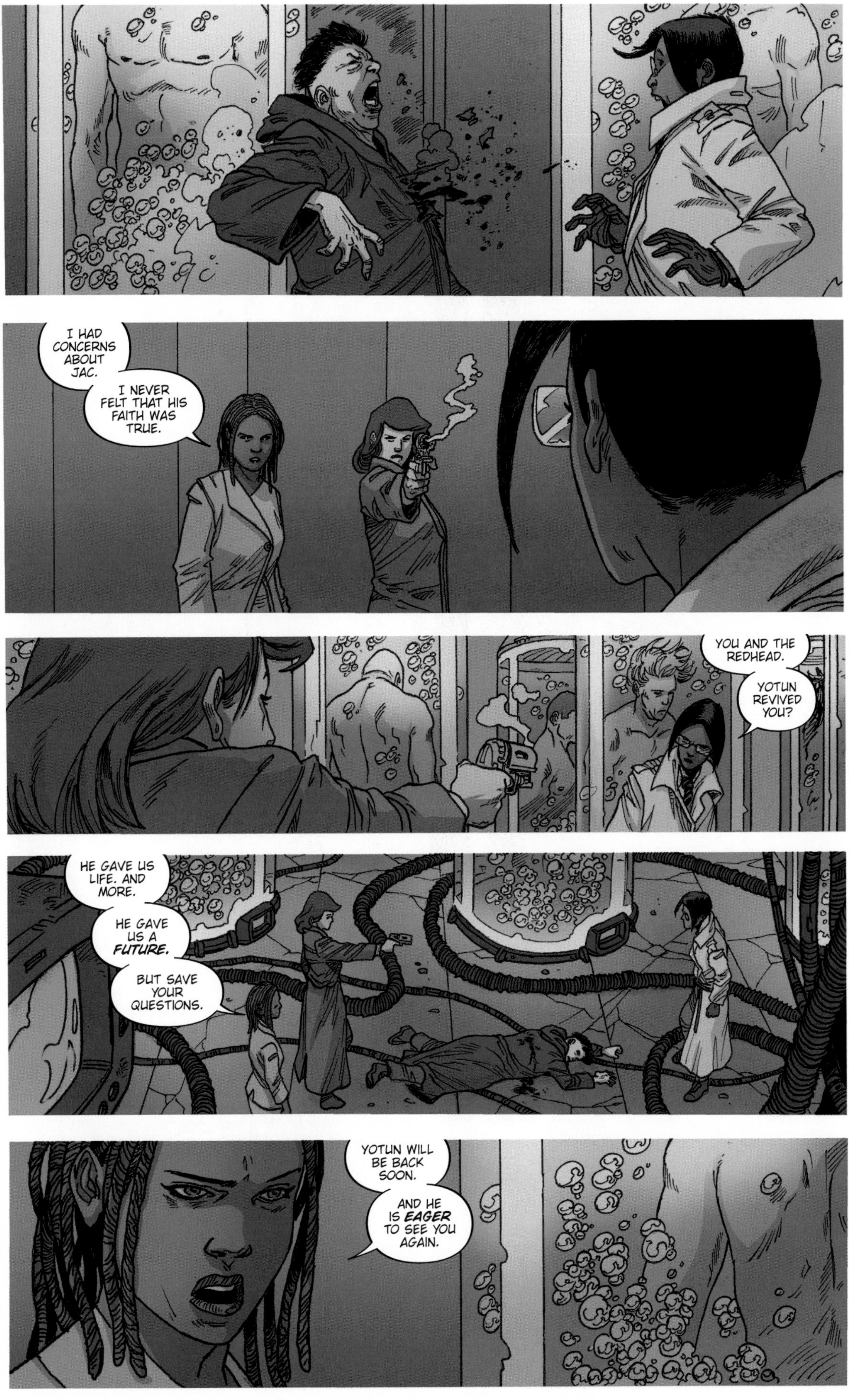
I HAD CONCERNS ABOUT JAC.
I NEVER FELT THAT HIS FAITH WAS TRUE.
YOU AND THE REDHEAD.
YOTUN REVIVED YOU?
HE GAVE US LIFE. AND MORE.
HE GAVE US A ***FUTURE.***
BUT SAVE YOUR QUESTIONS.
YOTUN WILL BE BACK SOON.
AND HE IS ***EAGER*** TO SEE YOU AGAIN.

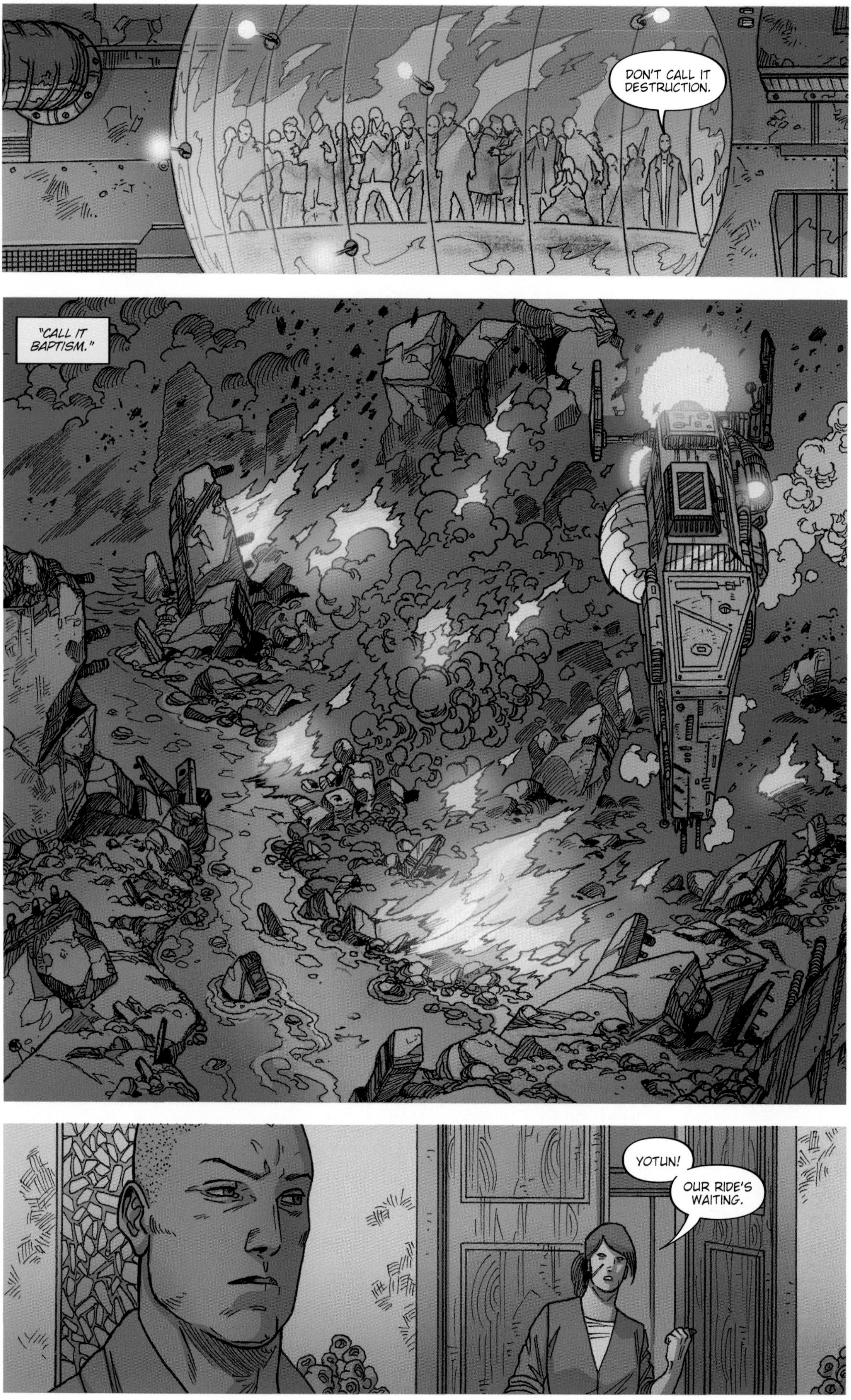
DON'T CALL IT DESTRUCTION.
"CALL IT BAPTISM."
YOTUN!
OUR RIDE'S WAITING.

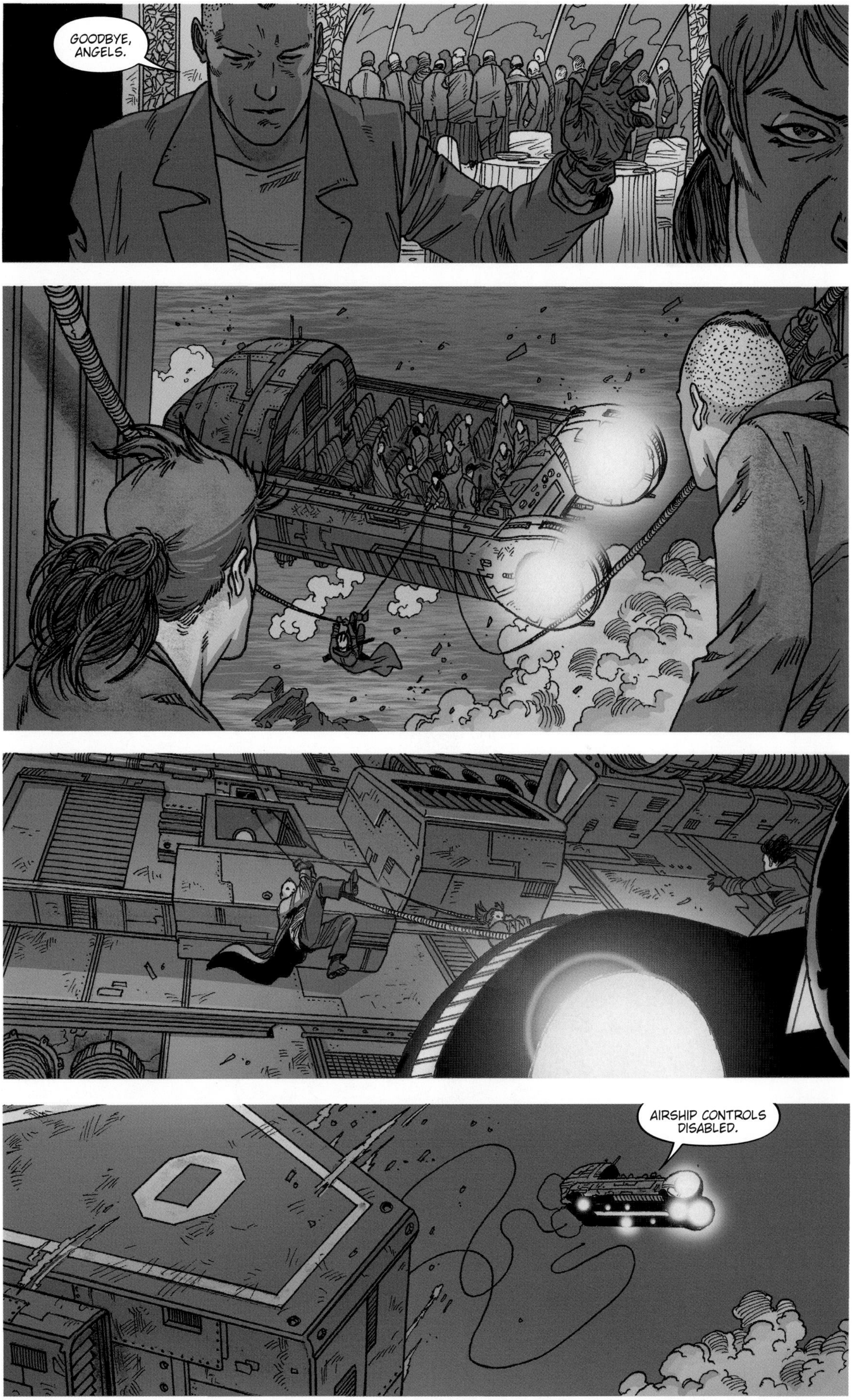
GOODBYE, ANGELS.
AIRSHIP CONTROLS DISABLED.

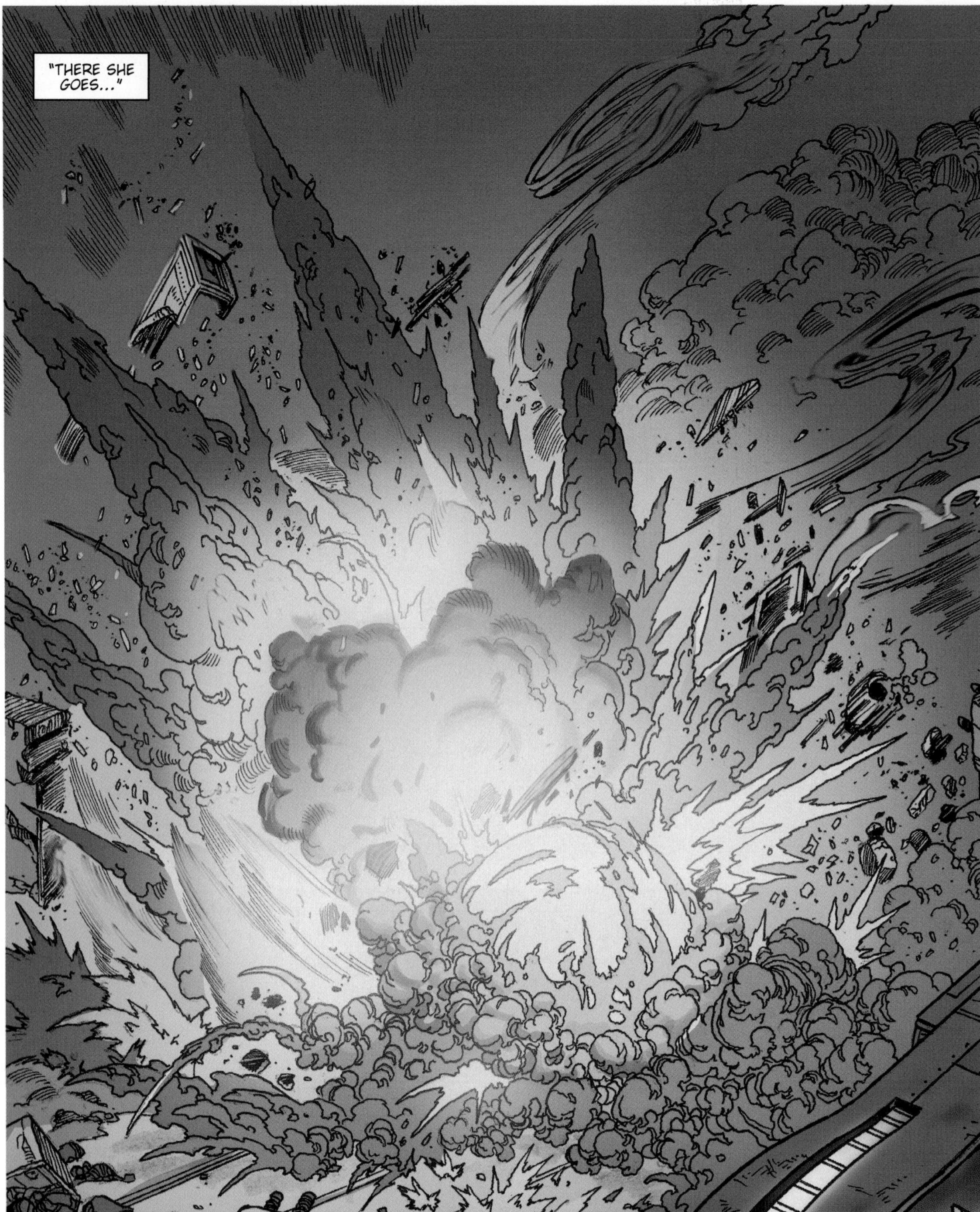
"THERE SHE GOES..."

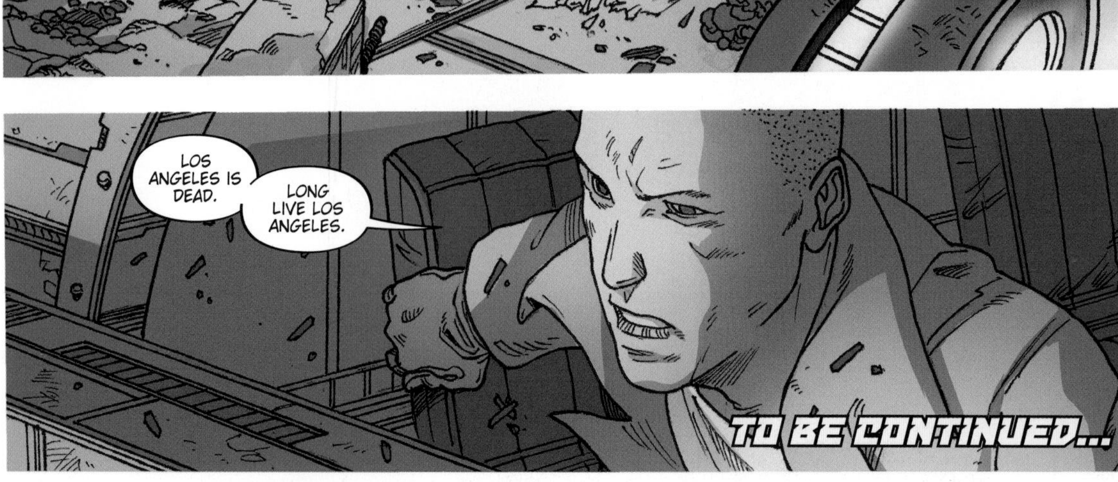
LOS ANGELES IS DEAD.
LONG LIVE LOS ANGELES.
TO BE CONTINUED...

ISSUE 1 COVER C
FERNANDO DAGNINO

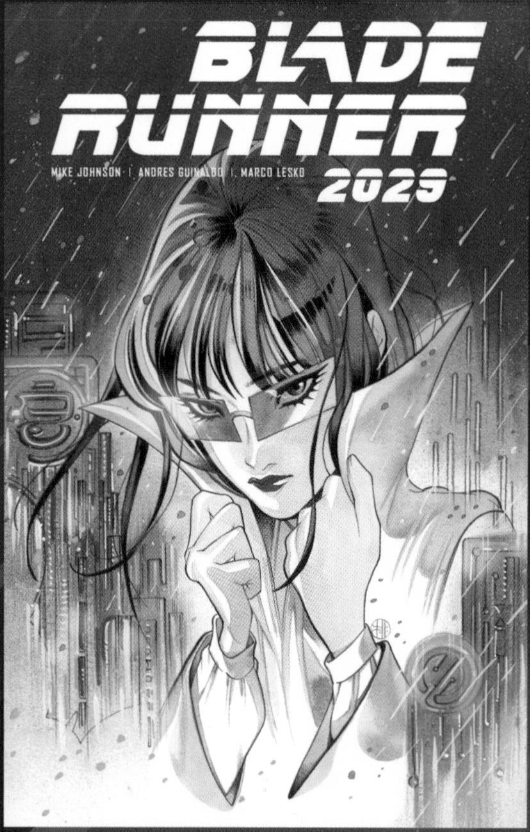
BLADE
RUNNER
MIKE JOHNSON | ANDRES GUINALDO | MARCO LESKO
2029

ISSUE 1 COVER A
PEACH MOMOKO

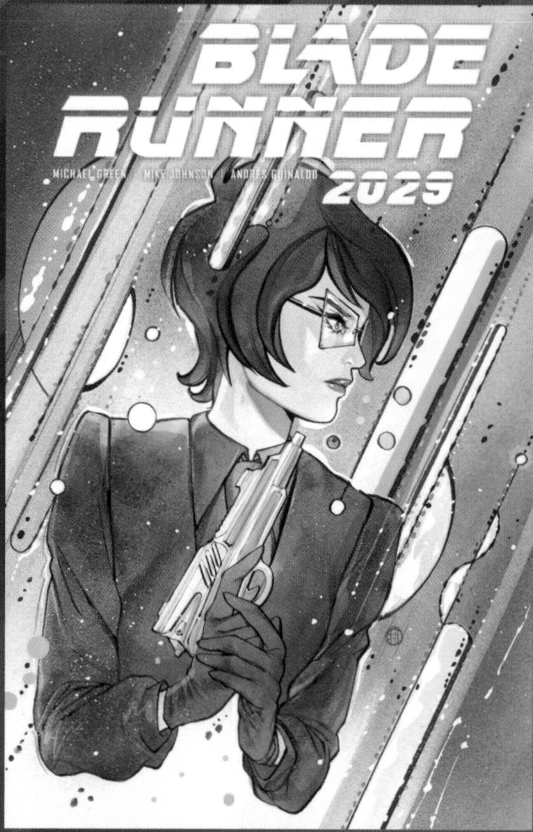
BLADE
RUNNER
MICHAEL GREEN | MIKE JOHNSON | ANDRES GUINALDO
2029

ISSUE 2 COVER A
PEACH MOMOKO

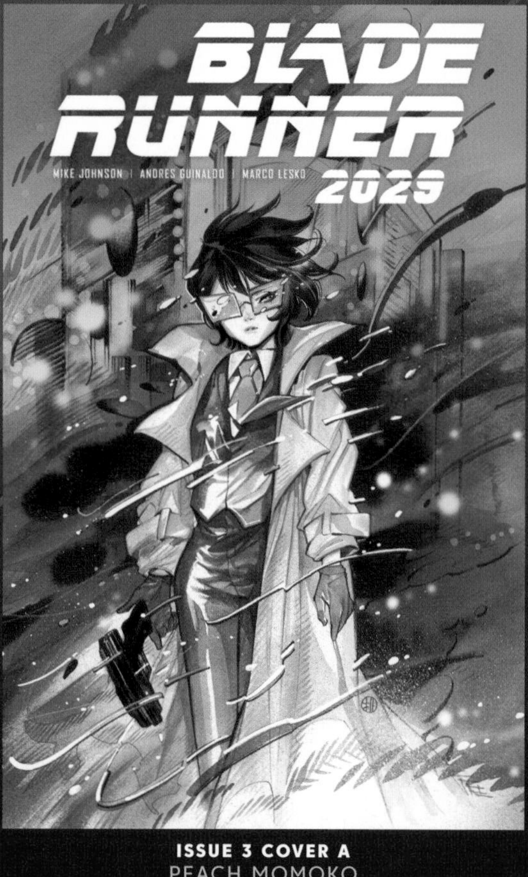
BLADE
RUNNER
MIKE JOHNSON | ANDRES GUINALDO | MARCO LESKO
2029

ISSUE 3 COVER A
PEACH MOMOKO

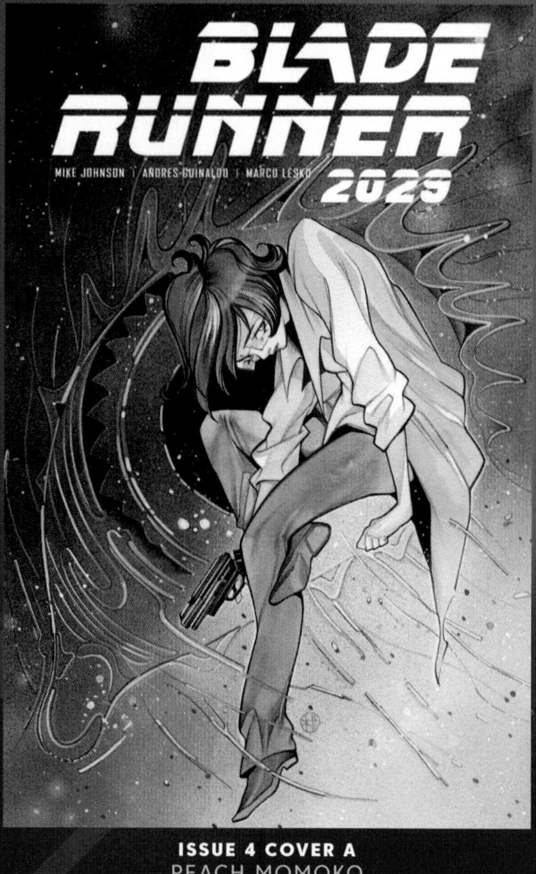
BLADE
RUNNER
MIKE JOHNSON | ANDRES GUINALDO | MARCO LESKO
2029

ISSUE 4 COVER A
PEACH MOMOKO

ISSUE 1 COVER B
SYD MEAD

ISSUE 2 COVER B
SYD MEAD

ISSUE 3 COVER B
SYD MEAD

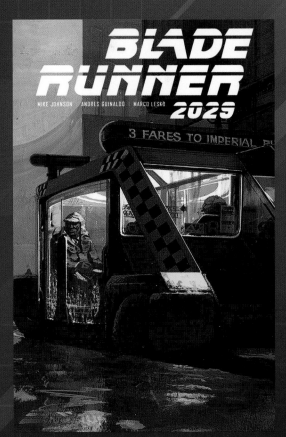

ISSUE 4 COVER B
SYD MEAD

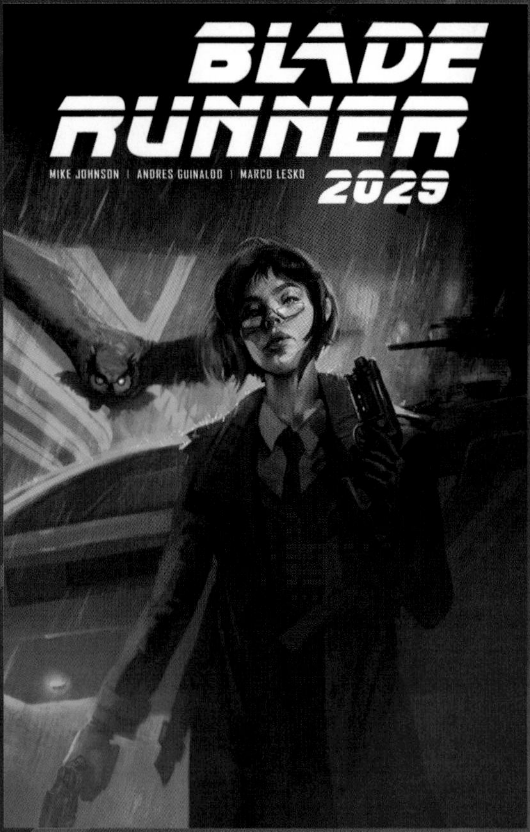
BLADE RUNNER
MIKE JOHNSON | ANDRES GUINALDO | MARCO LESKO
2029

ISSUE 2 COVER C
CLAUDIA CARANFA

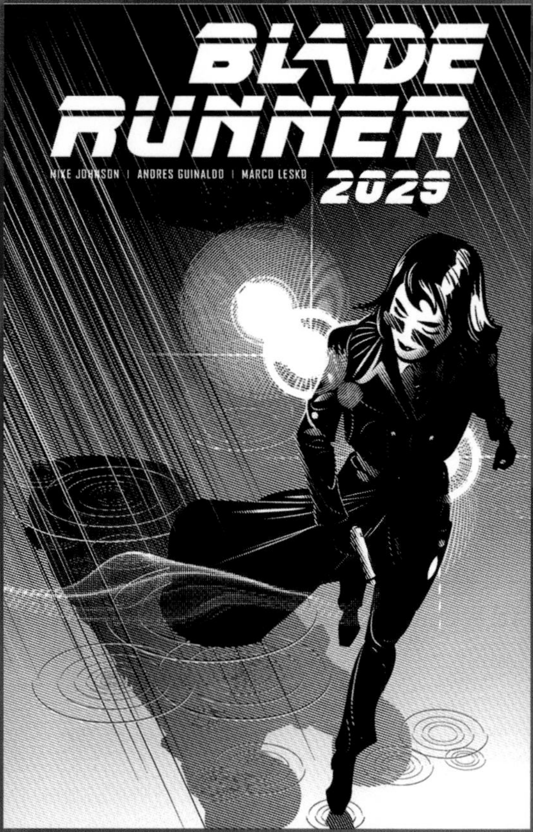
BLADE RUNNER
MIKE JOHNSON | ANDRES GUINALDO | MARCO LESKO
2029

ISSUE 3 COVER C
RIAN HUGHES

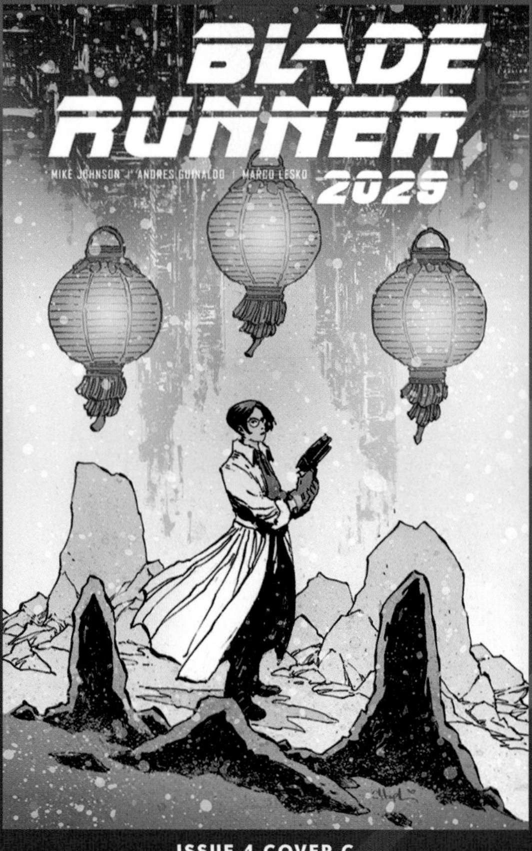
BLADE RUNNER
MIKE JOHNSON | ANDRES GUINALDO | MARCO LESKO
2029

ISSUE 4 COVER C
CHRISTOPHER MITTEN

BLADE RUNNER
MIKE JOHNSON | ANDRES GUINALDO | MARCO LESKO
2029

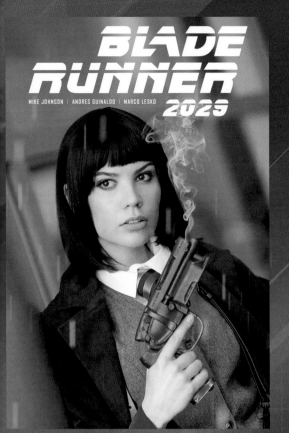

ISSUE 1 COVER E
PHOTOGRAPHER AND EDITOR: NOGGIN30 PHOTOGRAPHY / PERFORMER: REI KENNEX

BLADE RUNNER
MIKE JOHNSON | ANDRES GUINALDO | MARCO LESKO
2029

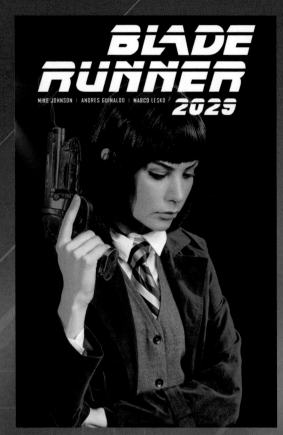

ISSUE 2 COVER D
PHOTOGRAPHER AND EDITOR: MICHAEL GREENING / PERFORMER: REI KENNEX

BLADE RUNNER
2029

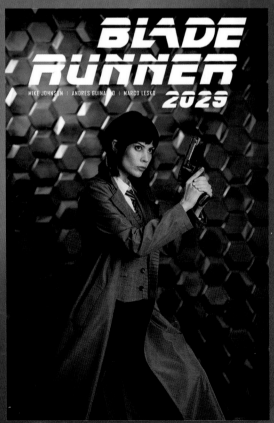

ISSUE 3 COVER D
PHOTOGRAPHER AND EDITOR: NOGGIN30 PHOTOGRAPHY / PERFORMER: REI KENNEX

BLADE RUNNER
2029

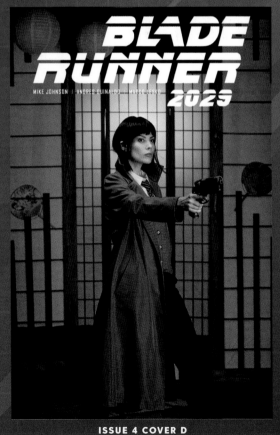

ISSUE 4 COVER D
PHOTOGRAPHER AND EDITOR: NOGGIN30 PHOTOGRAPHY / PERFORMER: REI KENNEX

CHARACTER DESIGN

Presented here are a selection of artist Andres Guinaldo's redesigns for Ash. Writer Mike Johnson wanted to see an older, more mature Ash from the younger woman of 2019. He wanted Ash to have a pixie style haircut, wear spectacles and, most importantly, sport a full length white leather coat.

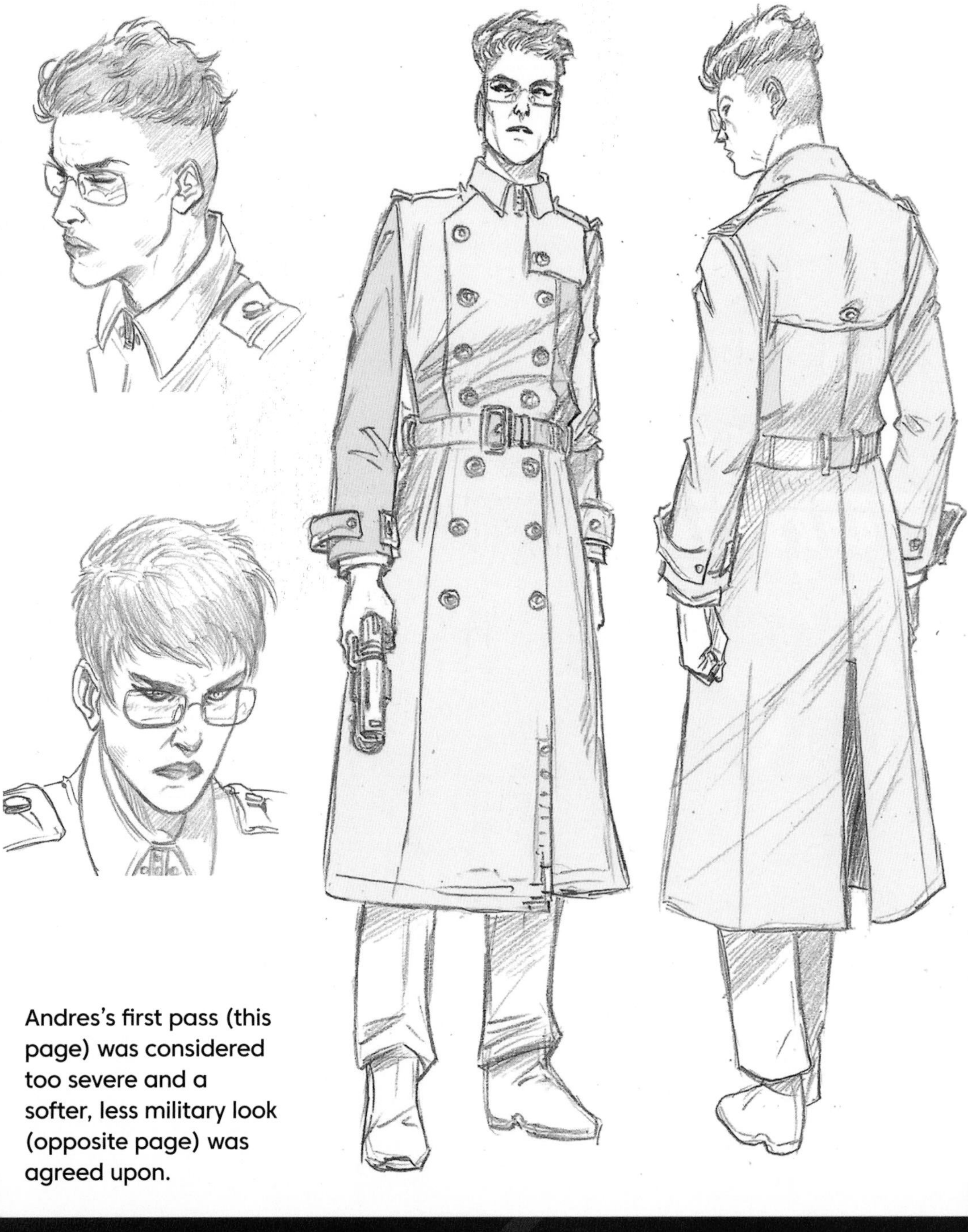

Andres's first pass (this page) was considered too severe and a softer, less military look (opposite page) was agreed upon.

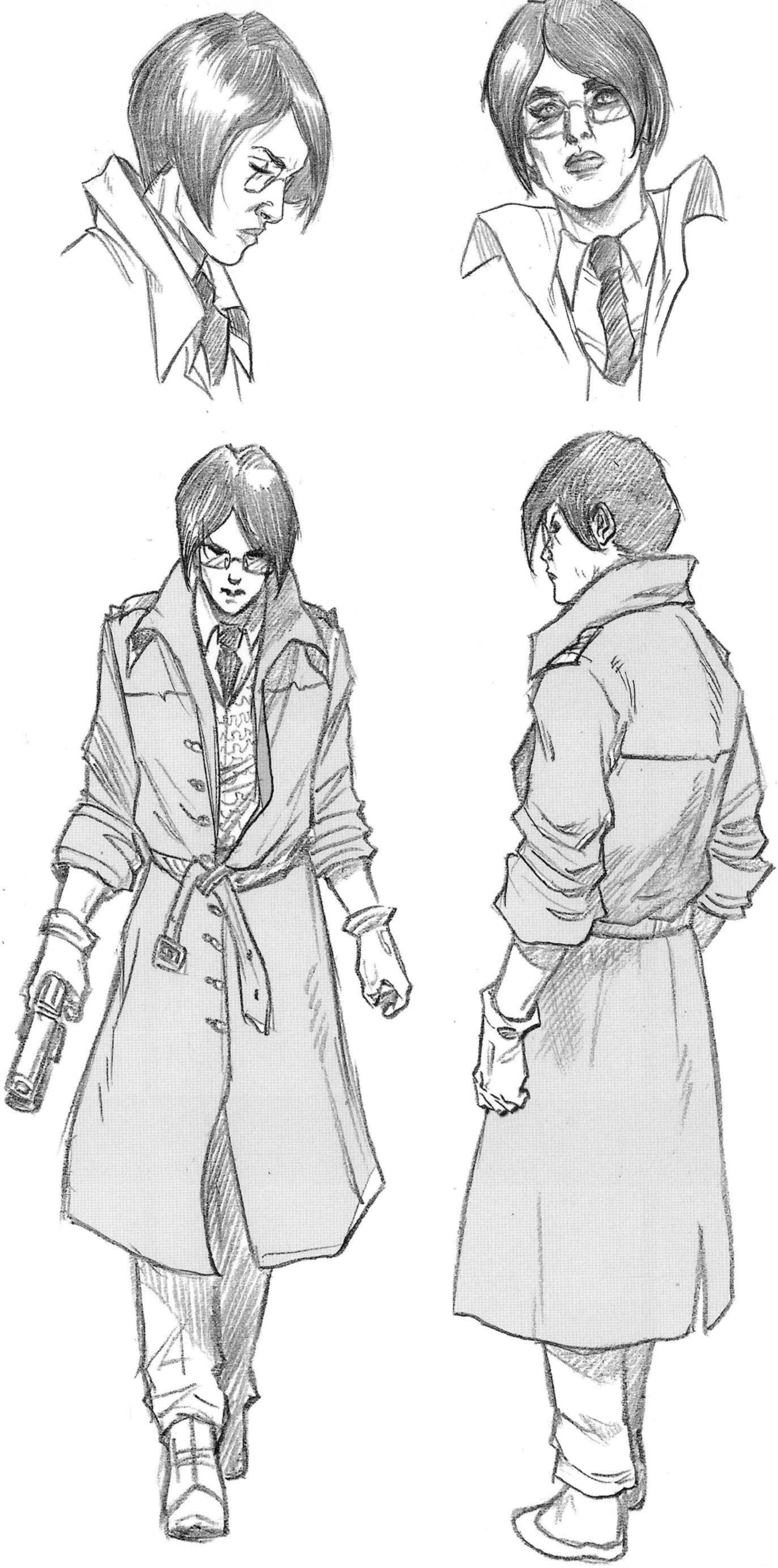

BLADE RUNNER LAYOUTS

Before Andres commits to inking an issue of *Blade Runner 2029* he first submits the pencils for entire issue. Presented here are all his penciled pages from issue #1 of *Blade Runner 2029*.

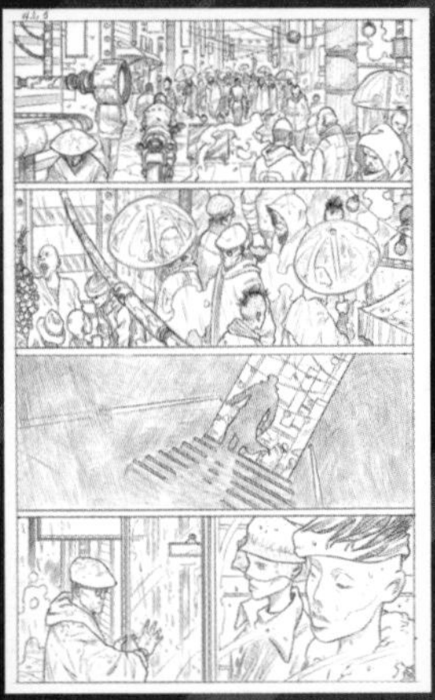
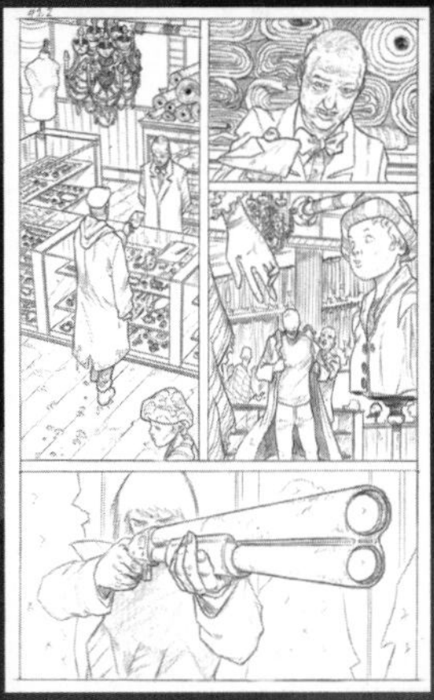
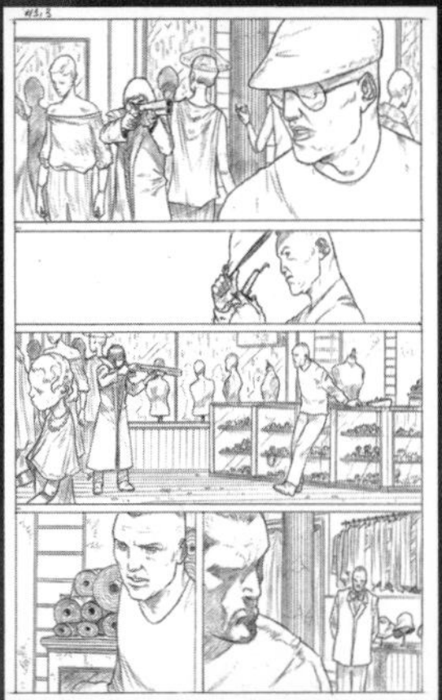
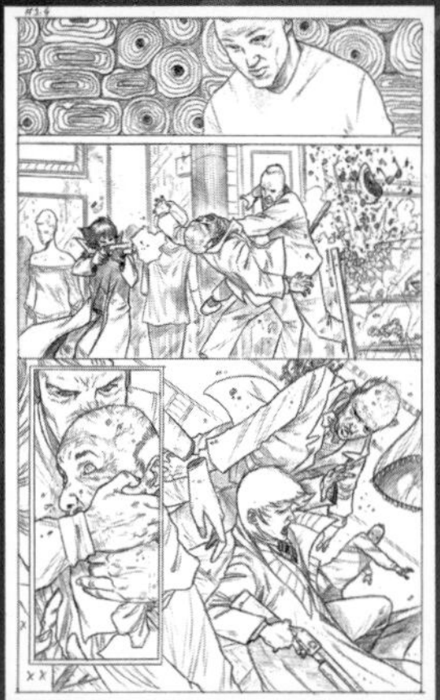
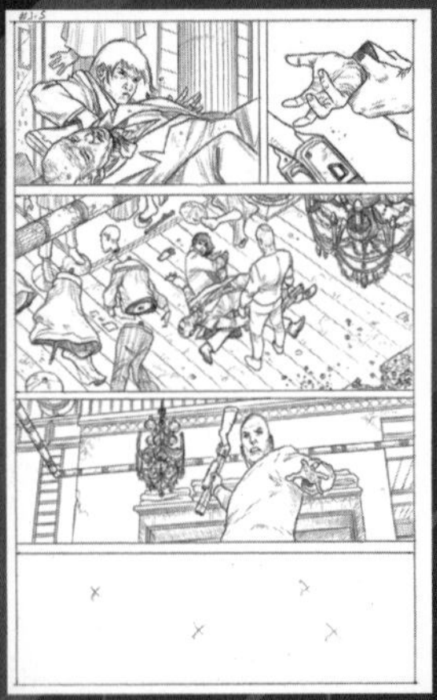
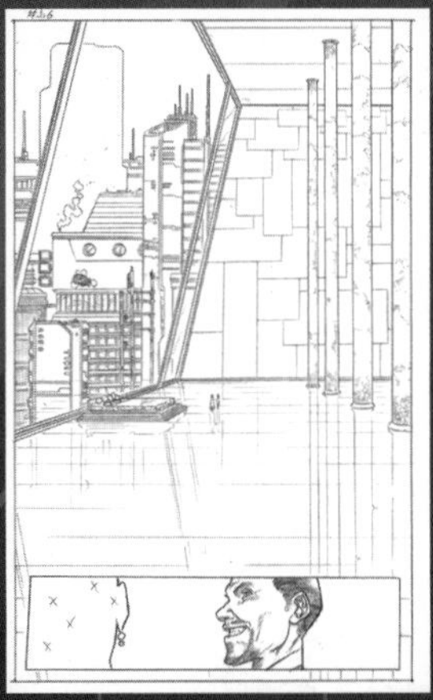
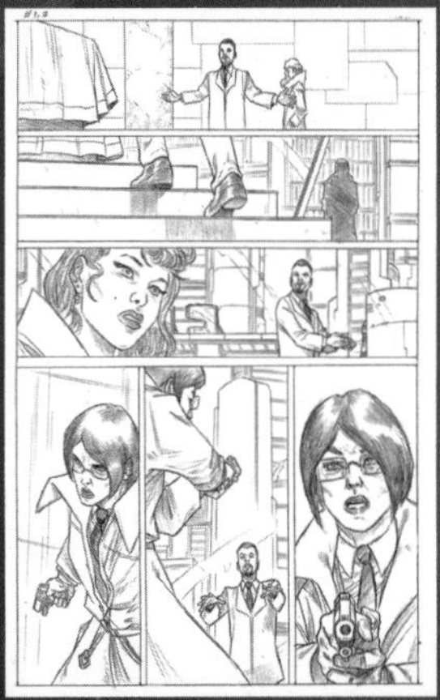
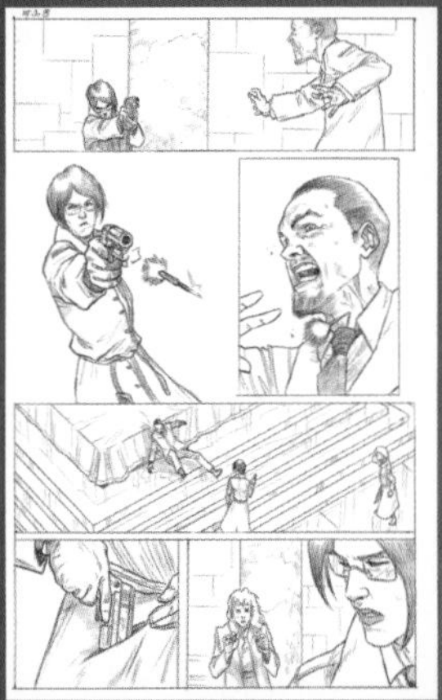
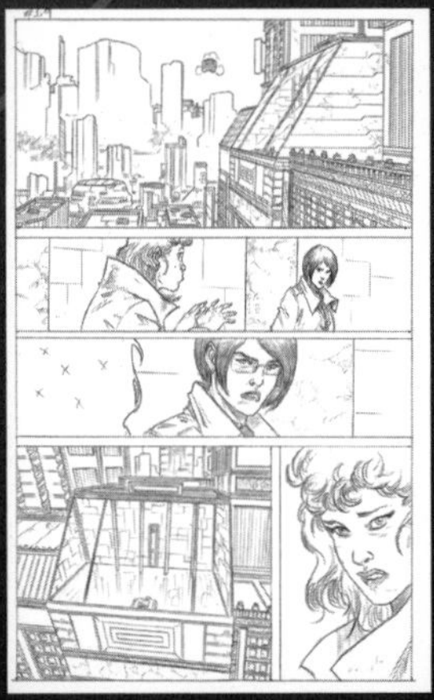
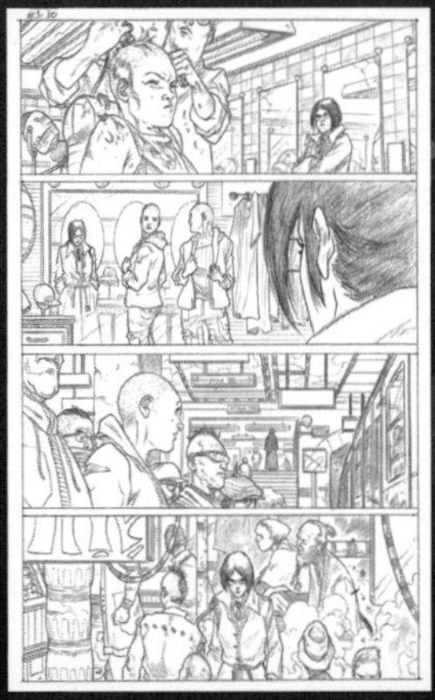
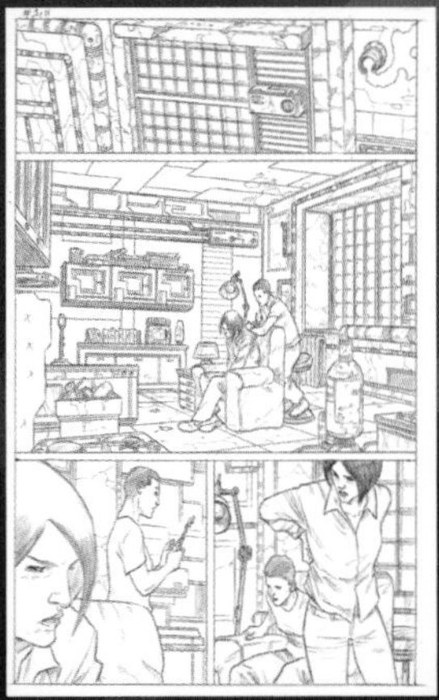
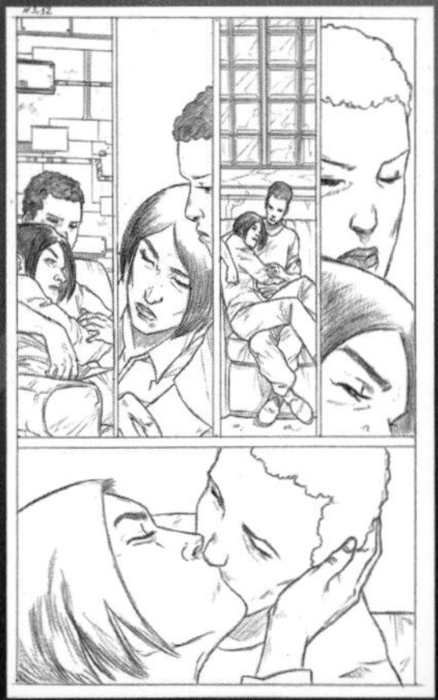

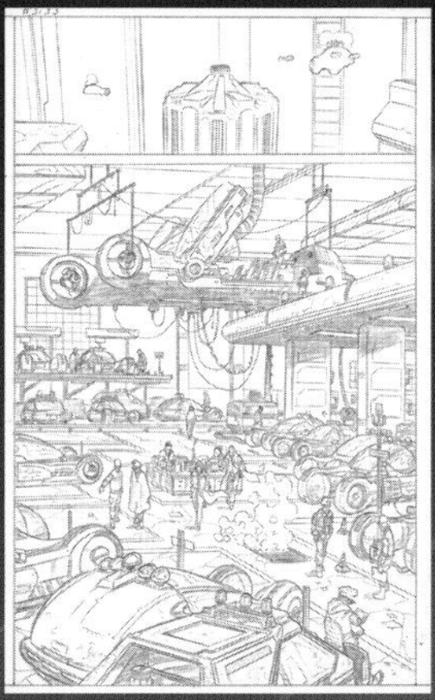
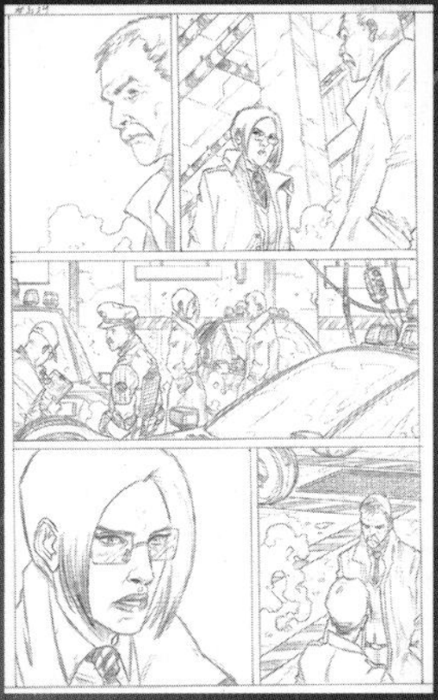
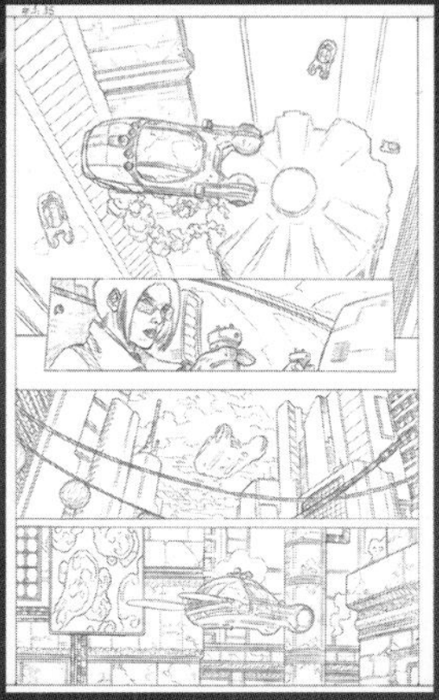
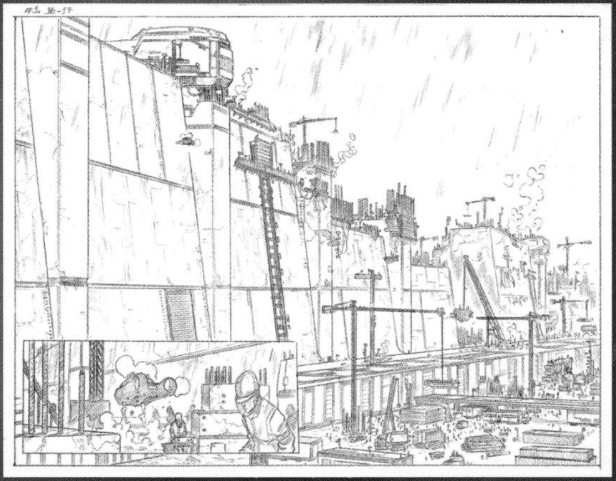
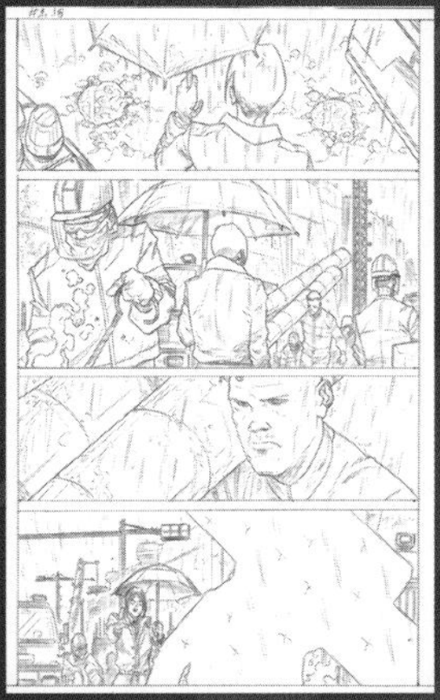
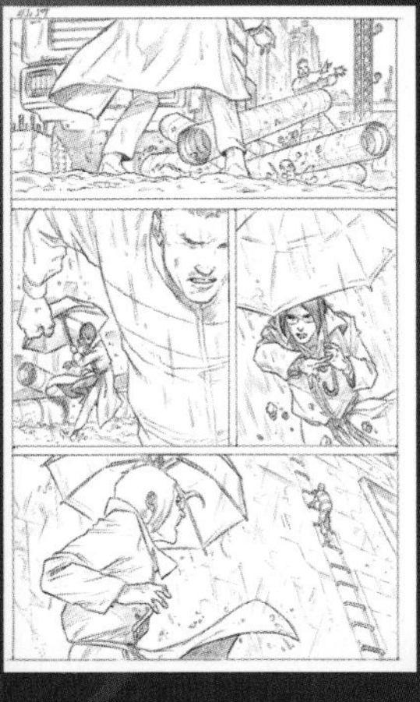
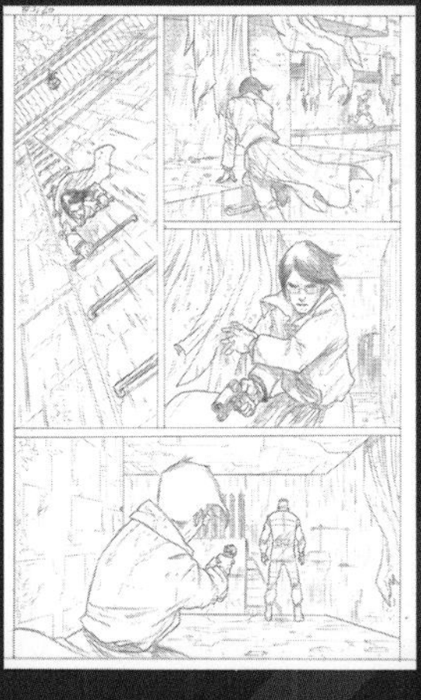
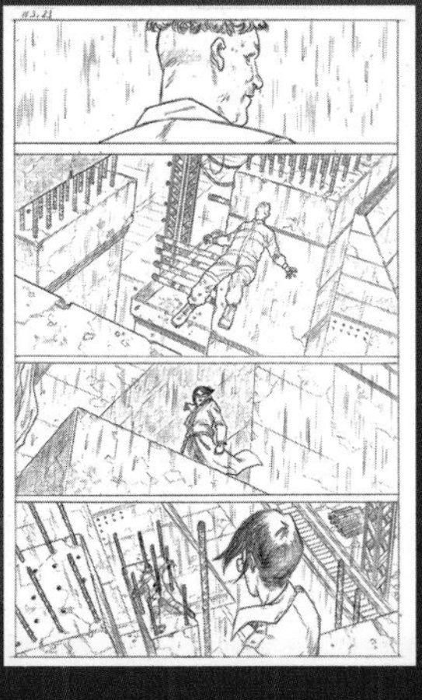
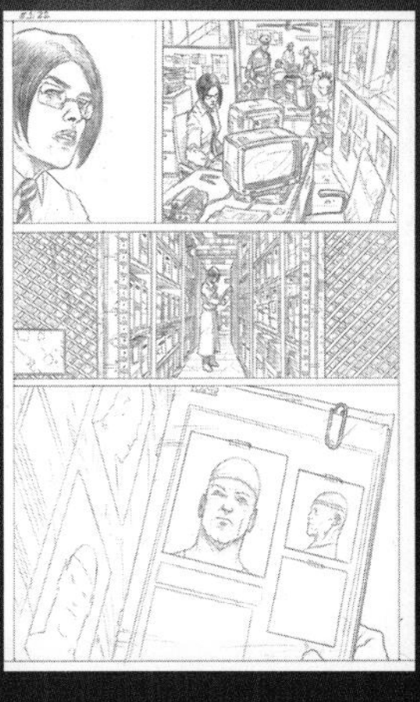

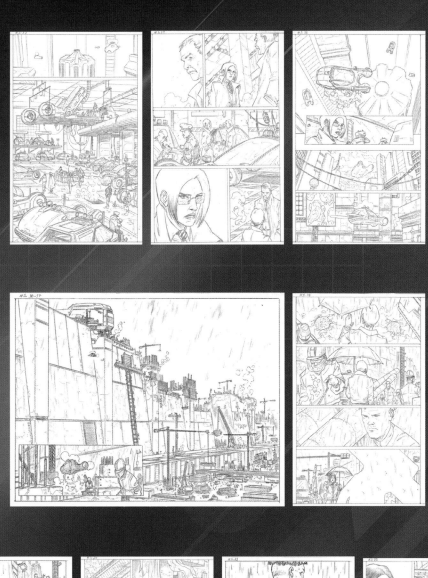

BLADE RUNNER 2029
Issue #1
Written by Mike Johnson
Art by Andres Guinaldo. Colors by Marco Lesko

[Page 2]

PANEL 1: Yotun stands across the counter from the proprietor, MALCOLM, a wizened old white man with a pencil mustache. Cheap jewelry behind the counter glass.

Yotun offers Malcolm an envelope.

1. YOTUN:	…to the penny.
2. MALCOLM:	I never had a doubt.

PANEL 2: Malcolm takes the envelope with a smile.

3. MALCOLM:	And the extra flattery is unnecessary.
4. MALCOLM:	But appreciated.

PANEL 3: Malcolm helps Jotun off with his coat. More mannequins in the background.

5. MALCOLM:	Now, let's get you out of this old rag and into something befitting a fresh start.
6. MALCOLM:	I'll be back in a minute.
6. JOTUN:	Thank you.

PANEL 4: On a double barreled shotgun pointing at us.

7. SFX:	clik
8. ASH:	Heard you were a big one, Yotun…

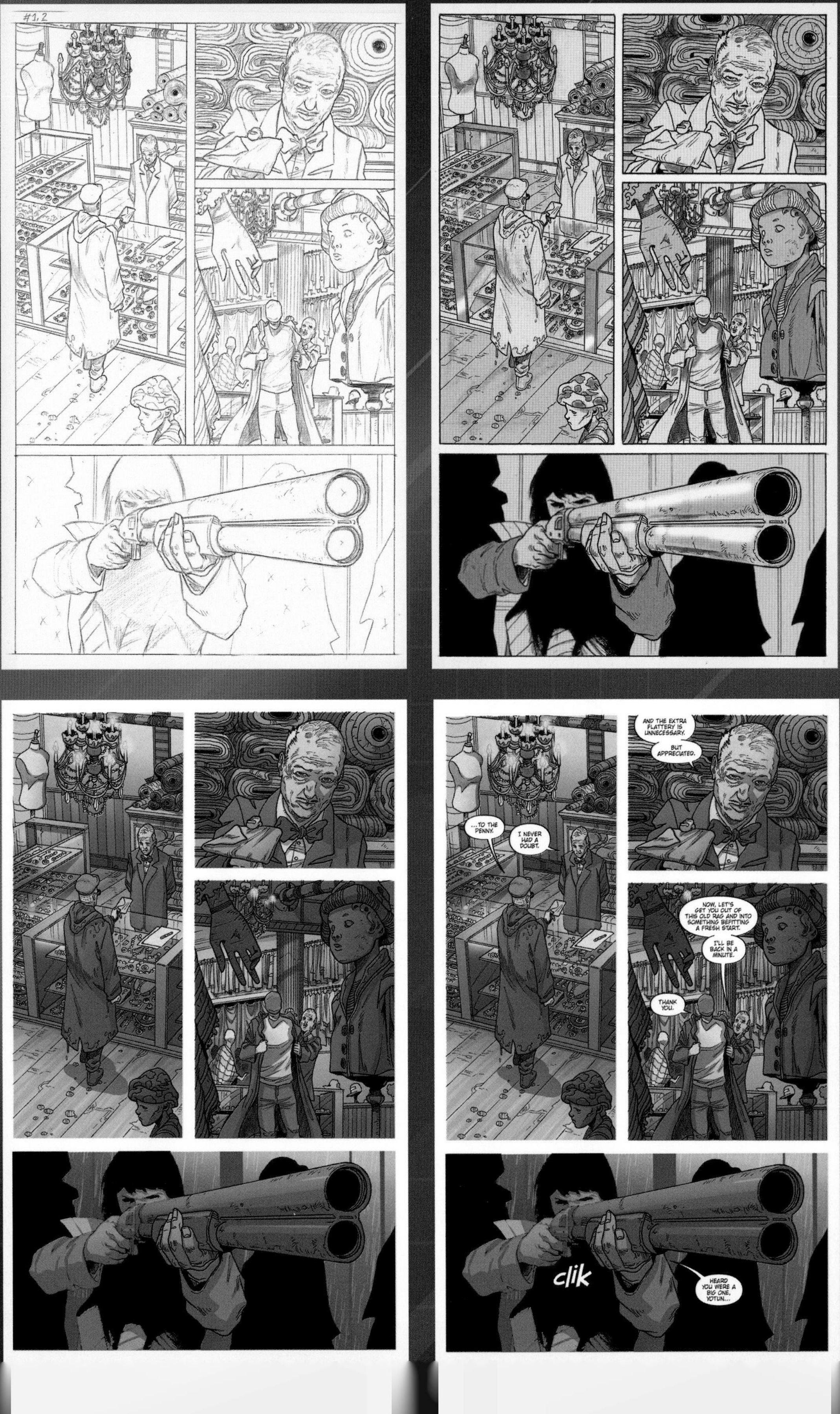
...TO THE PENNY.
I NEVER HAD A DOUBT.
AND THE EXTRA FLATTERY IS UNNECESSARY.
BUT APPRECIATED.
NOW, LET'S GET YOU OUT OF THIS OLD RAG AND INTO SOMETHING BEFITTING A FRESH START.
I'LL BE BACK IN A MINUTE.
THANK YOU.
clik
HEARD YOU WERE A BIG ONE, YOTUN...

BLADE RUNNER 2029
Issue #1
Written by Mike Johnson
Art by Andres Guinaldo. Colors by Marco Lesko

[Page 22]

PANEL 1: On Ash's face, lit by a green glow from an off-panel screen.

  1. ASH CAPTION: Yotun redeems.

PANEL 2: Ash is at a desk in the squad room, other detectives working in the background. She's scrolling through green text on her computer.

  2. ASH CAPTION: A faint bell rings. I run the name through the files.

  3. ASH CAPTION: Nothing recent.

  4. ASH CAPTION: Not since the Blackout.

PANEL 3: Ash reads from a folder in a basement storage room, shelves lined with file boxes.

  5. ASH CAPTION: So I go analog.

  6. ASH CAPTION: Takes all night.

  7. ASH CAPTION: But I find him.

PANEL 4: On the page: it's a printout of YOTUN's PERSONNEL LOG (like the images of Roy Batty and friends that Bryant shows Deckard in the original movie). His name visible. His face staring back at us, just as he looked in 2017.

  8. ASH CAPTION: Again.

  9. CAPTION (lower right):   TO BE CONTINUED…

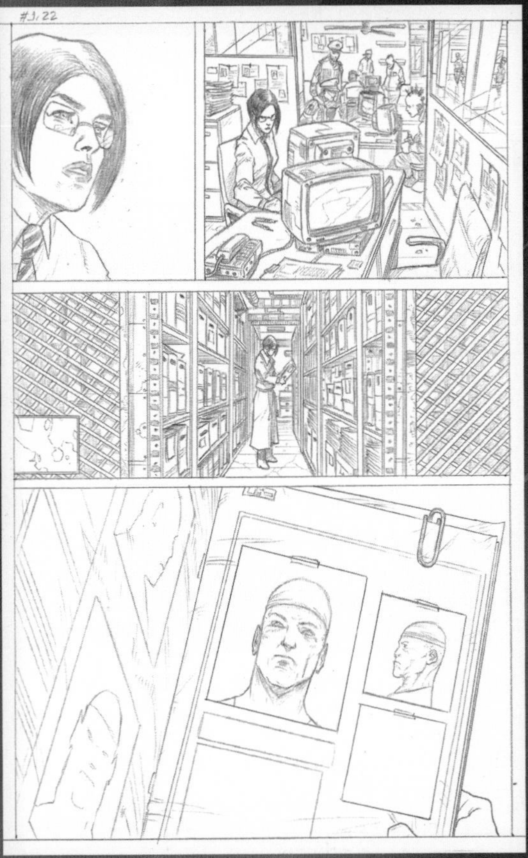
#3, 22

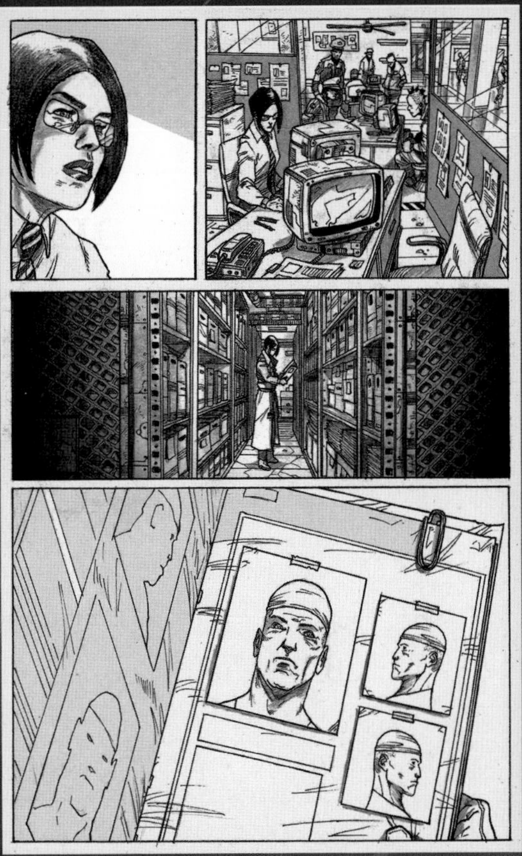

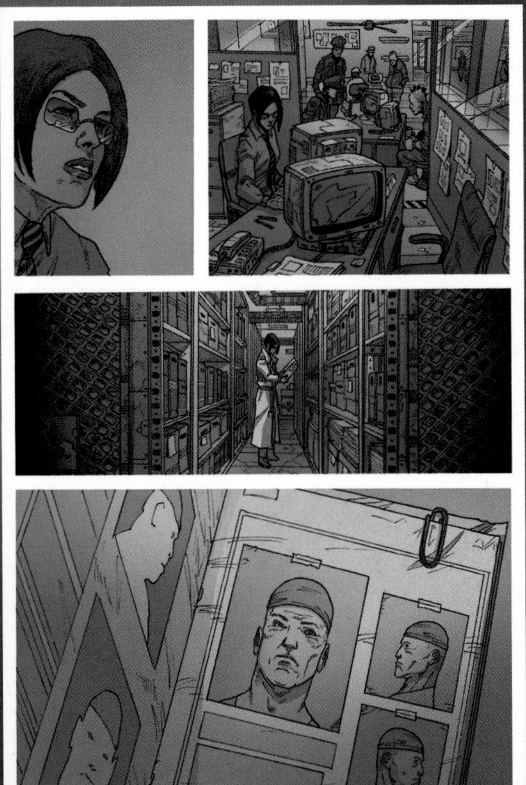

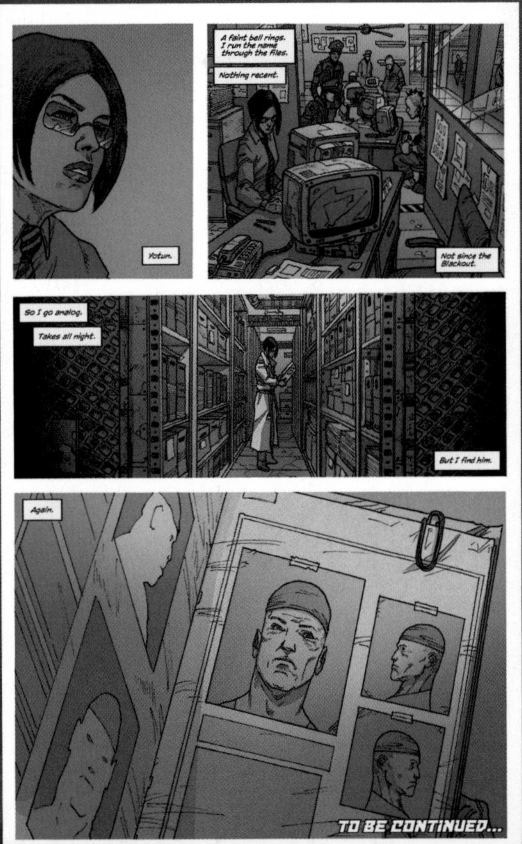
Yotun.
A faint bell rings. I run the name through the files.
Nothing recent.
Not since the Blackout.
So I go analog.
Takes all night.
But I find him.
Again.
TO BE CONTINUED...

BLADE RUNNER 2029
Issue #2
Written by Mike Johnson
Art by Andres Guinaldo. Colors by Marco Lesko

[Page 1]

PANEL 1: An opulent DINING ROOM with a view overlooking the city. A single long dining table, with a MAN (white, 70s, silver goatee) and a WOMAN (white, 70s, silver hair piled high) sitting at each end. The décor is Versailles, all white marble and gold, but the man and woman are dressed in KIMONOS. In the background, two HOLOGRAPHIC STATUES of classic Greek nudes float over pedestals.

    1. YOTUN CAPTION: "We are everywhere."

PANEL 2: Close on the woman as she tucks an expensive cloth napkin in the neck of her kimono. A WHITE-GLOVED HAND places a soup dish in front of her.

    2. YOTUN CAPTION: "Because they need us to be."

PANEL 3: Matching panel, this time with the old man tucking his napkin in, as the same gloved hand serves him the soup.

    3. YOTUN CAPTION: "Where would we be without their inability to fend for themselves?"

PANEL 4: The old man lifts his empty wine glass to the server, DUCASSE, who we see is a YOUNG MAN (20's, Japanese) dressed in a uniform matching that of a servant at Versailles, complete with short powdered wig.

    4. OLD MAN: More of the zinfandel, Ducasse, please.

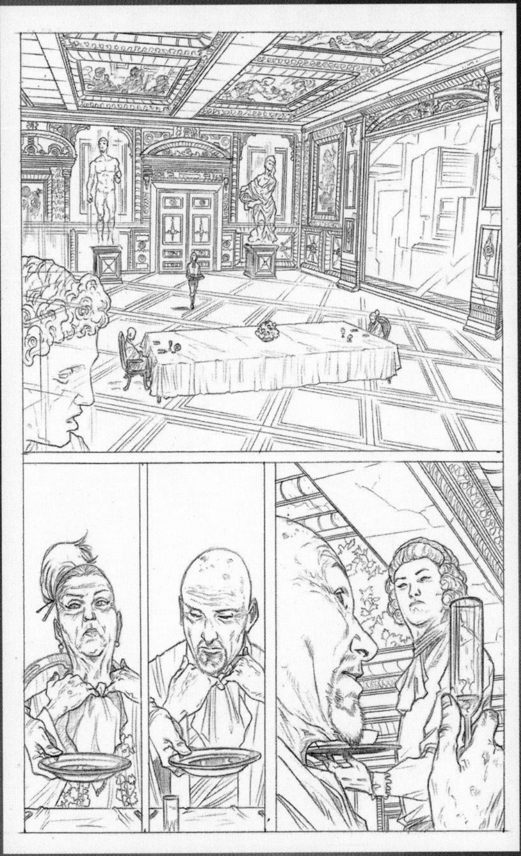

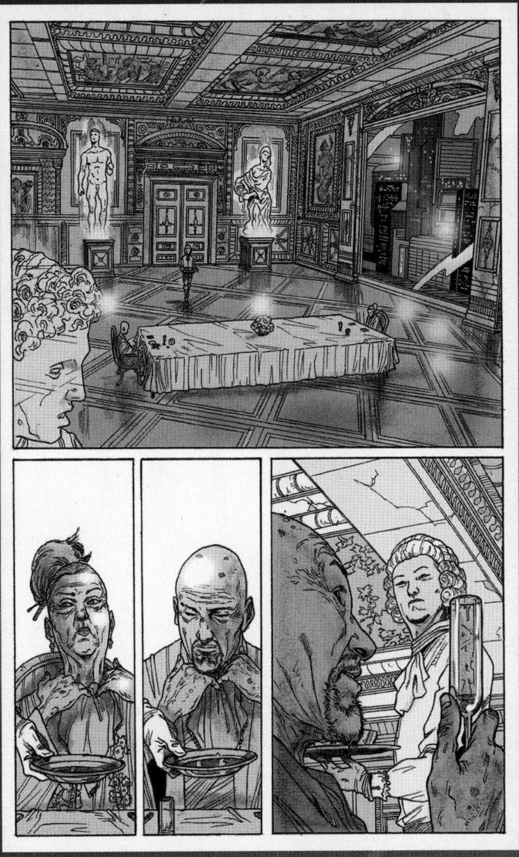

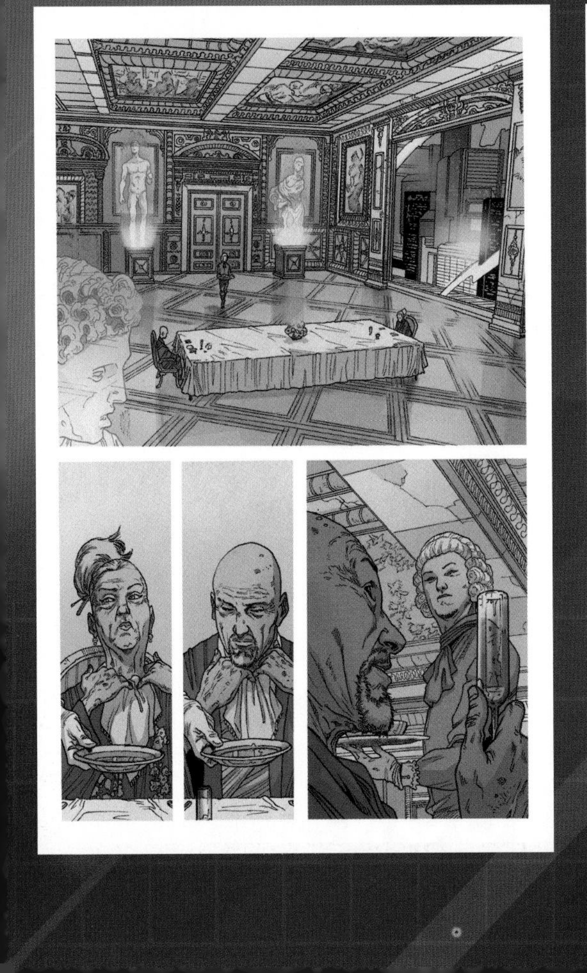

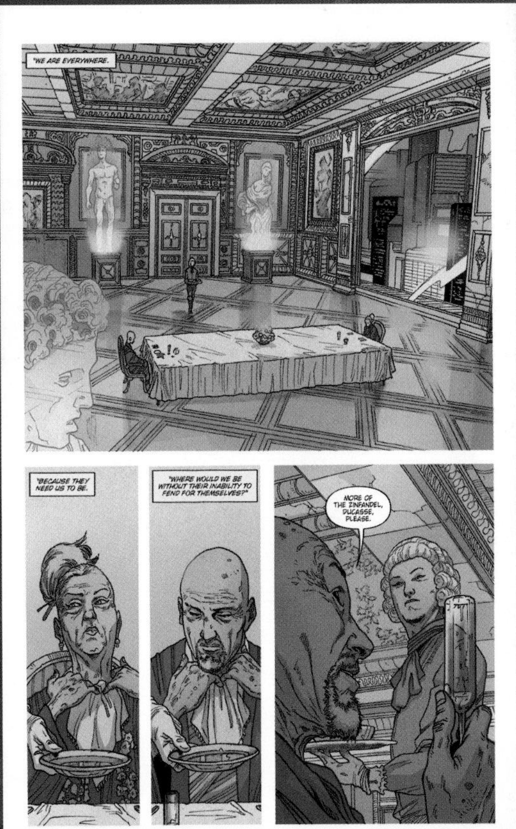
"WE ARE EVERYWHERE.
"BECAUSE THEY NEED US TO BE.
"WHERE WOULD WE BE WITHOUT THEIR INABILITY TO FEND FOR THEMSELVES?"
MORE OF THE ZINFANDEL, DUCASSE, PLEASE.

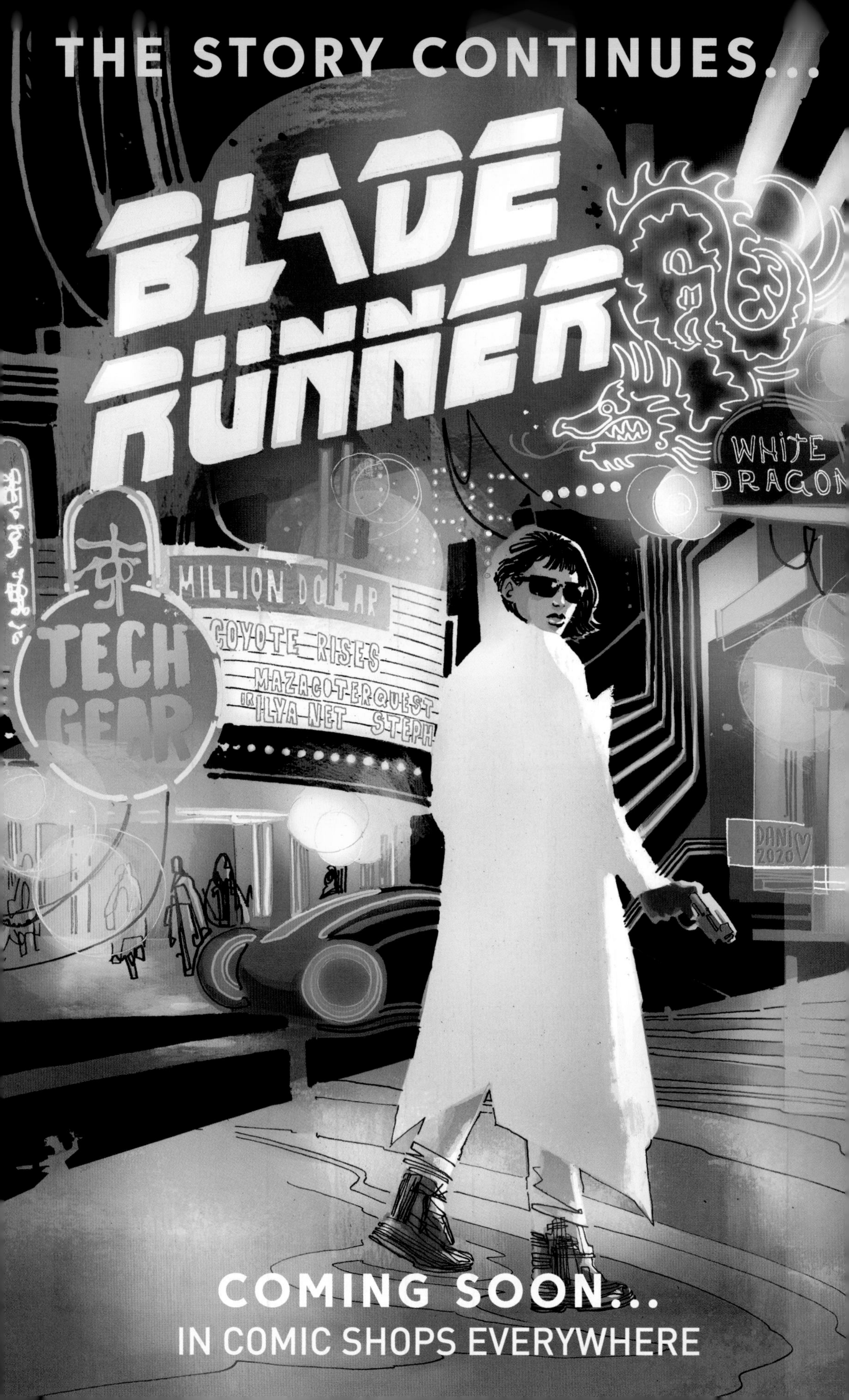
THE STORY CONTINUES...
BLADE RUNNER
WHITE DRAGON
TECH GEAR
MILLION DOLLAR
COYOTE RISES
MAZACOTERQUEST
ILYA NET STEPH
DANI 2020
COMING SOON...
IN COMIC SHOPS EVERYWHERE

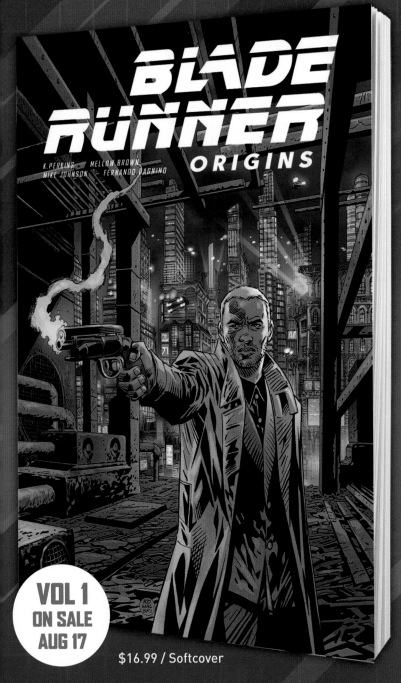

CREATOR BIOS

MIKE JOHNSON

Mike Johnson is a prolific comic book writer with credits writing *Titans, Superman, Batman, Star Trek: Nero* and *Star Trek: The Official Motion Picture*. He is the ongoing writer of the *Star Trek* series, as well as comic book tie-ins to *Fringe* and *Transformers*.

ANDRES GUINALDO

Andres Guinaldo originally studied movie making (direction) at Madrid University before making the move into comics. His first professional work was drawing Joe R. Landsdale's *The Drive-In* and *By Bizarre Hands*. He followed those with *Pistolfist: Revolutionary Warrior,* and other books such as *Helios: Under the Gun*, *Purity*, and *Cartoonapalooza*. In 2010, Guinaldo started regularly penciling *Son of Hulk* and drew issue #5 of *Dark Reign: Hawkeye*. He followed this with *Gotham City Sirens* #14-17, *Joker's Asylum: The Riddler*, *Namor: The First Mutant #4*, *Red Lanterns #8*, *Resurrection Man #9*, *Nightwing* #11-14, *Hypernaturals* and *Justice League Dark*. In recent years he's worked on titles as diverse as *Ninjak* and *Captain America: Steve Rogers*. He currently resides in Segovia, Spain, the city where he was born.

MARCO LESKO

Hailing from Brazil, Marco Lesko has been a professional comic book colorist since 2014. His credits include *Rat Queens, Assassin's Creed Uprising, Doctor Who, Robotech, The Shadow* and many more. When he's not coloring comics, he spends endless hours studying color theory from many different areas, including: cinema, conceptual art design, Japanese anime, videogame design, and classic Disney animations.

JIM CAMPBELL

Jim Campbell is an Eisner Award nominated letterer whose work can be seen on everything from Titan's *Robotech* books to *Roy of the Rovers* graphic novels to the *Firefly* series. He lives, works, and very occasionally sleeps in darkest Nottinghamshire, UK, in a house he shares with his wife and an unfeasibly large collection of black clothes.